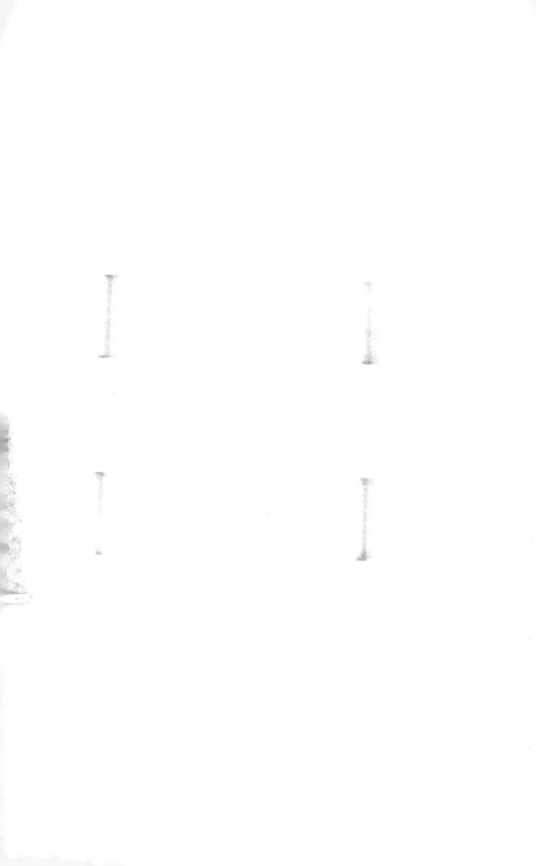

MUSIC AND RELIGION
IN THE WRITINGS OF IAN McEWAN

MUSIC AND RELIGION
IN THE WRITINGS OF
IAN McEWAN

IAIN QUINN

THE BOYDELL PRESS

© Iain Quinn 2023

All Rights Reserved. Except as permitted under current legislation
no part of this work may be photocopied, stored in a retrieval system,
published, performed in public, adapted, broadcast,
transmitted, recorded or reproduced in any form or by any means,
without the prior permission of the copyright owner

The right of Iain Quinn to be identified as
the author of this work has been asserted in accordance with
sections 77 and 78 of the Copyright, Designs and Patents Act 1988

First published 2023
The Boydell Press, Woodbridge

ISBN 978 1 83765 082 8

The Boydell Press is an imprint of Boydell & Brewer Ltd
PO Box 9, Woodbridge, Suffolk IP12 3DF, UK
and of Boydell & Brewer Inc.
668 Mt Hope Avenue, Rochester, NY 14620-2731, USA
website: www.boydellandbrewer.com

A CIP catalogue record for this book is available
from the British Library

The publisher has no responsibility for the continued existence or accuracy of
URLs for external or third-party internet websites referred to in this book, and
does not guarantee that any content on such websites is, or will remain, accurate
or appropriate

This publication is printed on acid-free paper

To Arianne and our family

CONTENTS

Acknowledgements	ix
Permissions	x
Introduction	1
1 The Question of Religion: An Atheist's Portrayal of the Church of England	23
2 The Value of Sublimity: Solitude, Voyeurism, and the Transcendental	77
3 From Gilbert and Sullivan to Mozart: Influences and Perceptions of Music in Society	125
4 'Don't Make Fun of the Fair': The Composer in Twentieth-Century Britain	169
Appendix	
Interview with Ian McEwan	211
Interview with Michael Berkeley	221
Bibliography	229
Index	237

ACKNOWLEDGEMENTS

I extend my very great thanks to all those with whom I have discussed this book. My wife, Arianne Johnson Quinn, has been a constant and inspirational source of support and our children have each contributed their own enthusiasm and encouragement. I have spoken about this book with many colleagues including Colin Andrews, Adam Cobb, Lori Gooding, The Very Revd Gary W. Kriss, Barbara Lee, Douglass Seaton, The Revd Canon Dr Nicholas Thistlethwaite, and Peggy Wright-Cleveland. Their knowledge and insights have made a significant difference to the outcome of this research, and I remain in their debt. I am also thankful to Paul F. Marty for inviting me to speak about the first chapter for our university lecture series. My early research interests in music and literature began as a result of conversations in Durham with Jeremy Dibble, Bennett Zon, and Francis O'Gorman when I was starting work on the research that led to *The Organist in Victorian Literature* (2017). Our continued conversations have provided me with sustained inspiration for this burgeoning area of study. I remain ever grateful that they prompted me to continue in a field that has been so deeply rewarding.

Much of the writing took place during the early months of the COVID-19 pandemic and I am grateful that Amy E. Armstrong of the Harry Ransom Center, The University of Texas at Austin, enabled me to continue as the Alfred A. and Blanche W. Knopf Fellow while providing valuable scans of documents from the Ian McEwan papers.

The publication of this book required several requests for permission to include copyright material and I am very grateful to The Revd Margaret T. Case for her grant support to the Florida State University Foundation and to the publishers and estates who assisted with this process.

I extend my sincere thanks to both Ian McEwan and Michael Berkeley for their willingness to be interviewed for this book.

Iain Quinn

PERMISSIONS

John Betjeman's poem *Exeter*, from *John Betjeman's Collected Poems*, reproduced with the permission of Hodder and Stoughton through PLSclear

Alan Bennett's *Allelujah!* and *The Habit of Art*, reproduced with the permission of Faber and Faber

Noël Coward's *Don't Make Fun of the Fair* © NC Aventales AG, 1951. Successor in title to The Noël Coward Estate. By permission of Alan Brodie Representation Ltd and the Noël Coward Archive Trust. www.alanbrodie.com / www.noelcoward.com

Philip Larkin's *Church Going*, reproduced with the permission of Faber and Faber.

Ian McEwan's *A Move Abroad: or Shall we die?* Published by Picador, 1989. © Ian McEwan. Reproduced by permission of the author c/o Rogers, Coleridge & White Ltd., 20 Powis Mews, London W11 1JN

Ian McEwan's *For You.* Published by Vintage, 2008. © Ian McEwan. Reproduced by permission of the author c/o Rogers, Coleridge & White Ltd., 20 Powis Mews, London W11 1JN

Ian McEwan's *The Imitation Game.* Published by Picador, 1981. © Ian McEwan. Reproduced by permission of the author c/o Rogers, Coleridge & White Ltd., 20 Powis Mews, London W11 1JN

Excerpts from various letters by Evelyn Waugh. © Evelyn Waugh, used by permission of The Wylie Agency LLC

Letters From Ian McEwan to John Updike, 2006–07. © Ian McEwan. Reproduced by permission of the author c/o Rogers, Coleridge & White Ltd., 20 Powis Mews, London W11 1JN

Letter from John Updike to Ian McEwan. © 2007 John H. Updike, used by permission of The Wylie Agency LLC

Interview of Michael Berkeley by Iain Quinn. © Michael Berkeley. Reproduced by permission of the author c/o Rogers, Coleridge & White Ltd., 20 Powis Mews, London W11 1JN

Interview of Ian McEwan by Iain Quinn. © Ian McEwan. Reproduced by permission of the author c/o Rogers, Coleridge & White Ltd., 20 Powis Mews, London W11 1JN

INTRODUCTION

*Music seeps into my novels because it's a fixed element of my interior life –
and the novel, pre-eminently, is an interior form.* (Ian McEwan)[1]

A Musician's Reading

In studying McEwan's writings, I shall be considering his work specifically
from a musician's perspective and as someone who has worked in the church
for thirty years. This book is both a complement and a departure to existing
writings. The major texts on McEwan by Dominic Head, David Malcolm, Kiernan
Ryan, Jack Slay Jr., and Lynn Wells[2] have covered many fields of literary
study and serve as important points of reference in this book. However, this
monograph will focus specifically on the musical and church references in the
novels and libretti of McEwan and therefore bridges literary and musical studies.
I shall be contextualising McEwan's work with other British writers including
references to Kingsley Amis, John Betjeman, Philip Larkin, George Orwell,
and especially Alan Bennett. The research of Robert Hewison, Daniel J. Levitin,
Adam Phillips, Oliver Sacks, Roger Scruton, Anthony Storr, and Barry Turner[3]
allows for further contextualisation of McEwan's distinct approach. Interviews
with Ian McEwan and his collaborator on two musical works, the composer
Michael Berkeley, are included in the Appendix. The book is divided into four
chapters, each of which is an individual study; *The Question of Religion: An
Atheist's Portrayal of the Church of England*; *The Value of Sublimity: Solitude,*

---

[1]   Iain Quinn, 'Interview with Ian McEwan' (2018).

[2]   Dominic Head, *Ian McEwan* (Manchester, 2007); Dominic Head, *The State of the
Novel – Britain and Beyond* (Oxford, 2008); Dominic Head (ed.), *The Cambridge
Companion to Ian McEwan* (Cambridge, 2019); David Malcolm, *Understanding Ian
McEwan* (Columbia, 2022); Kiernan Ryan, *Ian McEwan* (Plymouth, 1994); Jack Slay,
Jr., *Ian McEwan* (New York, 1996); Lynn Wells, *Ian McEwan* (London, 2010).

[3]   Robert Hewison, *Cultural Capital* (London, 2014); Daniel J. Levitin, *This is your
brain on music* (New York, 2016); Adam Phillips, *Unforbidden Pleasures* (London,
2016); Oliver Sacks, *Musicophilia – Tales of Music and the Brain* (New York, 2007);
Roger Scruton, *Our Church* (London, 2013); *England: An Elegy* (London, 2006);
Modern Culture (London, 2005); Anthony Storr, *Music and the Mind* (New York,
c.1992); Barry Turner, *Beacon for Change* (London, 2011).

2   *Music and Religion in the Writings of Ian McEwan*

Voyeurism, and the Transcendental; From Gilbert and Sullivan to Mozart: Influences and Perceptions of Music in Society; 'Don't Make Fun of the Fair': The Composer in Twentieth-Century Britain.

* * *

Ian McEwan is now in his mid-seventies and is one of Britain's most successful living writers. His novels have sold millions of copies around the world since he first published a set of short stories, *First Love, Last Rites*, in 1975. Eleven of his novels have been turned into screenplays for films with recent adaptations that include performances by Emma Thompson and Stanley Tucci (*The Children Act*, 2017), Benedict Cumberbatch (*The Child in Time*, 2017), and Saorise Ronan and Billy Howle (*On Chesil Beach*, 2017). For many, McEwan became a household name as a result of the 2007 film of his novel *Atonement* starring James McAvoy, Keira Knightley, and Vanessa Redgrave. The film was nominated for seven Academy Awards and won the Oscar for the Best Original Score, which was composed by Dario Marianelli. The medium of films released on an international scale has brought the stories of McEwan to a wide audience, while also presenting his descriptions and perceptions of modern Britain. The inclusion of *On Chesil Beach* in British high school examination syllabi created a new reception of him as an author of our time, typically writing about the current or near past while discussing numerous social issues. Coupled with his frequent contributions to newspapers and political television programmes, not least BBC *Newsnight*, McEwan has become a well-known figure in Britain, both for his novels and his opinions on religion, science, and politics. Lynn Wells suggests that 'McEwan has striven to exemplify the principled artistic behaviour by acting publicly in response to the problems of the times in which he is living, and by writing fiction that challenges readers to reflect on their own ethical responsibilities' and that he has a 'passion for human affairs and immense curiosity about the world, past and present'.[4] Dominic Head has commented that McEwan is at 'the forefront of a group of novelists who reinvigorated the ethical functions of the novel, in ways that embody a deep response to the historical pressures of the time'.[5] I agree with these points, especially having interviewed McEwan, and add that there is also a clear overlap between McEwan's own views and his fictional narratives. Head notes how McEwan's personal experience has been 'affected by a variety of key social and political changes, including: fading colonialism; the dissolution of the British class structure; educational reform; the transformation of family life; and the second wave of feminism'.[6] He further notes that McEwan continues a tradition associated

[4]   Wells, *Ian McEwan* (London, 2010), pp. 31, 21.

[5]   Dominic Head, 'Introduction', in Dominic Head (ed.), *The Cambridge Companion to Ian McEwan* (Cambridge, 2019), 1.

[6]   Head, *Ian McEwan* (Manchester, 2007), p. 5.

Introduction 3

with Iris Murdoch that is characterized by 'scrupulous thinking about the role of the novel and the novelist in the advancement of an ethical worldview'.[7] As McEwan himself has commented, 'fiction is a deeply moral form in that it is the perfect medium for entering the mind of another. I think it is at the level of empathy that moral questions begin in fiction.'[8] When considered through an interdisciplinary lens that measures his fiction not only through comparative analysis to other contemporary writers but to contemporary scholars and commentators, his fictional narratives demonstrate a strong understanding of the nuances of the fields being discussed. Depending on the reader's own knowledge of the fields, these fictional moments can be perceived as clichéd impressions, humorous, but most consistently, strikingly accurate, as is the case with his portrayal of the Church of England and music and musicians.

Considering McEwan's texts through a musical lens and as someone who has worked for the church for many years, I would agree with Dominic Head that there is 'deepening insularity' within the world of academic criticism concerning the novel. As Head notes, the novel 'remains an important cultural phenomenon'[9] and consequently the potential influence of a prominent author like McEwan is significant in terms of the topics and representations of society that are made. But it is Head's subsequent argument that has special resonance when it concerns how McEwan approaches topics like the Church of England and also music. Head challenges critics to 'take due cognizance of the sophistication evident in the novel and the expectation placed on readers' that leads to a 'dialogue between academic and non-academic enthusiasms'. This relates directly to the 'reader's sophistication' and potential awareness of topics which Head notes is 'rarely acknowledged'.[10] In the case of McEwan there is an obvious learning aspect for many readers, whether towards a scientific topic or something artistic. McEwan sheds light on potentially unknown specialised topics, but to the reader who knows the field his specific references add an additional layer to the narrative that is important to consider. Wayne Booth writes in *The company we keep; An ethics of fiction* about the nature of reading that involves a 'full otherness',[11] whereby there is a representation of lives other than our own. McEwan's portrayal of musicians as representative of otherness is especially interesting because of the complex nature of personal and professional dynamics that are also unavoidably connected to the music they perform and

---

[7]   Ibid., p. 9. Dominic Head, *The Cambridge Introduction to Modern British Fiction, 1950–2000* (Cambridge, 2002), p. 258.

[8]   Liliane Louvel, Gilles Ménégaldo, and Anne-Loure Fortin, 'An Interview with Ian McEwan' (conducted November 1994, *Études Britanniques Contemporaines*, 8 (1995), pp. 1, 3.

[9]   Head, *The State of the Novel – Britain and Beyond*, p. 1.

[10]   Ibid., pp. 8, 6.

[11]   Wayne Booth, *The company we keep; An ethics of fiction* (Berkeley and Los Angeles, 1998).

4   *Music and Religion in the Writings of Ian McEwan*

the experience of performance. Drawing on the writings of Edward O. Wilson, Judith Seaboyer notes how in *The Child in Time* and *Enduring Love*, McEwan enters into what Wilson terms the critical 'intellectual adventure'[12] of 'achieving a common ground through the science and the humanities'.[13] McEwan's writings could also be seen as a similar adventure into the world of music and indeed the church because the references are not fleeting but critically specific and nuanced and, in the case of music, more numerous than any other field of the humanities in McEwan's writings. Indeed, through his highly specific choices of composers, pieces, and performers, the reader with a knowledge of the field will encounter characters whose emotions, responses, and decisions are clearer and more easily explained and analysed.

McEwan's researches in advance of many of the novels that have a specialist nature, especially those concerning science and medicine (*Saturday*, *Solar*, *Machines Like Me*) or law (*The Children Act*), take the reader to often less typical surroundings. These researches form a counterpoint to his deep interest in classical music, not least instrumental and chamber music, and the greater nature of intellectual pursuit. References to specific musical works are carefully chosen to highlight a specific emotion or setting. A reader familiar with these pieces therefore reads the text through an added aesthetic lens as an aural environment is superimposed. The non-musician reader in turn encounters the 'sprightly argot'[14] of the field (as does Edward in *On Chesil Beach*) and the specifics of the setting. In *Lessons* there are the 'signature taps at the door – crotchet, triplet, crotchet, crotchet.'[15] The British terminology was even used in the US edition. The detailed description of the experience of attending a concert at the Wigmore Hall (*On Chesil Beach*) as discussed in chapter 2 is a notable moment for its degree of specificity.[16]

Research on Music and Text and the Place of McEwan

The field of word and music studies is constantly developing and the potential resources for future analytical study are very considerable. The founding of the International Association for Word and Music Studies in 1997, together with the WMS book series, has brought an enormous amount of research to the fore. However, the focus of studies to date has been almost exclusively on the musical setting of text rather than the portrayal of music and musicians within

---

[12]   Wilson, Edward O., *Consilience: the Unity of Knowledge* (London, 2001), pp. 6–7.

[13]   Judith Seaboyer, 'Ian McEwan: Contemporary Realism and the Novel of Ideas', in James Acheson, Sarah Ross (eds), *The Contemporary British Novel* (Edinburgh, 2005), p. 25.

[14]   Ian McEwan, *On Chesil Beach* (New York, 2007), pp. 17–18.

[15]   Ian McEwan, *Lessons* (New York, 2022), p. 145.

[16]   McEwan, *On Chesil Beach*, pp. 49–50, 152.

Introduction   5

texts. A notable exception to this is found in the research of nineteenth-century topics, particularly the monographs of Delia da Sousa Correa (*George Eliot, Music and Victorian Culture*, 2002), Phyllis Weliver (*Women Musicians in Victorian Fiction, 1860–1900: Representations of Music, Science and Gender in the Leisured Home*, 2000), and John Hughes (*Ecstatic Sound – Music and Individuality in the work of Thomas Hardy*, 2001). More recently, the *Edinburgh Companion to Music and Literature*, 2020, edited by Delia da Sousa Correa, and the *Routledge Companion to Music and Modern Literature*, 2022, edited by Rachael Durkin, Peter Dayan, Axel Englund, and Katharina Clausius have contributed immeasurably to this expanding field. However, the topic of literary representations of classical music in the later half of the British twentieth century remains unexplored. McEwan's significant writings on music allow for this area to be studied and contextualised. In terms of the broader field of word and music studies, the editors of the Routledge volume note that 'Much of the excitement [of the study of the field] stems from the realization that to unlock the secrets of what passes between the two arts, one has to place both in the context of the wider sociocultural and ideological shifts that have made them peculiarly what they are today. Not because music and literature are merely the product of specific sociocultural or ideological contexts, but because one cannot see what they are, what they tell us they have always been, unless one thinks through how they change, together, as times change.'[17]

This argument forms an interesting parallel to the nature of performance practice in music as musicians seek to recreate the original performing conditions for a particular piece. In order to understand the composer and their work a performer has to be able to situate an individual piece within a particular society and timeframe. In McEwan's writings, music is interwoven into daily lives and so this setting and context is presented to the reader. How believable a narrative might be and how close it might be to the contemporary world of a particular novel's setting is examined in this monograph. The *Routledge Companion* examines the 'universal, opera, form, and the popular' but the topics of performance practice, the artist in contemporary society, and the relationship between emotion and the performing musician that typify the portrayals of music and musicians in McEwan's writings are not included. As noted above, the field of study is so vast, this is unsurprising, but it does mean that McEwan's approach is uniquely fascinating in part because of the number of musical references across several texts. The editors of the *Routledge Companion* comment that a reader's experience when encountering music in literature will be dependent on '[a] private, personal interaction with … and understanding of, music and literature' and that the 'experience is highly individual', while asking 'does this matter?'. As a musician, I would stress that it matters very greatly. The reader may well have their own view when reading that a piece

---

[17]   Rachael Durkin, Peter Dayan, Axel Englund, and Katharina Clausius (eds), *The Routledge Companion to Music and Modern Literature* (Abingdon, 2022), p. 1.

6 *Music and Religion in the Writings of Ian McEwan*

of Mozart is being played but that does not mean their view aligns with the reason the musical character has chosen a particular piece to play or listen to by a particular performer. As such, the 'individual' response is dependent on the understanding of the material they encounter. The larger question of McEwan's approach to art and science is raised by Astrid Bracke, who questions 'dismissals of art and literature in favour of science' and that 'art is critiqued and frequently said to be lacking, yet in the end proves central and invaluable to the novels'.[18] The latter point resonates from a musician's perspective but the suggestion that there is a debate between art and science is problematic when considering the larger writings of McEwan because the only art form McEwan consistently describes across his larger output is music and the two are not in conflict. Within those descriptions he incorporates both highly positive descriptions as well as criticism, the latter typically of atonal music, but one does not present a challenge to the other.

I would argue that the reason for the lack of study in these areas in the past is that references to classical music, whether composers, pieces, performers, performances, or perceptions of the profession within literature are very often brief, vague, or problematic. This does not mean that they are necessarily inaccurate, but they are not detailed in the manner that McEwan's texts are. As an example, if an author refers to hearing 'Mozart on the radio', that statement does not clarify what sort of piece they are hearing (vocal, instrumental, etc.) or who is performing it. When McEwan provides all of that information the reader can see not only the bare facts of the narrative but the nature of the character being portrayed. An example of this can be seen in *Saturday*[19] when the surgeon, Henry Perowne, listens not just to a piece of Bach but a specific piece (*Goldberg Variations*) and, depending on his mood, he listens to interpretations by different performers. This level of detail adds to an understanding of his character. By a similar argument, a problematic narrative will raise eyebrows among musicians. Julian Barnes's novel *The Noise of Time* (2016) received a critical review of its musical content in *The New York Times*[20] by the musicologist Richard Taruskin, who noted that if Barnes had not named Shostakovich as the central figure, the story would have been simply reminiscent of the famous composer's life, rather than a portrayal that was a challenge for a musicologist to accept, especially one known for his research on Russian music. A similar, if comparatively slight, misunderstanding occurs in Lynn Wells's description[21] of the two composers in McEwan's writing – Clive Linley

---

[18] Astrid Bracke, 'Science and Climate Crisis', in Dominic Head (ed.), *The Cambridge Companion to Ian McEwan* (Cambridge, 2019), pp. 47–48.

[19] Ian McEwan, *Saturday* (London, 2005), p. 22.

[20] Richard Taruskin, 'Was Shostakovich a Martyr? Or Is That Just Fiction?', *New York Times* (26 August 2016) <https://www.nytimes.com/2016/08/28/arts/music/julian-barnes-the-noise-of-time-shostakovich.html> [accessed 8 June 2022].

[21] Wells, *Ian McEwan*, p. 149.

Introduction 7

(*Amsterdam*) and Charles Frieth (*For You*) – as bearing a resemblance to each other. Although there are character traits, not least narcissism, that they both share, they are in fact very different musicians. Clive's primary concern is to be taken seriously by his professional colleagues and he is broken when he cannot achieve that whereas Charles is an egotistical composer-conductor who is portrayed in near comic proportions. Charles is largely criticized for his personal life whereas Clive has the stigma of professional distrust of his earlier work. In a different vein, the 'socially repressive' world that Wells describes in *On Chesil Beach* by comparison to the 'libertine late capitalist world of *Amsterdam*'[22] does not acknowledge the free nature of the inner world of musical thought and performance that is central to the lives of the characters. Florence (*On Chesil Beach*) may seem to some inhibited but to others she is relatively free through her musical life. In this sense, in understanding both music and musicians within the realm of classical music in twentieth-century Britain, McEwan occupies an especially informed position. As a consequence, there are some relative surprises. For instance, McEwan's most well-known novel, *Atonement*, has very few references to music, whereas *Amsterdam*, *On Chesil Beach*, and the libretto for the opera *For You*, place music in a crucial narrative role. Overall, music appears more often in McEwan's later writings and from a musician's perspective the absence of research on this field is notable but equally predictable because of the breadth of potential research topics his work promotes. Many of McEwan's books have a specialist focus, several of them scientific in nature. This has provoked numerous interdisciplinary studies in vastly different fields to the extent that it is conceivable that the scholarship of one researcher on McEwan may not be immediately translatable to another. This could also be said of the field of words and music. Because there are so many texts that have been set to music, including some texts in settings by different composers, the possibilities for research and interdisciplinary scholarship are very considerable within the field of classical music alone.

The Nature of Questioning in McEwan's Writings

McEwan opens a window into many fields for the reader to explore and with an approach that suggests that many diverse topics are also easy to engage with. The appeal of elegant liturgy, the plush surrounds of the concert hall, and the dramatic world of the composer are portrayed within the context of other aspects of society so that they appear natural and unguarded. The supposed elitism of classical music is replaced with a narrative role that is as essential to the individual character as other aspects of their personality, emotions, and desires. But it is the degree of nuance in McEwan's writings that makes them stand out and also makes his writings especially intriguing. Richard Bradford

---

[22] Ibid., p. 96.

8 *Music and Religion in the Writings of Ian McEwan*

considers this point when he writes that 'McEwan's fiction shares this at once annoying and beguiling quality of elusiveness – except that the question of "What if?" recurs continually.'[23] This relates to the larger portrayal of characters that Wells observes when suggesting that McEwan believes in the role of fiction for 'improving our understanding and treatment of one another [with characters that] grapple with moral choices, and are placed in the hands of his readers for ultimate judgement.'[24] David Malcolm notes McEwan's 'trajectory from quite extreme moral relativism toward a clear moral focus'[25] over time. This development of approach coincidentally aligns with McEwan's increasing use of music over time. Claudia Schemberg suggests that 'McEwan's writing [is part of] a greater cultural movement which endeavours to open-mindedly address inescapable questions of value and which regard imaginative literature as an indispensable partner in this enterprise.'[26] McEwan has commented on this, suggesting that 'once you move inside a person, once you allow your reader direct access, then you are in a much more moral frame.'[27] When an understanding of the musical choices that occur through narratives is added to this layering of characters, values, and experiences then the perception of these characters and the larger narratives is by nature enriched.

The overwhelming majority of McEwan's characters are well-educated members of the middle class, although seldom with any great private financial means and certainly no detectable affluence. Despite different occupations, including a scientist (*Solar)*, a musician *(On Chesil Beach, Amsterdam, For You)*, and a surgeon *(Saturday)*, they are faced with moral, ethical, and personal dilemmas that bear easy believability and resonance to a contemporary audience. Classical music pervades nearly all of the narratives, not as a central theme (except in *On Chesil Beach, For You*, and *Amsterdam*) but as a necessary part of life's pleasures and, for some, essential needs. The combination of music and the unforgettable narrative moments, to which music is by nature also indebted, creates a specific space for McEwan to portray characters that can range from a verbally abusive conductor in *For You* to an idealistic violinist on *On Chesil Beach*. He does so in a manner that carefully places music as a powerful art form that relates to the emotions while also conveying a sentimentality and nostalgia towards a passing other world. This is mirrored in his approach to the Church of England along cultural and societal lines rather than theological ones. Through this approach he raises many questions about

---

[23] Richard Bradford, *The Novel Now* (Oxford, 2007), p. 23.

[24] Wells, *Ian McEwan*, p. 21.

[25] Malcolm, *Understanding Ian McEwan*, p. 15.

[26] Claudia Schemberg, 'Achieving "At-one-ment": Storytelling and the Concept of the Self in Ian McEwan's *The Child in Time, Black Dogs, Enduring Love*, and *Atonement*' (thesis) (Frankfurt, 2004), pp. 28, 30–31.

[27] Wells, *Ian McEwan*, p. 126.

Introduction   9

the role of deeper thinking in society. Roger Scruton's review of *Enduring Love* highlights the nature of this questioning:

> *Enduring Love* situates the conflict between science and religion in a context so original and startling, and at the same time so believable, as to force you to recognize that the conflict lies in you.[28]

Religion, the Church of England, Science

McEwan is a well-known atheist and has spoken about his views on faith in numerous interviews, including a televised discussion with Richard Dawkins.[29] His approach to religion within his writings can be divided into two categories: 1) His impressions and portrayal of the Church of England and its clergy, 2) His approach to religion from a scientific perspective. The latter point was largely absent from his novels until *Lessons*, although made explicitly clear in the publication of collected talks, *Science*. In *Lessons* he writes a blistering critique that extends into another area of this book, taste in music. Critically, he connects religion to art, but not positively in this specific reference that relates to science and the relationship with free enquiry.

> Christianity had been the cold dead hand on the European imagination. What a gift, that its tyranny had expired.

> It was not only science that Christianity had obstructed for fifty generations, it was nearly all of culture, nearly all of free expression and enquiry.

> Within the totality of human experience of the world there was an infinity of subject matter and yet all over Europe the big museums were stuffed with the same lurid trash [of religious art]. Worse than pop music.[30]

This otherwise contrasting approach between the portrayal of the Church of England and the church more broadly is important to note because while being highly critical of religion, he nonetheless portrays the Church of England with a degree of nuance that describes its multiple roles within British society.

McEwan's approach to the Church of England is therefore carefully assimilated. In the first chapter, I begin with an analysis of how the role of the Church of England functions within society as an Establishment presence. McEwan portrays it as part of the cultural fabric of society and as naturally present, and indeed accessible, as he does the world of classical music. In this sense, the acknowledged aspects of the church by those who do not actu-

---

[28]   Roger Scruton, 'Review of Enduring Love', *Sunday Telegraph*, 16 September 2001.

[29]   Richard Dawkins and Ian McEwan interview, Richard Dawkins Foundation for Reason and Science, online at <https://www.youtube.com/watch?v=o7LjriWFAEs> [accessed 17 December 2020].

[30]   McEwan, *Lessons*, p. 368.

Music and Religion in the Writings of Ian McEwan

ally attend give an impression of the role the church has come to play in the middle England identity consistently found in his writings. In chapter 1, I note the similarity between a passage in Henry James's account of a visit to Wells Cathedral in 1905 and McEwan's *Sweet Tooth*. Both observe the subtleties of liturgies and, irrespective of personal belief, introduce the reader to a specific ecclesiastical world.

McEwan advances the subject of religion in his novels through questioning, a measure of humour, and a particular understanding of the role that the Church of England and its leaders play in the public sphere. His narratives align with many other twentieth-century writers who maintain a sustained impression of the church that can be considered sentimental or nostalgic. In this respect, the loss or lack of faith by an author, and yet the continued reference to the church within their writings, is not unusual in the literary field, with Thomas Hardy being an obvious example. However, in portraying the church primarily as an institution that forms part of the cultural landscape of Britain there is an absence of reference in McEwan's writings (fictional and personal) to the specific relationship between the scientific world and the Church of England that has emerged in recent decades. In considering McEwan's commentaries on atheism this bears analysis, not least because of his regular public commentaries on scientific matters as well as his writing in *Science*.[31] Whereas the 'new atheists' (especially Richard Dawkins, Sam Harris, and Christopher Hitchens) adopted an adversarial role in their criticism of religion, leaders within the Church of England have consistently fostered an approach to science that has been one of sustained dialogue that is also far removed from creationist theology. In considering how to evaluate McEwan's doubting of religion, most especially in *The Children Act*, where a barrister asks if the Church of England could be considered a cult,[32] the significance of new atheists has to be considered.

A great deal of discussion has promoted new atheism since 9/11 and with it an all-inclusive brush that has tarnished faiths and denominations in the eyes of many. There is an undeniable populism to new atheism that is easily enhanced by criticism of organized religion, in part because most religious leaders do not generally feel the need to inject themselves into binary arguments. Hate and distrust can be extremely profitable along with a capitalist Darwinism in an age of the easy polemic argument. Prosperity theology has also served to bolster the arguments of new atheists because the aims appear contrary to the traditional role and identity of the church.

But the rise of atheism in its current form (and assuming it is not largely a matter of revisiting old arguments in a contemporary vein) has also been successful because religious institutions are themselves already wrestling with finer points of debate on an ongoing basis. This can either be seen as a strength or a weakness. The arguments within the church are nuanced as,

---

[31] Ian McEwan, *Science* (London, 2019).

[32] Ian McEwan, *The Children Act* (London, 2014), pp. 68–69.

Introduction 11

most obviously, successive reformations and schisms have shown. As a consequence, the polemics of new atheists often appear to believers not as contrary but simplistic, and to Ian S. Markham, whose book, *Against Atheism*,[33] methodically examines its flaws, little short of the fundamentalism they cry against. Markham notes, 'It is no coincidence that both the Christian fundamentalists of the early twentieth century and atheist fundamentalists of the early twenty-first century do not even try to understand their opponents. None of our atheist fundamentalists have studied theology'[34] and they readily lurch towards arguments that are by nature simplistic and relatable to a wide audience. Arthur Bradley and Andrew Tate view McEwan's writing as representing a 'fragile, sceptical and always questioning profession of faith [and the] possibility of secular transcendence' and that 'what fills the place of belief in God [in McEwan's writings is a] belief in family, love, scientific progress, and most importantly, art'.[35] Here, the balance between the church, sacred art and music, and the secular realm of music coalesces in McEwan's fictional writings and represents a specific dualism; his questioning of faith and yet his perception of a specifically British and Anglican church. As a consequence, the popular acuminate edge of new atheism is not found.

Moreover, the argument made by contemporary atheists consistently focuses on concerns about American conservatives, and this is a point McEwan reflects on in *Science*. He first presents familiar arguments, noting the large number of creationists who 'believe the cosmos is 6,000 years old, and are certain that Jesus will return to judge the living and the dead within the next fifty years'.[36] But his greater concern relates to the belief of end-time biblical prophecy described in Revelation, observing how the social scientist, J. W. Nelson, considered apocalyptic ideas 'as American as the hot dog'.[37] McEwan is concerned with how fundamentalist views are translated when violence is inflicted on others in the name of religion. His oratorio libretto, *or Shall we die?*, was written in a close time frame with Ronald Reagan's presidency. McEwan notes his despair with Reagan's acknowledgement of being 'greatly interested in the biblical prophecy of Armageddon'[38] and in the preface for *or Shall we die?* adds his frustration with the Cold War arms race and America's approach to Israel:

> The reluctance of the current US administration to pursue an even-handed policy towards a peace settlement in the Israel-Palestine dispute may owe as much to the pressures of nationalist Jewish groups as to the eschatology of

---

[33] Ian S. Markham, *Against Atheism* (Oxford, 2010).

[34] Ibid., p. 7.

[35] Bradley, Arthur, and Andrew Tate, *The New Atheist Novel: Fiction, Philosophy and Polemic after 9/11* (London, 2010), p. 16.

[36] McEwan, *Science*, p. 72.

[37] Ibid., p. 73.

[38] Ibid.

12   *Music and Religion in the Writings of Ian McEwan*

Christian fundamentalists. The precarious logic of self-interest that saw us through the Cold War would collapse if the leaders of one nuclear state came to welcome, or ceased to fear, mass death.[39]

In *Lessons* McEwan's scepticism about politicians in general is paralleled in his criticism of the Soviet situation as well:

A column asked what happened to Gorbachev's policy of openness. It was always a fraud. Someone wrote in the letters page that wherever there was nuclear power, east or West, there were official lies.[40]

Having made the statement in the preface for *or Shall we die?*, McEwan moves to the nature of the 'religious expression [of] joy, fear, love, and above all seriousness' that Philip Larkin who 'also knew the moment and the nature of transcendence' captured in 'Church Going,'[41] while observing the beauty of language found in the *Book of Common Prayer*. The significant pivot and seeming separation of the two identities is considerable but to someone who does not have an appreciation for the nuances of denominations, this can be easily missed. An important distinction needs to be made between the role of religion as seen through Christian conservative arguments (largely centred in the USA) and the specific nature of the Church of England as an institution in British culture that McEwan portrays in his fictional writing. The role of the church envisioned by conservatives such as Franklin Graham or Joel Osteen is vastly different from the image held by John Betjeman, Philip Larkin, Alan Bennett or Ian McEwan, none of whom could be considered under one banner, yet all of whom have written about the church as a presence in society. The question of how science, a notable interest of McEwan, could enter into this debate is important to consider. The first chapter of this book examines McEwan and his perceptions of the Church of England but in considering that analysis it is critical to include a discussion on how the worlds of science and the church currently coexist within the Church of England.

The physicist and lay preacher Tom McLeish considers the 'fundamentalist' doctrine that demonizes Darwinism and holds far 'greater currency in the USA than in the UK' as a 'largely sociological phenomenon.' He elucidates further stating that: 'Paradoxically, while promoted typically by those who make high claims about "the authority of scripture", it betrays a shallow disrespect for the richness of the Bible.' This is an aspect of what Rowan Williams, former Archbishop of Canterbury, terms a 'faithless kind of faith,'[42] and it is interesting to note that McEwan does not criticize the Church of England on theological

---

[39]   Ibid., pp. 90–91.

[40]   McEwan, *Lessons*, p. 29.

[41]   Ibid., p. 92.

[42]   Tom McLeish, *Faith & Wisdom in Science* (Oxford, 2014), pp. 240–241; Rowan Williams, 'Faith in the university', in S. Robinson and C. Katulushi (eds), *Values in Higher Education* (Cardiff, 2005).

Introduction   13

grounds in his novels but separates the two respective identities of religion and the church. However, there are parallels to be considered that give McEwan's work a greater contemporary context.

Echoing McEwan's characterizations of beauty, not least through music as well as the perfection of science, McLeish writes that 'when science recognizes beauty and structure it rejoices in a double reward: there is the delight both in the new object of our gaze and in the wonder that our minds are able to understand it.'[43] In understanding the similarities between the worlds of religion and science, both fields are to many filled with unfathomable depths and language that are their own. McLeish quotes Angela Tilby:

> Like priests in a former age, [scientists] seem to guard the key to knowledge, to have access to transcendent truths which the rest of us could never hope to understand. Many people feel that what they do is cut off from everyday life, that it is irrelevant and rather frightening, a form of magic.[44]

The 'key to knowledge' rests heavily on the use of language and, as noted above, McEwan expands the field of knowledge to many readers through references to specialised areas. Dominic Head notes McEwan's portrayal of the neurosurgeon Henry Perowne (*Saturday*) whose 'unprovable faith is part of his inhabitation of the present moment, the secular professional's equivalent of meditation.'[45] There is a leap of faith into the unknown that both the worlds of science and religion unavoidably share. There is also a well-established literary aspect within liturgies that extends beyond the Book of Common Prayer and bridges the worlds of religion and literature.

Clergy frequently approach the barrier of language and understanding through the texts of others, not least the poets. It is common for clergy across denominations to refer to texts beyond scripture in their preaching and teaching. Tom Wright, former Bishop of Durham, quotes T. S. Eliot (*East Coker*) and Malcolm Guite (*Easter 2020*) in his book *God and the Pandemic*.[46] Wright's explanation of the Eliot poem relates well to the church's approach to thoughtfulness in the twenty-first century. 'Eliot had realized that all the easy comforts for which we reach when things are tough are likely to be delusions. We grab at them – and perhaps we hope that God will quickly give them to us – so that we don't have to face the darkness. So that we don't have to "watch and pray" with Jesus in Gethsemane.' The bleak world of a supposedly naïve church often presented by the new atheists is to many believers not only contrary to their own experience, but anathema to scientists who are also believers. In *Let There Be Science*, co-authored by David Hutchings and Tom McLeish, it is observed that

---

[43] McLeish, *Faith & Wisdom in Science*, p. 102.

[44] Angela Tilby, *Science and the Soul* (London, 1992); McLeish, *Faith & Wisdom in Science*, p. 8.

[45] Head, *Ian McEwan* (Manchester, 2007), p. 194.

[46] Tom Wright, *God and the Pandemic* (London, 2020), pp. 54, 66.

14   *Music and Religion in the Writings of Ian McEwan*

'public conversation and ownership can help science maintain a conscience,'[47] and that this is an important aspect of the role of the church. This point resonates with a comment in McLeish's own text where he observes that 'The themes of reconciliation, communities of shared values and a primary engagement with the world are very ancient. But at the same time they speak urgently to our present predicament of public unease with science, and in particular with its unbalanced connection to economic values and minority interests.'[48] In this respect, the church can be a watchful presence but it is also a moral and ethical presence that new atheists frequently deny. McLeish's own comments also draw on a parallel concern between the respective institutions of science and religion. Specifically, that both must adopt a thoughtful stance in a modern world. The study of this significant field of middle ground between creationism and science has taken hold in the *via media* of the Church of England, and in this respect it will be interesting to see if McEwan broaches this in future writing. As Wells notes, his 'curiosity about the world, past and present'[49] is considerable and, as observed, there is a measure of overlap in his fictional and public work.

In assessing the development of the role of the Church of England in relation to science, the following initiatives can be considered. They contextualise McEwan's writings because of the comparative sentimental and nostalgic side of the Church of England that he instead brings forward, despite his strong interest in science. McEwan's portrayal of the Church of England is unquestionably a select one, not elitist, but nonetheless charged with a particular identity.

The ecumenical programme *Equipping Christian Leadership in the Age of Science* (ECLAS) explores science from the perspective of religious believers rather than in the historical adversarial approach. It is an example of the Church of England looking out through science rather than the scientific world solely looking in. Initially established in 2015 as a research programme by Durham and York Universities with the collaboration of the Church of England, funding for the programme has recently been extended.

In 2019, many cathedrals observed the fiftieth anniversary of the Apollo 11 moon landing with exhibitions, as a continuation of the *Scientists in Congregations* programme that is part of ECLAS. In addition to this specific research programme and the writings of David Wilkinson (*God, Time and Stephen Hawking*),[50] a co-founder of the programme, the research and blog posts of McLeish (https://tcbmcleish.wordpress.com) have also shed important light on this topic. The work of the Ian Ramsey Centre for Science and Religion at Oxford University continues the legacy of Ramsey's own researches in the

---

[47] David Hutchings and Tom McLeish, *Let There Be Science* (Oxford, 2017), pp. 188–189.

[48] McLeish, *Faith & Wisdom in Science*, p. 258.

[49] Wells, *Ian McEwan*, pp. 1, 21.

[50] David Wilkinson, *God, Time and Stephen Hawking* (Oxford, 2001).

Introduction 15

field. Ramsey was a former Bishop of Durham and chairman of the BBC's Central Religious Advisory Committee. The Faraday Institute for Science and Religion at the University of Cambridge has also initiated a programme called *Churches@Faraday* that seeks to encourage congregations to include science in their regular activities. There is an interesting parallel here with McEwan's earlier published comments that 'increasingly the talk of physicists has come to sound like theology [and science] might no longer be at odds with that deep intuitive sense ... that there is a spiritual dimension to our existence'.[51]

* * *

The inclusion of the societal role of the Church of England is an important point of relevance in McEwan's writings because as Karen Armstrong noted in her TED talk, 'My Wish: The Charter for Compassion', 'religion is extremely unpopular'[52] in Britain. As McEwan commented in a letter to John Updike following Tony Blair's final Prime Minister's Questions, an 'earnest question about the relationship between faith and the state' was asked, to the response 'Well, I can't be doing with that!'[53] As the Church of England has observed declining numbers of congregants in recent years along with many other denominations, Blair's comments speak to an increasing constituency and yet McEwan, a popular author, portrays a particular image of the church, its clergy, and its hymnody, with references that extend beyond the liturgy.

McEwan's portrayal of the church as specifically Anglican can also be seen in the plays of Alan Bennett as well as the writings of C. S. Lewis, Philip Larkin, Susan Hill, and the poetry of John Betjeman among others. He successfully draws on the emotive affection that many have for the church as an institution that is a continuing presence in society and the media (television and film), and one that serves a role that extends beyond the theological or indeed temporal. His narrative in *Sweet Tooth* highlights an understanding of the peculiarities of the denomination as well as the solace that it continually provides, often without questioning the individual. This is a point often completely lost in discussion of new atheism, where succinct answers to simple questions are typical. The role of the Church of England isn't confined to theological arguments and in this respect McEwan's approach is far more nuanced than the dialogue of new atheists.

The first chapter examines the nature of doubt in British society, especially when the transient nature of contemporary politics and the church collide. In this respect, the writings of McEwan concerning his libretto for the oratorio *or*

---

[51] Ian McEwan, *or Shall we die? A Move Abroad* (London, 1989), pp. 13–14.

[52] Karen Armstrong, 'Karen Armstrong: 2008 TED Prize wish: Charter for Compassion', online at <https://www.ted.com/talks/karen_armstrong_my_wish_the_charter_for_compassion> [accessed 1 November 2020].

[53] Letter from Ian McEwan to John Updike (24 June 2007).

16   *Music and Religion in the Writings of Ian McEwan*

Shall we die? align with the questioning of Dr David Jenkins,[54] then Bishop of Durham, and a powerful critic of the government of Margaret Thatcher, as well as the philosophers Bertrand Russell[55] and Roger Scruton.[56] Each writer questions the perceptions and consequences of the role of the church that McEwan brings to the fore in his narratives. In portraying Britain in an Anglican vein, McEwan is also portraying the view and sensibility that Scruton had long subscribed to in his own writing. Specifically, that the church is inseparable from the state and therefore from the people, irrespective of their beliefs. In depicting a society through fiction with the church as an institutional presence that is somehow unavoidable, McEwan's approach is especially intriguing considering his atheist background. Why discuss the church at all and especially through a sentimental lens? This is studied in chapter 1 through an examination of McEwan's image of the church as a sustained cultural and institutional relevance.

Specificity and Nuance

Throughout this book the highly specific descriptions of McEwan allow for a consideration of him as a serious thinker and evaluator of music, the church, religion, and their respective relationships to society. As a professional musician who has also worked in the church, I have observed how precise and thus wholly plausible McEwan's language and approach can be. Specific composers and musical works are referred to along with contemporary performers. Comments on church architecture, clergy, and hymnody show a particular understanding of the inner dynamics of institutions and those who encounter them in their lives. Although McEwan is under no obligation to portray any aspect of the musical or ecclesiastical worlds to his readers, he nonetheless brings forward perceptions of very specific fields. As noted above, the sacred world is considered primarily through an Anglican lens with the notable exception of *The Children Act*, which discusses the medical plight of a Jehovah's Witness. The world of the composer is considered with references to great British composers of the past such as Ralph Vaughan Williams, and a certain scepticism towards the field of atonal music that is redolent of contemporary criticism. The world of chamber music is described with detailed references to the Wigmore Hall. These impressions coalesce in a complementary fashion and would relate to many people who value a particular Anglican identity and are educated in the world and vocabulary of classical music. But they are at some distance from the thinking of people in other denominations and at a modest variance with the direction of classical music and the church in 2023. At first, that might seem a trivial point because the narratives are fictional but the dialogue and

---

[54] David Jenkins, *God, Politics and the Future* (Wilton, 1988).

[55] Bertrand Russell, *Why I am not a Christian* (London, 1957).

[56] Scruton, *Our Church* (London, 2013); Scruton, *England: An Elegy* (London, 2006).

Introduction 17

debate that McEwan presents relate very directly to our own time because many of the discussions remain current. As the relevance of Larkin's poem 'Church Going' is a constant point of reference, and questions over the programming choices on BBC Radio 3 and the BBC Proms are unabated, McEwan highlights very specific points of institutional and personal identity. However, what McEwan also manages to achieve is a capturing of a specific sentiment that, when aligned with his personal views, is clearly a matter of conveying a sense of value towards culture more broadly. He portrays a world where classical music is related to aspiration and higher thinking and the church as an institution that is as immovable as it is set apart from many. The modern composer is seen as a figure who has a distinct role, though often misunderstood, and in the UK is challenged by the unevenness of state support. As comments by the contemporary composers Simon Bainbridge and Howard Blake further clarify in chapter 4, this is an especially accurate portrayal of the profession as seen from the inside. Similarly, to follow Florence's exploration of repertoire in *On Chesil Beach* is to follow the development of a young musician's thinking process in detail and observe a maturing self that is highly critical and deeply committed to the artistic process. McEwan's narrative extends into the psyche of the young musician and the world of emotional intensity at play in daily life. As Kiernan Ryan notes in his book, *Ian McEwan*, when discussing the response of Cathy in *The Imitation Game*, her 'aspirations have found coded expression'[57] as she seeks to perfect her performance of the Mozart *Fantasia*, K. 475. Through her engagement with Mozart's music her aspirations not only have an outlet but a degree of meaning.

Individualism and the Emotional Engagement of Music

Whether taking walking tours in the Chilterns or asking for music to be turned off in restaurants, McEwan is someone who is averse to unnecessary or seemingly irrelevant noise. The nature and value of silence is a topic that occurs in both his personal commentaries and his fiction. The existence of near-obligatory enforced noise has been a topic for many years in Britain, and there are many societies that advocate for the removal of background music in restaurants, pubs, and shopping centres. Further, musicians have long campaigned that pollution of the aural environment has stifled not only an ability to appreciate music in a manner similar to earlier generations but also the ability to remain focused for that purpose. Among the most notable critics is the organist Dame Gillian Weir, whose comments are discussed in chapter 2 in relation to McEwan's own and those of Oliver Sacks. McEwan speaks to an audience that can remember a quieter existence, where silence was opened to music rather than obligatory music replacing music of choice. He discusses this environ-

[57] Ryan, *Ian McEwan*, p. 32.

18 *Music and Religion in the Writings of Ian McEwan*

ment in a positive light, noting its appeal. The reader, whether a musician or not, is brought into a place where music is appreciated in a manner above and removed from daily trivialities. The silence of anticipation, such as the moment before a concert begins or a musical phrase enters is valued in a serious way. This approach is not presented as an elitist focus but rather as a necessary comfort of the character's life and serving a purpose akin to an unlimited conversation of choice. In *On Chesil Beach* this is seen with a measure of escapism from a personal circumstance and indeed towards a (musical) life that is comparatively unconcerned with worldly relationships. However, in *The Children Act*, the reader can observe music at a sublime, almost transcendental level, both for a judge and a sick child. In this novel, three of the great institutions of life provide the central focus in a battle between law, science, and theology. All three are presented with questions during McEwan's narrative, including the unknown answer of how a child refusing a blood transfusion will respond to each of them. Critically, through this developing story, the judge for the trial continually returns to music as a source of solace and higher thought in her own private life. When the judge visits the sick boy in hospital, she briefly sings as he plays the violin (or guitar in the film adaptation). The therapeutic nature of this sharing of mutual passions brings a discernible joy to the boy that lifts him from his immediate health concerns and becomes a source of positive remembrance later in the novel. However, it is the judge's personal relationship to the music she performs that provides her with consistency and reassurance and, like the violinist in *On Chesil Beach*, the ability to communicate as a performer on her own terms during a period when her personal life is being threatened. Across the areas of law and science and in a setting in which theological concerns are paramount for a family, music is a continuing emotional and intellectual presence.

The nature of music as a source of intellectual solace is also found in the script of *The Imitation Game*, where a decoder at Bletchley Park returns once again to practise Mozart's *Fantasia* for piano, K. 475. It is a piece she struggles to perfect but nonetheless, like a code, it presents an intellectual challenge, in this case a personal, rather than professional, one. As discussed in chapters 2 and 3, there are considerable similarities in the role music plays in *The Children Act* and *The Imitation Game*. These chapters contextualise McEwan's writings most especially with the work of Daniel J. Levitin, Adam Phillips, Oliver Sacks, Roger Scruton, and Anthony Storr in assessing how the individual responds to classical music. I also draw on the writings of Alan Bennett in two plays, *The Habit of Art* (2010) and *Allelujah!* (2018), where the discussion of music and personal response is also portrayed. Through this analysis, conclusions are drawn on the importance of pivotal musical moments in McEwan's writings as he explores the critical nature of personal sublimity achieved through music that many encounter and the overpowering response to music that he portrays as accessible rather than elitist.

McEwan's characters engaged with music are often seen as both fallible and hopeful, and yet seek beauty and recognition in their work and their devo-

Introduction 19

tion to music, most typically music without words (absolute music). As a consequence, McEwan brings the reader into the character's world of individual response to absolute music as much as he describes the nature and value of artistic solitude. The value of music as a complementary presence to silence is portrayed not as the source of comfort that is popularly referred to, but as a known presence to artists that provides both an assurance as well as a response that can be emotionally overpowering or near transcendental. It is perhaps the intangible and personal nature of the response to music that makes challenges to the presence and relative accessibility of the arts in contemporary society especially important. For many, the 2020 pandemic signified an immeasurable loss to an emotional world. A world without live performance and immediate response to and from those around you. Susan Hill's comments[58] on trying to imagine the famous English cathedral cities without their cathedrals is apposite in this respect given the international fame of several of their choirs and the comfort many draw from attending services, whether regularly or as a visitor. The cathedrals are part of the greater cultural landscape, and at a basic level there is an expectation that they will always be present. The knowledge that they are *there.*

The topic of emotional response also relates to the number of references to pieces of instrumental or chamber music in McEwan's work and only rarely to opera or symphonic works. The appeal of the smaller ensemble or solo artist rests with the intimacy that he most values in his own musical preferences and which is found in a parallel form in the intricacy of relationships within the novels. These relationships are especially highlighted in *On Chesil Beach* where, beyond the central remembrance of an unconsummated wedding night, there is the development of the principal female character as a violinist leading a string quartet. Ultimately the reader is left with little doubt that her role as a musician allows her a reliable intimacy with musical friends that can remain unspoken. The dialogue is instead provided by the language of the music they perform. Near the end of her studies she decides which quartets she will perform and at what juncture in her life she will be mature enough to appreciate them. However, McEwan's portrayal of her as a musician does not focus solely on the performance aspect of her life but on her ability and that of the members of her quartet to embrace a musical dialogue that they can aspire to. It is this element that she endeavours to explain to her first husband. Although the playing may be virtuosic and the career of the quartet a great success, it is the reverence towards the music that brings an uncompromising approach from her. In this sense, McEwan portrays the artist as a custodian of purity with a higher calling.

---

[58] Susan Hill, 'At the still point of the turning world', in Stephen Platten and Christopher Lewis (eds), *Flagships of the Spirit – Cathedrals in Society* (London, 1998), p. 8.

The Composer in British Society

The final chapter examines the perception of the composer in British society. McEwan has many friends who perform classical music on the international stage and understands the subtleties and concerns of the music profession. His portrayal of an egomaniacal conductor and composer in his opera libretto *For You* will be a familiar description to any reader of Norman Lebrecht's well-known analysis of the professional classical music world, *The Maestro Myth*.[59] McEwan portrays a musician (Charles Frieth, *For You*) as a figure who is both morally and ethically flawed and comically irascible, driven by a narcissism that is apparent to everyone except himself. It is an image that was laid bare in comic fashion with Danny Kaye's performance conducting the New York Philharmonic in 1981 in a televised performance of the *Triumphal March* from Verdi's *Aida*. Facing the audience rather than the orchestra, he offered them an impression of what the orchestra usually sees or interprets from the conductor scowling at a trumpeter to mouthing 'I love you' to another member of the orchestra. The extremes of emotion are as believable as they are concerning, while the conductor manipulates one circumstance after another. The depiction is satirical but believable and demonstrates an inner knowledge of the field that is no less exacting than McEwan's enquiries into scientific matters.

There is a notable contrast to this characterization with the composer Clive Linley, in *Amsterdam*, who enters into a joint suicide pact with an old friend and has begun to doubt whether he might be compromising his own reputation for a final moment of fame and glory. Both narratives are tinged with the sadness of old age and regret, but each portrays a profession that is sometimes blissfully removed from quotidian concerns. The nature of soul searching that both texts capture is also found in Alan Bennett's play *The Habit of Art*, that centres around fictional conversations between Benjamin Britten and W. H. Auden. A comparative analysis draws on the similar presentations of the artist as both a figure of seriousness and comedy. McEwan's portrayal of an organist in *Atonement* as a 'jittery looking man ... playing for his own pleasure'[60] will similarly strike a familiar chord with readers who are knowledgeable of the often-solitary profession of the church organist.

This chapter further contextualises the research of Robert Hewison and Barry Turner with the writings of McEwan in examining how British culture has evolved in the second half of the twentieth century and early twenty-first century, with the resulting legacy on the artistic community. Turner's research in *Beacon for Change*[61] identifies both the great strengths of British artistic ingenuity and the formidable challenges in sustaining any lasting artistic legacy

---

[59] Norman Lebrecht, *The Maestro Myth* (London, 1991).

[60] Ian McEwan, *Atonement* (London, 2001), pp. 327–328.

[61] Turner, *Beacon for Change*.

beyond a generation. Hewison's *Cultural Capital* [62] reinforces the problematic balance between the government and the artistic world in a country where support for the arts is necessary but inconsistently delivered. In the context of this chapter, the topics of the earlier chapters are aligned with an analysis of how the necessary pragmatic nature of the music profession has collided with the world of politics and public expectation, most especially as a result of successive cuts to arts funding since the 1980s. However, it also demonstrates the nature of a profession that remains respected around the world. These points and the allied steadfastness and commitment of musicians across several generations are portrayed in McEwan's narratives with concisely argued points that touch on critical areas of concern to musicians. He also once again raises questions for the reader about the value of culture in society at large.

The many contrasting, though believable, figures in McEwan's narratives allow readers and scholars to consider the personal and emotional aspect of the musician to be seen through a multidimensional lens that has not been encountered elsewhere in twentieth-century British literature to the same degree. McEwan's ability to intuit sentiments that easily resonate with musicians places his contribution to the field of music and literature studies in a singular position among living writers discussing classical music in Britain. As someone who freely expresses his deep interest in the news, current politics, world events, and the arts, these narratives put forward definable circumstances that, though fictional, easily transfer for the musician from fiction to credibility within an entirely plausible narrative framework.

Summary

This book examines McEwan's narratives from the professional perspective of the fields he discusses in his novels and libretti with specific contextualisation of individual references. Singular statements often demonstrate multiple layers of understanding and shed light on McEwan as an enquiring and persuasive voice in the literary perception of British culture.

McEwan's writings illustrate a landscape of classical music, the church, religion, and the composer in society within Britain. This study will provoke questions for those who encounter these areas for the first time in his writings and provide a place of sustained enquiry for those who have experienced these fields firsthand, whether as listeners, performers, congregants, audience members or scholars across literary, musical or ecclesiastical fields. The intended readership for this book extends beyond McEwan studies and includes readers studying the church and classical music in contemporary literature.

---

[62] Hewison, *Cultural Capital.*

1

THE QUESTION OF RELIGION: AN ATHEIST'S PORTRAYAL OF THE CHURCH OF ENGLAND

An Understanding of Established Doubt

The relationship between the Church of England, the state and the public in Great Britain is as intricately woven as it is expected and, in many instances, presumed and taken for granted. Although McEwan is a professed and well-known atheist, his narratives and public comments on religion not only capture the nuances of life in the Church of England but align with the inquiring and questioning of many who would consider themselves members of the Established Church. This measure of perceptive comprehension has a special resonance because of the understanding that he demonstrates between the role of the church, its relationship to the larger Establishment and the public perception of these relationships. This chapter begins by examining the nature of doubt and scepticism in perceptions of the Church of England and demonstrates how McEwan's depiction of the church, its clergy, and its hymnody is often aligned with other writers. Critically, there is a larger question of how an atheist writer sees and portrays the Church of England and whether the doubt he expresses in fiction and in public commentaries is in fact part of the very nature of Anglicanism. In this respect, the 'What if?'[1] aspect of McEwan's writings that Richard Bradford notes is pervasive throughout McEwan's texts is found here in multiple instances.

McEwan's ability to capture the public perception of the Church of England places him alongside other prominent twentieth-century writers including Alan Bennett, John Betjeman, and Philip Larkin, who similarly saw the church as part of British identity that could potentially transcend or surpass the temporal theological debates that govern its public character. His writings dwell on the cultural and societal image of the Church of England as a presence within British society, whether in a nostalgic sense or with an awareness of current thought and writings. In this sense, McEwan's exacting perception and portrayal of the church relates no less specifically to his narratives than to the many scientific researches he has undertaken before several novels. Each

---

[1]   Richard Bradford, *The Novel Now* (Oxford, 2007), p. 23.

24   *Music and Religion in the Writings of Ian McEwan*

can resonate with an easy familiarity to the specialist reader, while presenting a larger narrative to the reading public that frequently depicts the church as a societal fixture. As McEwan is an atheist this is notable because although he doubts the role of religion in his public writings, he also captures the relative romanticism of an institution intentionally set apart in his fictional texts. It is the necessary aspect of being set apart that Norman Taylor criticized when he remarked that the modern liturgy of some churches means that 'today's clergyman often makes up his own special "hymn sandwich," and offers no further sustenance in the village church on the Lord's Day'.[2]

Part of McEwan's upbringing included membership of the Boy Scouts and he recalls the 'solemnity' of the experience of carrying a flag to garrison church events which his family was expected to attend.[3] Roger Scruton, born five years before McEwan, noted that his father had raised him in the Old Labour doctrine whereby England was 'in the hands of an unscrupulous upper class, which owned the factories, controlled the government, monopolized the judiciary and exploited the workers. This aristocracy was maintained by an education system designed to perpetuate social inequality, and by an Anglican Church which offered social promotion to the conformists and the snobs'.[4] The solemnity, routine, and measured conformity of McEwan, with attendance at church events and the singing of hymn texts that he did not believe in, draws on a similar perception of religion to Scruton in that it is an experience set apart.

The solemnity of the encounter also relates to the tenor of the texts employed in the 1662 Book of Common Prayer that is used in the services of evensong, which McEwan refers to in *Machines Like Me*.[5] As Scruton notes, the English invented a 'sacred language that retained the ancestral tone of Latin, while being the voice of the English people as they dialogued with God',[6] much as the sound of an organist in an English church improvising could be akin to the 'the Holy Ghost mumbling in an English accent'.[7] The use of a hymn in *or Shall we die?* denotes a seriousness of purpose with a typically uniform metre and measured performance style that can be likened to the familiar rhythms of the Prayer Book. Both are easily accessible to the churchgoer, even if in McEwan's case the experience of personal hymn singing did not extend consistently beyond childhood.

In Arthur Bradley's and Andrew Tate's *The New Atheist Novel: Fiction, Philosophy, and Polemic after 9/11*,[8] it is noted how Christopher Hitchens dedi-

---

[2]   Norman Taylor, *For Services Rendered* (Cambridge, 1993), p. 183.

[3]   Richard Dawkins and Ian McEwan interview (2 February, 2009), online at <https://www.youtube.com/watch?v=o7LjriWFAEs> [accessed 1 December 2022].

[4]   Roger Scruton, *England: An Elegy* (London, 2006), p. 25.

[5]   Ian McEwan, *Machines Like Me* (New York, 2018), p. 243.

[6]   Ibid., pp. 103–104.

[7]   Roger Scruton, *Our Church* (London, 2013) p. 110.

[8]   Arthur Bradley and Andrew Tate, *The New Atheist Novel: Fiction, Philosophy, and*

An Atheist's Portrayal of the Church of England 25

cated his book, *God is Not Great: The Case Against Religion* to McEwan, and that to Hitchens McEwan 'shows an extraordinary ability to elucidate the numinous without conceding anything to the supernatural'.[9] Bradley and Tate argue that McEwan is the 'leading exponent of the New Atheist Novel' and after 9/11 has become 'increasingly antagonistic towards militant religion'. But they also suggest that 'McEwan's fiction makes clear that this critique of the solipsism of religious extremism is also a defence of the morality of the novelistic imagination' and that the novel is a place 'where all of us like to imagine what it is like to be someone else'.[10] This latter aspect in fiction is unsurprising but it is especially interesting when advanced with their subsequent argument that 'as with Amis and Rushdie, the critique of religion – whether aesthetic, ethical or political – almost always turns out to be itself religiously inspired and indebted to a long-standing tradition of Christian apocalypticism'.[11] However, I do not see Amis and Rushdie advancing a similar agenda to McEwan, either in their public lives or in their writing, whether fiction or opinion pieces in the press. Rushdie's experience with religion is well known but his perception of the Church of England (discussed later in this chapter) has an air of affection for its traditions, not least in relation to the singing of hymns, arguably because it is connected to a particular image of England. But I would agree with Bradley and Tate that McEwan's writing represents a 'fragile, sceptical and always questioning profession of faith [and the] possibility of secular transcendence'. They suggest that in McEwan's writings 'what fills the place of belief in God [is a] belief in family, love, scientific progress, and most importantly, art'.[12] It is the questioning here that is important to consider because it pervades all of McEwan's writings. The church, like the concert hall, is not part of everyday life for most people, but McEwan portrays them with an effortless approach and certain appeal, and so the reader has the opportunity to consider them even if only as parts of a remote 'other' world in their perception. This is a key point because although McEwan expresses strong public views on the larger role of religion, he also describes the world of the Church of England with an affectionate tongue-in-cheek cynicism and wry amusement that can be seen in many other British writers, as will be discussed later. In this vein, there is a similarity to his own description of Larkin as 'an atheist who also knew the moment and the nature of transcendence'.[13]

   Polemic after 9/11 (London, 2010), p. 10.

[9]   Christopher Hitchens, *God is Not Great: The Case Against Religion* (London, 2007), p. 286.

[10] Bradley and Tate, *The New Atheist Novel: Fiction, Philosophy, and Polemic after 9/11*, p. 12.

[11] Ibid., p. 107.

[12] Ibid., p. 16.

[13] Ian McEwan, *Science* (London, 2019).

26 *Music and Religion in the Writings of Ian McEwan*

Dominic Head writes that McEwan is 'possibly the most significant of a number of writers, who had resuscitated the link between morality and the novel for a whole generation, in ways that befit the historical pressures of the time. Implicit in such a claim is the assumption that the novel is a significant form of cultural expression – by which I mean a special vehicle for an oblique form of social and cultural work – that is worthy of detailed study and public appreciation' but further that 'it is the bridge between notionally different readerships [popular and critical] that indicates McEwan's importance as a writer that has helped reinvigorate thinking about the novel'[14] and arguably topics contained within his texts.

In my 2018 interview with McEwan, he stated how he had lost interest in religion around the age of eleven and felt hymns to be dishonest, even though he had a fondness for particular tunes.[15] However, the fundamental contradiction of religion for McEwan was addressed by him in relation to personal morals in an interview with Richard Dawkins.

> I think we are instinctively moral beings ... even as an atheist I accept that it was quite a remarkable step to build a religion around the idea of love and turning the other cheek but I certainly didn't think that it needs a God to ordain our moral priorities for us.[16]

The comments stress both an acknowledgement of the higher calling of religion as well as McEwan's personal opinion, based on his own approach towards individual morality. But this does not subtract from his understanding of the sustaining perception of the church as an institution in England. It also doesn't extend to scepticism about the possibility of worthy church leaders who are themselves gifted and well-educated. Later in the interview with Dawkins he refers to a dinner with the Archbishop of Canterbury, Rowan Williams, and the comments stress McEwan's unease with the ineffable. But they also suggest a distancing between the nature of religion and an enlightened spirit of debate, which in fact most clergy are only too happy to engage in.

> He's a man of exceptional intelligence and given all the usual constraints of ever raising the matter of someone's faith ... it was a great relief to go nowhere near religion at all and instead we talked about poetry about which he knows quite a lot and takes a great deal of pleasure from.[17]

The observation that it was a 'great relief' to avoid a discussion of religion resonates with the difficult position held by any senior cleric and especially one as visible as an archbishop. When Justin Welby became Archbishop of Canterbury in 2013 and started to express views on poverty, inequality, social justice,

---

[14] Dominic Head, *Ian McEwan* (Manchester, 2007), pp. 1, 2.

[15] Iain Quinn, 'Interview with Ian McEwan' (2018).

[16] Richard Dawkins and Ian McEwan interview.

[17] Ibid.

An Atheist's Portrayal of the Church of England   27

high-interest lending, and the use of food banks in Britain, he found himself having to state that he was not 'too political',[18] even though the work of the church is generally acknowledged to be at least partially focused on helping the poor. In this sense, church leaders could be considered as more aligned to the sovereign than to the political world, although being removed from its role as a voice for the voiceless, the church has often run aground on the recurring concern about 'relevance in society' that drew easy jokes in a dialogue (below) in *Yes, Prime Minister*. The challenge for the archbishop is summarized by his predecessor, Rowan Williams:

> Every archbishop, whether he likes it or not, faces the expectation that he will be some kind of commentator on the public issues of the day. He is, if course, doomed to fail in the eyes of most people. If he restricts himself to reflections heavily based on the Bible or tradition, what he says will be greeted as platitudinous or irrelevant. If he ventures into more obviously secular territory, he will be told that he has no particular experience in sociology or economics or international affairs that would justify giving him a hearing. Reference to popular culture prompts disapproving noises of 'dumbing down'; anything that looks like close academic analysis is of course incomprehensible and self-indulgent elitism.[19]

However, there is a robustness to the criticism of faith in Britain. As McEwan notes, it was something that Voltaire found appealing because there was a certain 'absence of religious absolutism and divine right'[20] (McEwan). Voltaire attended Isaac Newton's funeral and was astonished that a scientist could be buried in Westminster Abbey.[21] In a more recent interview with *The Guardian*, McEwan endeavoured to contextualise a societal sentiment about Christian religion in Britain in the second half of the twentieth century. He maintained that (for those who had grown up in a primarily moderate Anglican environment) the end of the last century appeared to have signalled a changing of national identity and this in turn had a bearing on the practice of religion with particular concern to the rise of fundamentalism in a post 9/11 culture:

> Jonathan Freedland: Simon Schama said the other day that it is [*sic*] one of the great surprises of the twenty-first century is the persistence of religion. He referred to his own grammar school teacher who in what he describes as the idealistic time of postwar Britain said 'you know the one thing we can take for granted is that by the end of the twentieth-century nationalism and

---

[18] Justin Welby, 'Archbishop of Canterbury: I am not too political', *The Guardian*, online at <https://www.theguardian.com/uk-news/2018/dec/02/archbishop-of-canterbury-i-am-not-too-political-justin-welby> (2 December 2018) [accessed 17 December 2020].

[19] Rowan Williams, *Faith in the Public Square* (London, 2015), p. 1.

[20] McEwan, *Science*, p. 58.

[21] Ibid.

religion will be almost gone, they will have receded, and here we are in 2014 where there are these domestic cases [of terrorism] which turn on religion … are you yourself surprised by what I've called the persistence of religion?

Ian McEwan: I wouldn't use the word persistence [about religion]. It was like a sort of recrudescence. I think we were all celebrating the end of the Cold War and we didn't notice actually there was something else beginning to form around us.[22]

The nature of public discussion, like the public interview above, and the culture of doubt and questioning has a specifically British identity and McEwan's fictional portrayals adhere to common popular perceptions that are further reinforced by the media. Moreover, there is strong historical precedent for the nature of the British as a strong, questioning people and to consider McEwan's place as a commentator and indeed thinker about religion, historical context is critical.

With the English Reformation and in particular the Act of Supremacy of 1534, Henry VIII not only asserted authority over the church in England but also largely removed the senior clergy from positions of ultimate power. With the argument that Rome was trying to exert influence on a future English succession, Henry had determined that the church post-Reformation would always be part of the aristocratic vein of society but in a tempered fashion. However, the degree of self-confidence that Henry exerted was nothing new. As Diarmaid MacCulloch has noted, the idea of England as an exceptional country with a chosen people can be traced back as far as Bede and his *Ecclesiastical History of the English People* (AD 731). But it is also, as Rowan Williams observes, a country in which Bede repeatedly complained about the 'reluctance of British Christians to preach the gospel to their neighbours'.[23] MacCulloch's suggestion that religion had fundamentally shaped the English soul is drawn from his interpretation of the history of the church in England. The idea that England was a country set apart from others was bolstered by Pope Gregory's decision to send Augustine on a mission to England (rather than first to other countries) and Bede's description of the then-diverse English people as one large community (gens Anglorum). To Williams, the church offered 'an intelligible common identity to groups that might otherwise be at war'.[24] Bede had inspired Alfred the Great and the references in the Palace of Westminster to the 'Heart of the Queen [being] in the hand of God' together with coronation anointments have sustained this image. Henry had prayed to God for a son

---

[22] 'Ian McEwan on Religion in the Twenty-First Century', *The Guardian*, 2014, online at <https://www.youtube.com/watch?v=L-qNht38CeE> [accessed 17 December 2020].

[23] Rowan Williams and Benedicta Ward SLG, *Bede's Ecclesiastical History of the English People* (London, 2012), p. 3.

[24] Ibid., p. 26.

An Atheist's Portrayal of the Church of England 29

and saw the birth of Edward as a confirmation of his decision to separate from Rome.[25] This was further reinforced after the Restoration with new boundaries concerning dogmatic faith, and England ultimately became a country where certain beliefs were considered essential to an understanding of Christian faith and others were left to science. Although Henry had challenged the authority of Rome, this did not mean that the English Reformation had any sympathy for doubters but rather argued for a return to earlier practices.

The return of Charles II to Britain (1660) and the Restoration included visible signs of loyalty to the Crown with the display of the royal coat of arms in paintings that appeared inside churches. These were often painted by a local artist and thus not always especially refined. The use of the lion and unicorn in images was often unusually virile, a point of artistic interpretation in heraldic works known as being pizzled. This prominent depiction of genitalia did not seem to overly concern eighteenth-century churchgoers, although the Victorians did not share the same view. However, the broad perception of the church related to society was allied to the notion that the church was and is in some sense the property of the people, and that it was better to have a sovereign as a leader than a foreign pope. Most obviously it showed that the people and the church were as one, albeit with vague lines of influence in both directions. The self-confidence that had begun with Bede considering the English as a chosen people and a connection to Israel and the Old Testament would find a musical alliance in the oratorios of Handel and later Mendelssohn which, sung in English, further reinforced the idea that the English language also had its own supremacy.

The degree of resolve to hold religion through the church in some sense accountable to public will is part of a long-developing trend. If a member of the Church of England promoted critical views of the denomination, it would not be perceived as unusual or necessarily unwelcome in the twentieth or twenty-first centuries. Questioning is part of the culture, even if the answers are not always welcome. That degree of easy access within a society of relatively free speech enables McEwan to move in and out of discussions about the church within his fiction while being critical of the larger role of religion in his media interviews and public commentaries. It is part of a larger sense of Enlightenment thinking that enables McEwan to engage or disengage with religion without issue because it is a similar degree of unaffected public response that hinders the influence of the Archbishop of Canterbury, as noted above.

The architects of churches of the eighteenth century, especially Christopher Wren and his assistant Nicholas Hawksmoor, employed light so effectively that an openness was blazingly and indeed beautifully shining an illumination onto religious practice that can still be witnessed by observing the buildings today.

---

[25] Diarmaid MacCulloch, *How God Made the English* (TV programme), BBC Television (2012), online at <https://www.youtube.com/watch?v=pHALnYbGS1o> [accessed 17 December 2020].

30   *Music and Religion in the Writings of Ian McEwan*

It was a sustained and, to some remains, a continuing Enlightenment. Wren's small masterpiece of St Stephen Walbrook in the City of London is a supreme example, with the use of light and a self-supporting dome itself something of a worldly leap of faith, whereas Hawksmoor's St George's Bloomsbury includes not only Near Eastern influences but the use of a statue of George I atop the steeple.[26] The architecture fosters the sense of awe that in *Machines Like Me* McEwan notes is absent in Holy Trinity, Clapham.[27] (The reference to this particular church is notable because of its association with the nineteenth-century Clapham Sect of evangelicals which E. M. Forster refers to in his discussion of his great-great-grandfather, Henry Thornton.) Dustin Friedman argues that eighteenth-century evangelicalism associated with Holy Trinity 'set in motion a historical trajectory that led secular modern intellectuals to retreat into their own privacy, a position exemplified by Forster's contemporaries in the Bloomsbury Group' with *A Passage to India* demonstrating a 'politically relevant alternative' to both Clapham's 'rationalized religiosity' and Bloomsbury's 'secular insularity'.[28] As such, McEwan's portrayal of both this church and the larger Church of England is further expanded with the impression of the church as a place of reference for ongoing debate even if, as a physical structure, a particular edifice might be unimpressive.

Rather, McEwan's perception of a church that can inspire an individual is enveloped in an image of a building that is more than simply functional. As such, like Betjeman and indeed Larkin, the furnishings really do matter to McEwan and consequently the church is portrayed as more than an institution that can be challenged on theological grounds but rather as one serving a distinctive cultural role. Indeed, he characterizes a confidence in the British identity that extends beyond theology and towards seeing the Established Church in a largely accepted cultural vein. The Church of England is increasingly uninterested in a structured identity but increasingly focuses on an expression of openness. As Susan Hill observed, 'Dogmatism does not seem a very useful approach, or one that appeals much to our way of thinking ... we are born to ask questions'.[29] Larkin's poem, 'Church Going', speaks to the questioning nature of identity in relation to British churches because the physical buildings are admired for their architecture even though many are suspicious about the sacraments that take place within them.

---

[26]   These points are discussed in the fifth part of Richard Taylor's six-part BBC series *Churches: How to Read Them* (2010), which examines the history of church architecture.

[27]   McEwan, *Machines Like Me*, p. 45.

[28]   Dustin Friedman, 'E.M. Forster, the Clapham Sect, and the Secular Public Sphere', *Journal of Modern Literature*, 39:1 2015, 19–37.

[29]   Susan Hill, 'At the still point of the turning world', in Stephen Platten and Christopher Lewis (eds), *Flagships of the Spirit – Cathedrals in Society* (London, 1998), p. 9.

An Atheist's Portrayal of the Church of England 31

McEwan's approach towards the church and indeed the clergy is one of otherness but, like Larkin, he discerns the nature of physical space that is sacred being different from the normal world outside the church. A place that is 'too reasonable' does not immediately stretch the imagination or capture the mystique of a sacred space, but the furnishings help to embody the sense of 'awe'.

> Once I am sure there's nothing going on
> I step inside letting the door thud shut.
> Another church: matting seats and stone
> and little books; sprawlings of flowers cut
> For Sunday brownish now; some brass and stuff
> Up at the holy end; the small neat organ;
> And a tense musty unignorable silence
> Brewed God knows how long. Hatless I take off
> My cycle-clips in awkward reverence.[30]

The complete Larkin poem is laced with a notable curiosity about the church and the goings-on therein but concludes with a stanza beginning 'A serious house on serious earth it is'. Although Larkin clearly knows the names of all of the church furnishings there is also the 'tense' silence and the 'awkward' reverence that highlight both an atheist discomfort and, perhaps equally, a nonconformist or at least a non-Establishment unease. In a similar fashion to McEwan, there is a clear understanding of what the church seeks to achieve through its physical presence in communities, but it is met with suspicion and the 'unignorable silence'.[31] It can be argued that the 'unignorable' aspect is what might catapult the role of the church into the novels of any writer. The buildings, like the popular hymns, are part of the larger cultural identity for many.

The postwar culture also ushered in another era for the church. McEwan's comments to Dawkins (above) speak to his suspicion about religion in general, and this was an increasingly prevalent sentiment in Britain after two world wars. However, the question of the contemporary ethical and moral roles of the church is brought to the fore, most especially in *The Children Act*, where the central narrative concerns whether a young Jehovah's Witness is able to receive blood for a necessary operation, and in *or Shall we die?*, which includes a preface and a hymn in a Victorian style, both of which specifically criticize the role of clergy. Although during the war and postwar (World War II) years there was an initial increase in church attendance and groups that had a tangential connection to the church, like choral societies and the scouts, thrived, the identity of the church began to shift towards a new age. The building of the new cathedral in Coventry in 1951 after the old cathedral was almost completely destroyed by bombing and ultimately the reimagining of Britain through the Festival of Britain (1951) set in motion a relative enlightenment

---

[30] Philip Larkin, *Collected Poems* (London, 1988), p. 97.
[31] Ibid.

32   *Music and Religion in the Writings of Ian McEwan*

through recovery in a postcolonial age. The final damning of an empire spirit came only six years later with the Suez crisis (1957). This gradual age of transformation would ultimately lead a comparatively socially liberated Western Europe of the 1970s, and one of wealth for some in the 1980s, to a continual questioning of the role of the Anglican church that, prior to the coronation of 1953, was still heavily rooted in the previous century in terms of customs and hierarchical structure and influence. As the importance of and availability of radio and television continued to expand, so too did the multiple opportunities for commentaries to be heard. What followed was an increasingly passive and uninterested public approach to church attendance and personal religious association, which resulted in a consistent decline in the number of weekly congregants. As McEwan writes in the preface to *or Shall we die?*, 'the average Briton rarely sees the inside of a church, and is so far removed from matters of that sort that he hardly bothers to call himself an atheist'.[32] However, as the Church of England is embedded in the heart of Establishment culture, not least with the sovereign as Defender of Faith, the presence of the Lords Spiritual in the House of Lords, and the recommendation of individuals to the episcopacy from the Prime Minister's office, the public presence and relative influence of the Church of England unavoidably extends beyond the number of parishioners in pews. It is this cultural awareness, especially in *Sweet Tooth, or Shall we die?*, and briefly in *The Children Act* that McEwan portrays as readily as he does concerts at the Wigmore Hall in *On Chesil Beach*. This gives readers an impression of a society in which various cultural elements are side by side and equally relevant to characters and the larger narrative. Indeed, in considering the broad church aspects of the Church of England, it can be suggested that McEwan portrays an impression of a perceived common culture that many of his particular characters experience. In a musical vein, the role of classical music appears as a positive force within the lives of those who are not themselves professional musicians and as a source of betterment and comfort.

The common answer given by many people in Great Britain when asked about their faith, 'I'm C of E' (Church of England), does not indicate regular or even occasional attendance of a church, nor does it necessarily indicate a strong adherence to the teachings of the church. This has enabled several writers to discuss the church without discussing theology or even current debates within the church. It is this casual and convenient approach to religion that Muriel Spark alluded to in *The Bachelors*. When speaking of a Roman Catholic priest who was previously an Anglican she writes, 'He was brought up in a big rectory and he broke away from the Church of England. It's true you don't have to go to church to believe in God. I agree with that. Father Socket knows psychology'.[33] Doubt of Christianity in general also plays a role in Graham Greene's *Stamboul Train*, where Mr Opie comments that 'the patient leaves the psy-

---

[32]   Ian McEwan, *Preface. A Move Abroad* (London, 1989), p. xvi.

[33]   Muriel Spark, *The Bachelors* (Edinburgh, 2015), p. 127.

An Atheist's Portrayal of the Church of England   33

cho-analyst with the power, as well as the intention, of making a fresh start ... from that point of view ... confession to the psycho-analyst seems to be more efficacious than confession to the priest.'[34] In both cases, there is an interest in enlightened thinking and religion plays only one part in the tapestry of life irrespective of the personal beliefs of the authors. In this respect, McEwan's comments on the perceived moral weakness of clergy in *or Shall we die?* – 'there never seems to be a priest lacking to bless the executioners'[35] – draws on a perceived vacuity or spinelessness on the part of clergy that derives from a ministry that, to him, should have a higher standard and not simply be one of the intellectual options for a worthy life. Spark and Greene both offer a cynical view in these specific narratives whereas McEwan's approach is both sarcastic and critical. Similar sentiments about the seemingly apathetic approach of parishioners are described in Alan Bennett's *The Laying on of Hands*. The cultural aspect that McEwan mocks is further extended by Bennett who infers that attending church is effectively like joining another club of affinity. Like McEwan's overarching doubt in priests, Bennett questions the nature of attending a church when personal belief isn't certain.

> It's true that looking down from the pulpit on his flock Sunday by Sunday Father Jolliffe sometimes felt that God was not much more than a pastime; that these were churchgoers as some people were pigeon-fanciers or collectors of stamps, gentle, mildly eccentric and hanging on to the end of something. Still, on a scale ranging from fervent piety to mere respectability these regular worshippers were at least like-minded: they had come together to worship God and even with their varying degrees of certainty that there was a God to worship the awkward question of belief seldom arose.[36]

The relative reticence of some clergy with regard to evangelism is similarly found in the description of Serena Frome's father, an Anglican bishop, in *Sweet Tooth*[37] who appears to move from his home in the cathedral precinct to the cathedral and back again. At no point in the novel is the bishop described as having engaged in any sort of outreach into the community, an observation that is also absent in McEwan's other references about the church. The question here is not whether this is a believable depiction of every member of the clergy, as obviously it is not, but whether Bennett and McEwan are portraying a character that is beyond belief or plausible to a large popular readership. A further similarity between Bennett and McEwan can be seen in hymn references, as noted later.

* * *

---

[34]   Graham Greene, *Stamboul Train* (London, 1978), pp. 118–119.

[35]   McEwan, *or Shall we die? A Move Abroad*, pp. 10–11.

[36]   Alan Bennett, *The Laying on of Hands* (London, 2018), p. 25.

[37]   Ian McEwan, *Sweet Tooth* (New York, 2012), pp. 2–3.

34   *Music and Religion in the Writings of Ian McEwan*

McEwan's questioning of the role and responsibility of religion presents the reader of *The Children Act* with the powerful dilemma of whether a terminally ill boy should accept a transfusion and break from the teachings of his faith. However, the challenge to the reader is not just to question the deliberations of the doubter of a specific faith but of faith in general. The central argument of whether faith can control a person's decisions could equally be discussed in relation to abortion or euthanasia for the chronically ill who are in pain. Provocatively, McEwan brings the role of religion out of the smaller community of Jehovah's Witnesses and immediately to the fore in a question that strikes at the heart of the Establishment. Further, the question is asked in the privileged environment of a courtroom. As a barrister probes a (medical) consultant with knowledge of the boy's health concerning the integrity of the minor's wishes, the consultant responds:

> 'His views are those of his parents. They're not his own. His objection to being transfused is based on the doctrines of a religious cult for which he may well become a pointless martyr.'
>
> 'Cult is a strong word. Mr Carter,' Grieve said quietly. 'Do you yourself have any religious belief?'
>
> 'I'm an Anglican.'
>
> 'Is the Church of England a cult?'
>
> [The judge] looked up from her note-taking.[38]

This exchange serves multiple ends and bluntly highlights McEwan's larger scepticism through several complementary arguments. He begins with the assertion that religious views are largely handed down from one generation to another. That in turn suggests an immediate weakness from an atheist's perspective because it infers a lack of individual thought or an absence of parental trust. He then infers that martyrdom is 'pointless' whereas that is not the belief of those who choose to martyr themselves or those who have been martyred without a choice. In the same sentence religion and futility are side by side. In questioning whether the consultant has a religious belief, McEwan raises the spectre of a centuries-old understanding that those who work in medicine are typically nonbelievers. This in turn casts into doubt the measure of sincerity a medical professional can have in a chosen faith, thus undermining any answer that is affirmative. When the consultant responds that he is an Anglican, McEwan's barrister does not ask the most obvious question 'how often do you attend church?' or 'what is the name of your parish?' but instead asks 'Is the Church of England a cult?'. Were the consultant to answer 'yes' he would be unavoidably stating, among other things, that the sovereign, as supreme governor of the Church of England, was head of a religious cult. As such, although a critical

---

[38]   Ian McEwan, *The Children Act* (London, 2014), pp. 68–69.

focus of faith in *The Children Act* studies the beliefs of Jehovah's Witnesses, the reader is obliged to consider the possibility that the Established Church could be equally critiqued, censured in public and, most critically, doubted. Further, this is not an exchange in a pub or a park but a courtroom, where facts are expected to prevail. Doubt is brought to the fore.

In *Lessons* this censure is taken to another level and, again, an end-of-life decision is being considered and with specific reference to the Church of England.

> The Church worthies in the Lords, the archbishops, fought it – the possibility of choosing the moment of your own death. They hid their theological objections behind lurid tales of greedy relatives wanting to get their hands on the money. The divines were beneath contempt.[39]

Therefore, the question in examining McEwan's approach to religion and specifically the church is not primarily an issue of his own belief or unbelief but the portrayal and assessment of these questions in his writings. Further, the commentaries and narratives about the life of the church (especially in *Sweet Tooth*) developed in McEwan's writings and commentaries raise the critical question of whether his own voice as a popular writer intuiting popular sentiment is resonant throughout much of British society at the contemporary point of his writing because of not only its plausibility but its believability. To what extent can it be said that Britain is a sceptical or doubting culture or from an atheist's perspective simply an enlightened sceptred isle that has consistently challenged authority since Magna Carta? Is McEwan part of the popularity of doubt that leads celebrities to describe themselves as atheists, as if that is an essential characteristic of their lives to know? Debates on atheism are typically polarized and change few minds as a result, with the supporters of atheism and religion little interested in crossing to the other side. There is also historical context for members of society relating in a popular vein to the church irrespective of whether they attend services themselves. It can be argued that as much as Trollope's stories easily sit alongside the discussions in nineteenth-century church presses and pamphlets – *The Parish Choir*[40] journal being an obvious example – and in turn are easily relatable to a contemporary reader, the commentaries of McEwan, Bennett, Betjeman or Larkin adeptly assess a public impression of the church in modern Britain. In this respect, McEwan's grasp of the subtleties of argument between politics, religion, and society and the specific observations he has may provoke the reader to ask whether the culture of Christianity in England is unavoidable, even to an atheist, because it is also almost entirely inescapable.

The English philosopher and public commentator Roger Scruton offered a concise analysis of the Anglican church in England in the second half of the twentieth century:

---

[39] Ian McEwan, *Lessons* (New York, 2022), p. 379.

[40] A journal published by the *Society for Promoting Church Music* from 1846 to 1851.

English churches tell of people who for several centuries have preferred seriousness to doctrine, and routine to enthusiasm – people who hope for immortality but do not really expect it, except as a piece of English earth. The walls are covered with discreet memorials, placing the dead at the same convenient distance that they occupied when living. The pews are hard, uncomfortable, designed not for lingering and listening but for moments of penitence and doubt. The architecture is noble but bare and quiet, without the lofty aspirations of the French Gothic, or the devotional intimacy of an Italian chapel. More prominent than the altar are the lectern, the pulpit, the choir stalls and the organ. For this is a place of singing and speaking, in which Biblical English passes the lips of people who believe that holy thoughts need holy words, words somehow removed from the business of the world, like gems lifted from a jewel box and then quickly returned to the dark.[41]

Scruton highlights many aspects of a perceived Englishness in the Anglican church approach that is mirrored in the literary portrayals of Bennett, Betjeman, and Larkin as I shall discuss. It is a portrayal of a specific ecclesiastical identity that appears comfortable with itself. That measure of comfort, depicted most especially in *Sweet Tooth* with the charmed setting of the bishop's residence,[42] can also assume a degree of complacency or even indolence that is not beyond censure, as Evelyn Waugh noted to John Betjeman in a letter that questioned the sincerity and gravitas of the Established Church:

> I don't believe your wretched clergy have any faith themselves. I met a number of protestant chaplains in the war. None showed any special knowledge ...
>
> One deep root of error is that you regard religion as the source of pleasurable emotions & sensations [a view Betjeman rebuffed] and ask the question 'Am I not getting just as much out of the Church of England as I should from Catholicism?' The question should be 'What am I giving God?' ... I wouldn't give a thrushs [sic] egg for your chance of salvation at the moment.[43]

Waugh took umbrage at what could be considered Betjeman's sentimental and romanticized view of the church where more enthusiasm was shown in church furnishings than theology. But it is the same approach that McEwan seizes upon and the church is placed in a role that can be observed from a distance and then, to quote Scruton, 'quickly returned to the dark.'[44]

However, with the sense of comfort and establishment of role, there is also a specific perception of what the church is identified for. There is a ready self-confidence that faith in the institution is itself unshakeable because it would be representative of a lack of faith in a cultural institution and, although this is not

---

[41] Scruton, *Our Church*, p. 39.

[42] McEwan, *Sweet Tooth*, pp. 2–3.

[43] Mark Amory (ed.), *The Letters of Evelyn Waugh* (New Haven and New York, 1980) (9 January 1947 and May 1947), pp. 244, 250.

[44] Scruton, *Our Church*, p. 39.

An Atheist's Portrayal of the Church of England   37

a universal opinion, it is nonetheless one that McEwan reinforces and for which there is historical context. In *Sweet Tooth*, McEwan writes about a bishop and the liturgy in a tone that is strikingly reminiscent of Henry James's comments in 1905 on a visit to Wells Cathedral:

> The Bishop sat facing me, enthroned in a stately Gothic alcove and clad in his crimson band, his lawn sleeves and his lavender gloves; the canons, in their degree, with still other priestly forms, reclined comfortably in the carven stalls, and the scanty congregation was select; it was unexceptionably black-coated, bonneted and gloved. It savoured intensely in short of that inexorable gentility which the English put on with their Sunday bonnets and beavers and which fills me – as a mere taster of produced tastes – with a sort of fond reactionary remembrance of those animated bundles of rags which one sees kneeling in churches in Italy.[45] (James)

> and there he was [the bishop] in distant splendour, saying nothing at all on that particular day. Underlings, grand enough in their own right, undeterred by the feeble turnout conducted the service with all the brio of unshaken faith. One fellow with a nasal voice preached the sermon, a sure-footed exegesis of the Good Samaritan parable.[46] (McEwan)

The sense of grandeur, remoteness and sartorial concern, and above all confidence, are considered in both texts, with McEwan's bishop in his cathedra, presumably wearing a cope and seen in the context of junior clergy, who have an air of superiority to themselves as well. Despite the small congregation, there is no shortage of clergy and in James's portrayal it is much the same. James's observations concerning the congregation dressing well for church still apply in the twenty-first century and the 'gentility' of the service is quite possibly now more restrained than it was for James. However, the element of mystique to services and, to a visitor, the choreographed nature of liturgy has a relative captivation that is not so removed from the world of the arts that the church is connected to through music, paintings, and most obviously architecture. McEwan's affinity for art in general and his particular appreciation for music cannot be overlooked in his descriptions as they capture an understanding of the mystery in place.

Mythos and Logos

Karen Armstrong has discussed the value Greeks placed on acquiring knowledge through both *mythos* and *logos*, and that neither was considered superior but rather equal. While *logos* was essential for understanding practical concerns, *mythos* helped people comprehend life's challenges. Armstrong notes

---

[45]   Henry James, *Cathedrals and Castles* (London, 2009), p. 39.

[46]   McEwan, *Sweet Tooth*, p. 295.

38   *Music and Religion in the Writings of Ian McEwan*

that today we live in a society where myth is met with suspicion.[47] This has partly occurred through an increased dependency on *logos*, but *mythos* and the nature of understanding is still very prevalent in the nature of the church and extends far beyond theological matters, even though they form a root to subsequent dialogue. This nature of introspection, enquiry, and betterment can be seen in the many affinity groups that churches host where theology or even scripture is seldom discussed, as well as in sermons that dwell on secular texts that have nothing whatsoever to do with scripture but enable the mind of the congregant to ponder a greater perspective of life. In the Introduction and later in this chapter I discuss aspects of the church and clergy that are absent from McEwan's novels in order to further contextualise what he has included. It is important to state that in presenting the church through an often-romantic lens of traditional liturgy, McEwan is also fostering an image that draws on the nature of *mythos* and an expansion of the mind to consider areas that support deeper understanding. The nature of traditional hymns, services of evensong, and cathedral life in general intentionally relates to the value of self-enquiry and deeper thinking rather than the many superficial aspects of daily life. In *A Taste for Death*, P. D. James described evensong as 'that most neglected aesthetically satisfying portion of the Anglican liturgy'.[48] There is an intentional opacity because historically religion is not something just thought but is undertaken towards a greater understanding. As Armstrong[49] notes, the more you persevere with a task, the deeper the understanding of it and so when the former prisoner in *Machines Like Me*[50] starts attending daily evensongs at a cathedral on his release, he is not simply repeating an experience but deepening one.

Considering these points, there are several critical aspects to the relationship between the church and society that bear consideration in assessing McEwan's contributions as a popular writer to the public perception of the church.

The Media and Public Perception

McEwan's depiction of the church in *Sweet Tooth* unquestionably aligns with many popular perceptions of the Church of England. These can appear to be clichéd because of the dominant presence of the Church of England in the media, although that does not mean that they are unrepresentative of a constituency found within the church. As a church musician, what is most notable to me about the above Henry James description of attending a service in an English cathedral is how little has changed in the larger liturgical aesthetic. It is therefore unsurprising that with such a sustained identity, various other media

[47]   Karen Armstrong, *Religion* (London, 2019), pp. 4–5.

[48]   P. D. James, *A Taste for Death* (London, 1986), p. 385.

[49]   Armstrong, *Religion*, pp. 13–14.

[50]   McEwan, *Machines Like Me*, p. 243.

An Atheist's Portrayal of the Church of England   39

should have noted and reinforced a particularly familiar image. In considering this, I begin by discussing the legacy of a television programme that for many years defined a familiar image of the church in contemporary society.

The BBC television programme *Songs of Praise* began with a broadcast from Tabernacle Baptist Church, Cardiff in October 1961 and it is now the longest-running programme of its type in the world. It is based on a programmatic formula that includes large choirs and occasional soloists singing favourite hymns interwoven with discussions about personal views of faith, often from figures who are well known to the public. It is believed that more people watch the programme than attend Sunday services although this is difficult to ascertain with any certainty because many denominations do not publicly disclose weekly attendance. Certainly, more people watch the programme than attend an individual church on a Sunday. However, central to the programme is the singing of hymns and the personal and communal satisfaction gained from doing so. When McEwan refers to the cabinet singing as 'they might a hymn by Hubert Parry'[51] in *The Cockroach*, it is with this sense of impassioned delivery. The avoidance of theology or even a detailed analysis of the texts is part of the dynamic of the programme as people respond to the hymns on their own terms. A pronounced example of this somewhat casual approach to religion is similarly seen at weddings where the text 'Dear Lord and Father of mankind' is sung because people enjoy singing it, even though it has little relevance to a service of Holy Matrimony. This is not a debate of the sacred and secular in society but rather an example of what is often a very blurred line and which has typically been highlighted in television and film, thus reinforcing the public perception. In this respect, what might at first seem to be a clichéd approach by McEwan is more accurately described as a popular understanding and, it could be argued in a romanticized vein, an appreciative understanding. McEwan's interests in the church include traditional hymn singing, beautiful buildings, and the disciplined liturgy that is consistently the realm of the cathedral but not necessarily the modern parish church that to McEwan, in the case of Holy Trinity, Clapham was comparatively unimpressive.[52]

The legacy of film and television narratives that portray the Church of England in the traditional vein that McEwan consistently refers to is significant in British media alone with little offence observed by the press and public. This is arguably because of the easy believability of so many sketches and scenes that draw on a pastiche of the modern church. Rowan Atkinson's frequent portrayals of priests, most famously a stuttering cleric in the film *Four Weddings and a Funeral* (1994) and as the Archbishop of Canterbury for *Comic Relief* (2013), have borne an easy familiarity between a fine line of predictable awkwardness and occasional over-eagerness that now so often defines the modern priest in contemporary media.

---

[51]   Ian McEwan, *The Cockroach* (London, 2019), p. 43.
[52]   McEwan, *Machines Like Me*, p. 45.

40   *Music and Religion in the Writings of Ian McEwan*

In contrast to the well-meaning nature of *Songs of Praise* there is also a critical comical perspective of the church with the evisceration of appointments to bishoprics in *Yes, Prime Minister* (1986). Faith and the legitimacy of candidates are called into question. More critically, the discussion highlights a perception of the Church of England in the social terms that McEwan draws on in his description of the bishop in *Sweet Tooth*,[53] and the removed world of evensong in *Machines Like Me*.[54] In the latter there is no social stigma to a former prisoner attending evensong because the church is perceived as being socially aware and yet paradoxically detached enough from society to maintain a unique position of cultural relevance.

'In the Church of England the word Modernist is code for non-believer.'

'An atheist?'

'Oh no, Prime Minister,' he replied wickedly. 'An atheist clergyman couldn't continue to draw his stipend. So when they stop believing in God they call themselves modernists.'

'How can the church recommend an atheist as Bishop of Bury St Edmunds?'

'Very easily. The Church of England is primarily a social organisation not a religious one. It's part of the rich social fabric of this country and so bishops need to be the sort of chaps who speak properly and know which knife and fork to use. They are someone to look up to.'

'So being a bishop is simply a matter of status. Dressing up in cassock and gaiters.'

'Yes, Prime Minister. Though gaiters are now worn only at significant religious events – like the royal garden party.'[55]

In *Sweet Tooth*, the bishop's daughter, Serena, speaks of her father's ascent to the episcopacy with a description that bears strong resemblance to the intentionally comedic exchange above, while she notes the considerable advantages of being politically savvy within the church.

Our father's belief in God was muted and reasonable, did not intrude much on our livesand was just sufficient to raise him smoothly through the Church hierarchy.[56]

In the popular television series *The Vicar of Dibley*, Dawn French, as the vicar of a fictional Oxfordshire village church, brings a spirit of believability to the fallible as well as pragmatic nature of the priest in a small community. The

---

[53] McEwan, *Sweet Tooth*, pp. 2–3.

[54] McEwan, *Machines Like Me*, p. 243.

[55] Jonathan Lynn and Antony Jay, 'The Bishop's Gambit', *The Complete Yes Prime Minister* (London, 1988), pp. 219–220.

[56] McEwan, *Sweet Tooth*, pp. 1–2.

An Atheist's Portrayal of the Church of England   41

relative eccentricities of priests and their parishioners can be seen throughout the late twentieth and early twenty-first centuries in the campaigns of individuals and community groups the length of Britain, who have protested about topics such as bell-ringing rehearsals at a parish church that interrupted their television watching or a vicar of my own acquaintance in the Welsh town of Pontypridd who used to instruct wedding guests to throw confetti outside church property so that the council would remove it instead of the vicar being obliged to clean it up later in the day. Dawn French's portrayal is in many respects subdued compared to some in real life.

Michael Palin leading a school chapel hymn that begins 'O Lord, please don't burn us' (*The Meaning of Life*, 1983), set in the sentimental style of a Victorian hymn, successfully encapsulates the sense that the church – which in the British media as well as in McEwan's writings nearly always refers to the Anglican church – is sufficiently familiar to society that its characters and liturgies can be the ready subject of comedy. Keith Waterhouse's humorous version of the Christmas carol 'While shepherds watched their flocks by night' at the opening of his short novel *There is a Happy Land*, is a similar spoof because it assumes the original text is already known.

> While shepherds watched their turnip tops
> A-boiling in the pot,
> An angel of the Lord came down
> And scoffed the blinking lot.[57]

'O Lord, please don't burn us' has particular relevance to McEwan's libretto in *or Shall we die*? with Berkeley's musical setting drawing on a familiar Victorian style of hymn. This is discussed further in this chapter in relation to the church and the Cold War. Both hymns are used to merge the familiar with the unexpected. The music sets the tenor and reception of the text in a style the public easily recognizes and the turn of narrative towards the cynical or critical becomes all the more potent. Fundamentally, both draw on the nature of hymn singing as a typical communal force for good and this is important because it stresses the larger societal engagement in hymn singing that often surpasses individual beliefs.

More recent television series such as *Rev.* (2010–2014) and *Fleabag* (2016–2019) have given the clergy an edgier appearance, albeit largely removed from liturgy and yet still extremely believable. Theology is only broached in the safest of environments and when, in *Fleabag*, a pseudo-confessional experience leads to a sexual encounter, then reverence is once more put back in the box and the priest is once more 'relatable'. To the leaders of the Oxford Movement, who in the nineteenth century sought to reimagine the church and draw on historical models, what is now considered 'nice' and 'relatable' would have been curiously weak points of engagement. As noted above, McEwan's portrayal of a bishop

---

[57]   Keith Waterhouse, *There is a Happy Land* (London, 1957) p. 1.

42 *Music and Religion in the Writings of Ian McEwan*

in *Sweet Tooth* who holds a particular social position relates closely to the *Yes, Prime Minister* image of the clergy rather than the relatively softer approachable personalities that *Rev.* and *Fleabag* foster. But by presenting the church in a traditional light, McEwan is also aligned with many in the artistic world who find a route to spirituality, rather than a specific denomination, through artistic engagement. When surrounded by the beauty of buildings, art, and music, they find the experience transformative, at the very least from everyday life. In this regard, Hitchens's comments that McEwan 'shows an extraordinary ability to elucidate the numinous without conceding anything to the supernatural'[58] aligns with an approach to describing the church in terms that are not theological but cultural.

Hymns, Community, and Belonging

The adoption of Blake's/Parry's 'Jerusalem' at meetings of the Women's Institute, as well as being a perennial favourite of the Last Night of the Proms, has very little, if anything, to do with religion but rather empowerment and reinvigoration of the shared value of community. It is perhaps for this reason that when the conductor Mark Elder questioned whether to remove patriotic music from the *Last Night of the Proms* in 1990 with an impending Gulf war looming, the decision was met with more befuddlement than anger and the argument that – rather like a church that will not change its liturgy to conform with a secular event – the notion of patriotic singing surpasses temporal circumstances. Also, the singing of patriotic hymns was an annual cultural event that meant something to the British public and provided a sense of community that largely surpassed a connection to a forthcoming war. A spirit of community surpassed politics. Many in Britain will have been unaware that the music to be sung at the *Last Night of the Proms* was being discussed or that the conductor who suggested a change in the repertoire was removed from conducting the concert, such was the prevailing surety of a tradition and the pseudo-religious comfort of a thoroughly Anglican identity. There was never a serious doubt that the music would have been omitted. More recently, the question of whether 'Land of hope and glory' would be sung in the online Proms season during COVID-19 (2020) drew on the subject of Britain's colonial past and provoked a blunt response from the Prime Minister, Boris Johnson. 'I think it's time we stopped our cringing embarrassment about our history.'[59] It is also a coincidence that the cabinet that comes to mind in *The Cockroach* when there is a reference to hymn singing in a style akin to the vigorous singing of a hymn (tune) of Parry[60] is the cabinet of Boris Johnson, thus drawing the worlds of fact and fiction into

---

[58] Hitchens, *God is Not Great: The Case Against Religion*, p. 286.

[59] 'Boris Johnson "cannot believe" BBC Proms decision', online at <https://www.bbc.com/news/entertainment-arts-53902065> [accessed 17 December 2020].

[60] McEwan, *The Cockroach*, p. 43.

one. Either Johnson's statement is considered offensive because it bypasses serious discussion and reassessment of the past, or it draws on the same sentiments that were considered in 1990 with the discussions surrounding Mark Elder, whereby a value placed on communal singing was above immediate criticism. Both arguments have problems, but McEwan's reference to the singing of a hymn on a bandstand on the beach at Dunkirk in *Atonement*[61] reinforces the sense of communal and national sentiment that hymn singing can provide. The history of this perception is tied to larger social structures and in this respect McEwan acknowledges the positive removal of social barriers that hymn singing also enables.

It is highly improbable that William Henry Monk, the editor of *Hymns Ancient and Modern* (1861), would have imagined that his setting of Henry Francis Lyte's text 'Abide with Me' would continue to be performed not only in churches but also in brass band concerts in the north of England that were associated with former collieries. Indeed, the hymn is played by a brass band at a funeral in the 1997 film *The Full Monty*. Music conveys sentiment and singing in groups reinforces a sense of belonging, even between members of the cabinet in *The Cockroach*.[62] As Scruton notes, the brass band movement that began in the nineteenth century was, like the Labour movement, associated 'with Nonconformist religion (and with the Salvation Army in particular), with temperance, self-help and the campaign for an extended franchise' and the use of hymn arrangements bolstered a sense of belonging. Scruton notes that 'the bands were also more than associations, gathering to themselves an extraordinary social ambience which was unmistakably English in its subdued pageantry and phlegmatic togetherness'.[63]

The blurring of lines between the sacred and the secular can also be seen in the use of non-scriptural texts which have found their way into many denominations and services. Often the scriptural and non-scriptural can be side by side, simply because of a relative emotional attachment. I attended a summer wedding in the Cotswolds in 1991 which included Handel's 'Zadok the Priest', Edgar Bainton's 'And I saw a new heaven', and Henry Mancini's 'Moon River', even though none had particular relevance to a service of Holy Matrimony. The first piece was written for the coronation of George II in 1727, the second piece is based on a Revelation text, and the third piece is obviously secular. The relatively liberal use of texts, including in some services of *Lessons and Carols* that do not incorporate scripture at all, is especially broad in the late twentieth and early twenty-first centuries and often draws on sentimental associations rather than theological ones. In this sense the church has itself drawn heavily on the cultural aspects of larger society which McEwan, Bennett, and Betjeman have intuited, not least in the emotional role of music in the Church of England.

---

[61] Ian McEwan, *Atonement* (London, 2014), p. 248.

[62] McEwan, *The Cockroach*, p. 43.

[63] Scruton, *England: An Elegy*, p. 146.

44   *Music and Religion in the Writings of Ian McEwan*

Established Comfort, Personal Affection, and Evensong

When McEwan refers, in *Machines Like Me*, to Holy Trinity, Clapham as 'a huge brick Age of Reason shed', being a church 'too reasonable a place to evoke much awe' although its 'clean lines and sensible proportions were soothing'[64] he encapsulates a view of many who see the church as a primarily consoling institution, providing a measure of solace to communities large and small. The contrasting descriptions of the modern edifice as 'soothing' by comparison to one that inspires 'awe' is a dramatic one that shows McEwan's understanding of the different constituencies of preference and style within the Church of England. These observations draw on the sentiment that an austere-looking building does not capture the imagination in the same way that an older and more ornate edifice could. Susan Hill's comments about the role of cathedrals – which arguably have among the most impressive edifices of all – speak to the central societal and cultural role that the church embodies, irrespective of whether someone is a believer or, in McEwan's case, an atheist.

> Durham. Westminster. Wells. Norwich. Exeter. Salisbury. Canterbury. St Paul's. Picture them. Click. Picture them gone. The idea of their absence is an absence in the heart; not an airy emptiness, a leaden one. It is a deadness. To think of the world without these cathedrals, without all cathedrals, is like a bereavement. It is painful. The loss of the buildings themselves, the grandeur the beauty, is unimaginable – the mind veers away from it. But think of the world without the great palaces. Surely it is just the same?
>
> We know, deeply, instinctively, that it is not. Destroy all the churches? Is that not the same?
>
> We know that it is more. And that it is not merely a question of size. Nor of the fear of thunderbolts.[65]

McEwan's comparison taps into the nature of association that different groups have with different points of heritage, but in the case of churches which are often used for public meetings as well as civic carol services, the role is a distinct one. Christopher Rowland writes of the unifying nature that the cathedrals similarly provide within communities. It can be suggested that this especially applies in the smaller cities where the cathedral is a dominant physical presence and often has a professional as well as volunteer staff of several dozen people. In this sense, the cathedral can be viewed as a mirror of the community outside its walls.

> Cathedrals have been transmitters of British culture, and as such have nurtured a much broader relationship between English society, culture and so-

---

[64]   McEwan, *Machines Like Me*, p. 45.

[65]   Hill, 'At the still point of the turning world', p. 8.

An Atheist's Portrayal of the Church of England   45

ciety on the one hand and the Church which bears witness to Christ on the other.[66]

The cathedral cities are, as Blake called them in *Jerusalem*, 'the friends of Albion'. McEwan draws a line between the religious doubter of postwar Britain and the gentle believer with a devoted affection for the subtle role the church fulfils. This sentimental appreciation for buildings and hymns is conveyed repeatedly by Betjeman, not least in his many programmes for television. His observations are laced with a comfortable and, in many respects, panacean glow with the church representing a beacon within communities as if its very presence has an ameliorating quality. Later in *Machines Like Me*, McEwan captures the sense of solace for a former prisoner attending services, initially because of a personal benefit and then, on release from prison, by choice: [If you went to services you had] 'more time out of [your] cell if you came on as all religious. A lot of us were on to it and the screws [prison guards] understood but they didn't care. I put myself down as Church of England and started going every day to evensong. I still go every day [now that I've been released from prison] to the cathedral [for evensong].'[67] Initially being seen as religious had a benefit but his exposure to the liturgical world provided him with something that he ultimately continued with on release and not just occasionally but 'every day'. The relative isolation of a cell had been supplanted by the anonymity that attending a cathedral service often provides. Sometimes a service in the same building can also offer relatively contrasting experiences. At Durham Cathedral, like many other cathedrals, it is possible to sit in a small congregation near the choir for evensong and see the faces of other congregants sitting opposite. But it is also possible to sit in the nave, rows apart from another person and come and leave without speaking a word or motioning a gesture to another person. It is an entirely unforced engagement with the church and when McEwan draws attention to the Church of England in *The Children Act*[68] and a barrister asks if it is a cult, a key point is missed by the inference that all denominations are somehow the same. Putting aside the provocative use of the word 'cult', there is a marked difference in the expectations of Jehovah's Witnesses and Anglicans regarding matters of medicine and a way of life. Whereas either believer may laugh off the suggestion that they are part of a cult, the courtroom exchange suggests a parallel can be drawn.

This pattern of regular or occasional attendance at the non-sacramental service of evensong, a service that on a weekday typically does not involve preaching, is common at cathedrals throughout the UK. In recent years there has been a marked increase in attendance. The appeal of the service rests with both the beauty of the experience, not least the opportunity to hear sacred

---

[66] Christopher Rowland, 'Friends of Albion', in Stephen Platten and Christopher Lewis (eds), *Flagships of the Spirit – Cathedrals in Society* (London, 1998), p. 30.

[67] McEwan, *Machines Like Me*, p. 243.

[68] McEwan, *The Children Act* , p. 72.

46   *Music and Religion in the Writings of Ian McEwan*

choral and organ works performed at an impressively high level, and the relative anonymity that attending the service affords, at a time when a private life is increasingly removed, with attention devoted to social media and an encroaching state. People can come and go and not be troubled by conversations unless they choose to and with a degree of solitude that can easily be likened to a private viewing at a museum or gallery. In this sense the ready criticism of the church maintaining a 'museum culture' is perhaps valid but the rationale behind the criticism fails to observe the potential benefits that attract many. While a confirmed atheist, McEwan nonetheless grasps the cultural legacy of a service that is treasured by a devoted following. I suggest this speaks to an especially British appreciation of the service, which is encapsulated in a comment that Stephen Fry, an atheist, made regarding his participation in an online service of evensong during the 2020 COVID-19 pandemic.

> I know it might seem strange coming from a godless heathen atheistical swine like me, but I do love a good evensong service. I've contributed to this one (speech not song, you'll be relieved to hear) – the music is SUBLIME.[69]

It is quite possible that the study assumes there is an overarching understanding that evensong is still part of the diurnal routine of the nation, but are the congregants present to 'worship' or simply to 'experience' a service or are these to be viewed as an essential and predictable union? In this sense, McEwan's reference to evensong accurately grasps the fact that the service is seen primarily along cultural lines for many in the first instance which, coincidentally, is far more palatable for an atheist to digest in any event, albeit within a fictional context. This is not a criticism of the study but an observation that the study itself shows the broad reach of the service almost irrespective of a specific commitment to a particular faith. Evensong is meaningful to many while being offensive to very few because the broader theological questions are typically left at the door, not least with the absence of preaching. Indeed, clergy who attempt to explain readings of scripture before they are read are often frowned upon for interrupting the historic flow of the service. An example of this broad appeal can be witnessed with the significant number of people who attend the service and practise another faith or no faith at all. This larger question of the appealing otherness of evensong can be considered in comments by the composer John Tavener in terms of his impressions of the contemporary church.

> I think what we're seeing in religion is a change in direction from the spoken and literal to the unspoken and symbolic.[70]

The 'unspoken' and 'symbolic' aspects will relate more to a reader of McEwan's novels who is familiar with Church of England liturgy than one who is not,

---

[69]   Stephen Fry, Twitter, 19 May 2020.

[70]   Andrew Palmer, 'John Tavener', *Encounters with British Composers* (Woodbridge, 2015), p. 440.

An Atheist's Portrayal of the Church of England

but the inclusion of these references is typical of his presentation of musical matters in the secular world as well. Specific works and composers are referred to in *On Chesil Beach*, just as the life of a bishop is described in *Sweet Tooth*, with an approach that infers these references need no introduction. In the case of evensong and the diurnal round of cathedral liturgies, Betjeman's poem of 1937, *Exeter*, draws on the same trope. Evensong is presented as being familiar and its language one that is known. To that end, it can be suggested that, though an atheist, McEwan in fact introduces readers to a liturgical world that if not he then his characters can relate to.

> The doctor's intellectual wife
>   Sat under the ilex tree
> The Cathedral bells pealed over the wall
>   But never a bell heard she
> And the sun played shadowgraphs on her book
>   Which was writ by A. Huxléy.
>
> Once those bells, those Exeter bells
>   Called her to praise and pray
> By pink, acacia-shaded walls
>   Several times a day
> To Wulfric's altar and riddel posts
>   While the choir sang Stanford in A
>
> The doctor jumps in his Morris car,
>   The surgery door goes bang,
> Clash and whirr down Colleton Crescent,
>   Other cars all go hang
> My little bus is enough for us —
>   Till a tram-car bell went clang.
>
> They brought him in by the big front door
>   And a smiling corpse was he;
> On the dining-room table they laid him out
>   Where the *Bystanders* used to be —
> *The Tatler*, *The Sketch* and *The Bystander*
>   For the canons' wives to see
>
> Now those bells, those Exeter bells
>   Called her to praise and pray
> By pink, acacia-shaded walls
>   Several times a day
> To Wulfric's altar and riddel posts
>   And the choir sings Stanford in A.[71]

---

[71] John Betjeman, 'Exeter', in *Collected Poems of John Betjeman* (London, 1970), pp. 41–42.

48 *Music and Religion in the Writings of Ian McEwan*

The reference to the cathedral choir singing Stanford in A draws on the popularity of Charles Villiers Stanford's majestic setting of the evening canticles (*Magnificat and Nunc dimittis*) in the key of A major that is sung by cathedral and parish choirs around the country. For the reader who knows the music, an immediate aural landscape is created as is the image of a timeless tradition in the service of evensong and indeed the belief of a continuing tradition. For the reader familiar with evensong, the former prisoner's attendance at evensong in *Machines Like Me* brings this liturgical world to mind. But it is also the balance in the larger poem of the everyday life of the canon's wives in the shadow of a great cathedral that is mirrored in different literary perspectives, whether Goldsmith's *The Vicar of Wakefield*, George Eliot's *Scenes of Clerical Life*, Trollope's Barchester novels or McEwan's *Sweet Tooth*, where the central protagonist, Serena, is the daughter of a bishop. The everyday aspect is not introduced to the reader but presented as if it is familiar and, in some sense, relatable. McEwan approaches scientific matters with a degree of explanation but in the case of the church, as well as classical music, there is a relative presumption of understanding. It is the 'reader's sophistication' that is 'rarely acknowledged'[72] that Dominic Head comments on and McEwan both introduces the potential unknown as well as demonstrating knowledge of it to those for whom it is familiar. In comparative instances, the cathedral world is portrayed by McEwan as being relevant to both the former prisoner (*Machines Like Me*) and a bishop (*Sweet Tooth*).

However, beyond the immediate liturgical space, McEwan also describes the nature of a clerical life and the subdued surroundings that some senior clergy experience. His portrayal is in the same spirit as Betjeman's *Exeter* and instantly recognizable with life in a cathedral precinct.

> [we lived in a] comfortable Queen Anne house. It overlooked an enclosed garden with ancient herbaceous borders that were well known, and still are, to those who know about plants. So, all stable, enviable, idyllic even. We grew up inside the walled garden, with all the pleasures and limitations that implies.[73]

The touch of sublimity on earth that McEwan describes mirrors an impression that Coleridge had of a church's role in 1830. The 'idyllic' nature combined with the enclosed world set apart from the public at large was both remote and necessary. The model church of Coleridge being 'sufficiently' interesting is also similar to the narrative in *Machines Like Me*[74] and the preference towards churches that were, at first sight, impressive to consider. So too is the nature of a world that is 'stable' (McEwan), 'continuous' (Coleridge), and potentially 'enviable' (McEwan).

---

[72] Dominic Head, *The State of the Novel – Britain and Beyond* (Oxford, 2008), pp. 8, 6.

[73] McEwan, *Sweet Tooth*, pp. 2–3.

[74] McEwan, *Machines Like Me*, p. 45.

That to every parish throughout the kingdom there is transplanted a germ of civilization; that in the remotest villages there is a nucleus, round which the capabilities of the place may crystallise and brighten; a model sufficiently superior to excite, yet sufficiently near to encourage and facilitate imitation; *this* unobtrusive, continuous agency of a Protestant Church Establishment, *this* it is, which the patriot, and the philanthropist, who would fain unite the love of peace with the faith in the progressive amelioration of mankind, cannot estimate at too high a price.[75]

The 'enviable' aspect also refers to the impression of privilege enjoyed by senior clergy with housing that is not only set apart from the larger community but also very attractive. The cathedral precinct offers an image that is beyond the norm and in Ely and Winchester, as two examples, the cathedral precincts are closed each evening, following monastic traditions and the nature of protecting religion at all costs. It is even subtly, though unintentionally, reinforced in the verse of the Victorian hymn, 'All things bright and beautiful', such was the prevailing climate of order and class distinction:

The rich man in his castle,
The poor man at his gate,
God made them, high and lowly,
And ordered their estate.

It is the aspect of the church as a constant presence whether for worship, prayer or solace that Betjeman and McEwan allude to so successfully and, to a reader familiar with Anglican traditions, comparatively effortlessly. In Betjeman's case in *Exeter*, it is the portrayal of a church that is part of the everyday life, where magazines are referred to as easily as Stanford's evening canticles along with the local doctor and the little bus. To a reader who is unfamiliar with the nuances of Anglican church life this nonetheless becomes part of the patchwork of the larger narrative and in that sense it is no less critical an element in McEwan's references and perceptions in *Sweet Tooth*, where the description of the life of a bishop is portrayed as completely and indeed appealingly natural.

The church of the late twentieth century was and remains, in both cathedral and much parish life, rooted in both the Prayer Book language of the sixteenth century and the hymnody of the nineteenth century. Service leaflets for carol services frequently ignored textual revisions of hymn texts and instead included earlier versions, typically extracted from the popular volumes of *Carols for Choirs* published by Oxford University Press, the first volume of which appeared in 1961. The popularity of *Carols from King's*, which is broadcast around the world from King's College, Cambridge on Christmas Eve each year, has further promoted the association of Anglican worship with older eras. Although new works have been commissioned on an annual basis for many

---

[75] Samuel Taylor Coleridge, 'On the Constitution of the Church and State', in Stephen Potter (ed.), *Selected Poetry and Prose* (New York, *c.*1951 (repr. 1964)), p. 467.

50 *Music and Religion in the Writings of Ian McEwan*

years, the aesthetic sentiment and tenor of the King's service has only changed modestly. However, this has been no accident as the beauty of the language has consistently been recognized as one of the great legacies of literature and the church, most especially with Myles Coverdale's translations of the psalms. The language of the Prayer Book has permeated much conversational speech in the same way that Shakespeare can be heard each day without an awareness of an attributable reference. It is the historical impression of the Church of England that McEwan draws on and there are no references to anything new, in terms of liturgy or liturgical spaces, in a positive light. The 'soothing'[76] architecture of Holy Trinity, Clapham is a solitary example of a modest comment on a church that is not historic. Rather it is described as something accessible but nonetheless somewhat lacking in consequence or indeed relevance through this particular lens. But as a writer who also has strong connections with contemporary arts, not least with his collaborations with the composer Michael Berkeley on *or Shall we die?* and *For You*, there is an absence within McEwan's writings of commentary on the arts in sacred spaces in the second half of the twentieth century that could move beyond this impression of the modern sacred space. In music terms, the references to Benjamin Britten in *On Chesil Beach*,[77] *The Children Act*,[78] and *Amsterdam*[79] do not refer to his relatively well-known sacred works but his secular works. There are also no references to Walter Hussey's many commissions in Northampton or Chichester, or the commissioning of Jacob Epstein's *Majestas* in Llandaff Cathedral. Most notably, there is no reference to the new cathedral in Coventry with its numerous commissions, all of which have a significant cultural relevance. These points are especially intriguing because McEwan has not only worked with a leading composer but also written a libretto about a composer, *For You*, and a novel with a composer, *Amsterdam*, both of which lay bare the challenges of contemporary artists in modern Britain. Rather, McEwan has kept the portrayal of the church in a niche image that, though instantly recognizable, is nonetheless a very specific impression of the Church of England that does not include its broader reach in the artistic world.

From The Act of Supremacy to the 'Niceness' of Clergy

McEwan's portrayal of clergy ranges from a bishop in his comfortable surroundings in *Sweet Tooth* to the weak advocate for peace in *or Shall we die?*. As noted above in the first section of this chapter, the difficulty of taking a stance, even if a priest is the Archbishop of Canterbury, is fraught with public censure.

---

[76] McEwan, *Machines Like Me*, p. 45.

[77] McEwan, *On Chesil Beach* , p. 51.

[78] McEwan, *The Children Act*, p. 119.

[79] Ian McEwan, *Amsterdam* (London, 2005), p. 133.

An Atheist's Portrayal of the Church of England   51

The nature of constant criticism that places the senior clergy in a visible position might be considered, in an increasingly secular society, as little different from other public commentators. However, the relationship that the Church of England has to the state places the senior clergy in a unique position.

In relation to the Act of Supremacy the church was born not only from a reformation but an awareness of nationalism and this continues to be reinforced. State occasions such as royal weddings and funerals reinforce the place of Anglican clergy in positions of power and privilege. By comparison, clergy of other Christian denominations rarely provoke sustained public discussion. Through a relationship with the sovereign that is further reinforced by the presence of the Lords Spiritual in the House of Lords, the church is also inextricably linked to both the political establishment and, still more specifically, the monarchy. But in practical terms, there is little the clergy can do to bring about change, for the very reason of quick censure that Rowan Williams referred to (above).[80] It is here that McEwan's criticism of the clergy in the preface to *or Shall we die?* – 'Before the slaughter [of war] there never seems to be a priest lacking to bless the executioners'[81]– is contradictory to the role the public increasingly anticipates from the contemporary priest at a parish level or even at a senior level, as Rowan Williams notes. Far from being lofty and removed, the local vicar is increasingly expected to fulfil a role that is closer to a non-judgemental social worker. In discussing the challenges facing religion in modern Scotland, Steve Bruce raises the now necessary presumption of 'niceness' on the part of the local religious leader.

> the reduction of Christianity to 'niceness' has the ironic effect of making serious Christian organisations appear mean-spirited and self-interested and, well, not Christian. Any idea that the chief end of man might be to glorify God … or that loving thy neighbor might involve telling him that unless he changes his ways he will go to hell, has been quite forgotten.[82]

Bruce further notes that when Pope Benedict pointed out that very few of the traditions we associate with Christmas have any basis in scripture, his comments were reported negatively in the press. The *Daily Mail*'s headline was 'Killjoy Pope crushes Christmas nativity traditions'.[83] Bruce goes on to say that 'clergy who refuse to provide religious offices to people who are patently unin-

---

[80]   Williams, *Faith in the Public Square*, p. 1.

[81]   McEwan, *or Shall we die? A Move Abroad*, pp. 10–11.

[82]   Steve Bruce, 'Serious Religion in Secular Culture', in *Scottish Gods* (Edinburgh, 2014), p. 133.

[83]   Martin Robinson, 'Killjoy Pope crushes Christmas nativity traditions: new Jesus book reveals there were no donkeys beside crib, no lowing oxen and definitely no carols', *Daily Mail*, 21 November 2012, online at <https://www.dailymail.co.uk/news/article-2236195/New-Jesus-book-reveals-donkeys-crib-lowing-oxen-definitely-carols-Christmas.html> [accessed 17 December 2020].

52 *Music and Religion in the Writings of Ian McEwan*

terested in the religion in question are reported as mean-spirited. Ditto ministers who refuse to let church halls schedule yoga and meditation groups on the grounds that, if the original justifications for those activities are taken seriously, they are tools of the opposition.'[84] Thus, the popular critical approach, not least adopted by new atheists, that the church does not stand up to various injustices, is not a simple argument because the public and more specifically the press, who in an increasingly secular society have an increasingly louder voice, have continually censured the degree of effectiveness and influence clergy are able to exert.

The sum total of this expectation is that a Christian leader in modern Britain is able to preach the gospel on Sunday mornings but is not to 'use' their position in society to change minds. This is a difficulty for any cleric who believes that the gospel should be preached publicly and energetically. It is in part for this reason that David Jenkins, Bishop of Durham in the 1980s, was such a striking public presence because he upset the natural order of public perception of the Establishment and challenged those who would not usually be called on to answer difficult theological questions. That he did so from a cathedral pulpit in a county (Durham) that suffered hardship as the consequence of government policy in closing collieries added still further to the media appeal and resulting attention.

The modern cleric has to walk a fine line because the public perception rests heavily on visiting the church when it suits them and largely ignoring or criticizing it the rest of the time. In 2019, the idea of the church serving a current or future multipurpose space took pronounced departures with a golf course installed in Rochester Cathedral and a fifty-foot helter-skelter installed at Norwich Cathedral, both with the hope of attracting a younger crowd. The twentieth-century development of church shops and cafeterias has also nurtured a role for the church as a meeting place without the burden of religious thought. This brings to mind once more McEwan's comment in *Machines Like Me* on some churches being 'too reasonable a place to evoke much awe'[85] because the air of mystique is temporarily absent or set apart. The surrounding architecture of a cathedral might be very impressive and inspiring to many, but the multipurpose aspect is increasingly deemed essential. People visit a cathedral but do not necessarily stay to worship. However, this is not to suggest the environment does not have a powerful impact on them, merely by its presence. But to an atheist it is easy to direct a cynical argument that the administration of the church has either become rudderless or in some sense has lost faith in itself. McEwan's attention to hymn singing (*Atonement, The Cockroach*), evensong, and the 'idyllic' (*Sweet Tooth*) nature of the cathedral setting draws on the cultural aspects that are appealing to someone who views the church at a remove but understands that it is in some way an identifiable component in

[84] Steve Bruce, 'Serious Religion in Secular Culture', p. 132.
[85] McEwan, *Machines Like Me*, p. 45.

An Atheist's Portrayal of the Church of England   53

life because to be without the great edifices would be, in Susan Hill's opinion, a leaden 'absence in the heart' and a 'deadness'.[86]

The Church as the Other

A steady trope in Steve Bruce's chapter 'Serious Religion in Secular Culture' is the analysis that 'as Christianity has become less popular it has also become less well-known and to most outsiders it has become reduced to a parody of the golden rule: God is nice, proper Christians are nice, and anyone who does or says anything which is not nice cannot be a Christian.'[87] However, some of this dilemma has been caused from within the church, or more specifically from administrative circles, and begs questions about the lasting impact of potential miscalculations such as the secularization of sacred space. The concerns noted above regarding Pope Benedict and a Christmas that might not have favourite traditions included relate very largely to the nineteenth century, when most of the popular traditions such as Christmas trees and decorations took hold and simply remained popular. The same could be said of the popularity of Christmas carols and indeed of *Lessons and Carols* as a church service that began around the 1880s. This was by no coincidence the same era that saw the after-effects and liturgical changes that were influenced by the Oxford Movement. The legacy of the Movement is an undeniable turning point in the approach to High Church liturgy and the nature of mysticism in the English church. To a cynic, let alone an unbeliever, the aesthetical endowments of High Church liturgy with incense, vestments, occasional or regular use of Latin, are by nature the cause of cries of Popery and, more critically, the Other. Many of these constituent parts are commonplace today and McEwan's narrative in *Sweet Tooth*[88] speaks to a setting of disciplined liturgy that is well executed and, to a modern reader familiar with the Anglican world, instantly recognizable. But to an atheist the unexplainable becomes unintelligible and uncritical in a modern age that is suspicious of a spiritual life beyond scripture and has little interest in theology, dogma, church hierarchy, or the sartorial side of liturgy. As such, though McEwan gives an accurate depiction of a contemporary setting he also illuminates the Other aspect of it all, much as his criticism of the government in fiction and in public commentaries highlights a complementary aspect of those in authority being removed from reality. However, the sense of necessary social standing that the senior clergy often emanate and of which the bishop in *Sweet Tooth* is a typical part stems from an older understanding of the social role senior clergy were expected to have. Hurrell Froude, a priest and a leader of the Oxford Movement, expressed the necessary position as follows:

[86] Hill, 'At the still point of the turning world', p. 8.
[87] Bruce, 'Serious Religion in Secular Culture', p. 131.
[88] McEwan, *Sweet Tooth*, p. 295.

A modern high Churchman has been taught from his youth to identify the Church and the Establishment – to suppose that the respectability of the Clergy is the result of their connexion and intercourse with the higher classes, – and that in the event of any change which should render the clerical profession distasteful to the wealthy and well-connected, the Church must necessarily sink into insignificance.[89]

The leaders of the Oxford Movement saw a clear difference in the role of bishops and the clergy of lower orders. Whereas the bishops were responsible for providing a resistance to the state, the lower orders were to identify with the laypeople. McEwan's portrayal of the family life of the bishop in *Sweet Tooth* relates to this removed impression and, though now increasingly dated, denotes how the life of a bishop was quite simply very different from the average parish priest. Thus, McEwan highlights the class structure even within the church in a case of double othering. The church is set apart and so too are the clergy defined by particular roles and perceptions within it.

However, McEwan is far from alone in keeping the church within a specific image. Alan Bennett's 1995 television series, *The Abbey*, includes an extended tour of Westminster Abbey as both an historic monument and a place of daily worship. It is not simply an author's tour of favourite points of interest but also a late-twentieth-century commentary on the role of the Abbey in contemporary life. Bennett's script expands upon the impression of writers from James, Betjeman, Larkin, and McEwan of an institution that represents a particular image of the church seen through a British lens. The three-part series is a curious mix of admiration and critique and in this respect the tenor of the documentary also has a very British pivot between the historical, cultural, and moderately circumspect. As much as Bennett points out important tombs – the second episode is titled 'Whom would you like to be seen dead with?' – he also questions how the Abbey might be a reflection of England, complete with a readiness to elevate certain figures above others through celebrated memorials, not least in literature and music, and the English fondness for societies and clubs. This further points out the prevailing class structure that the bishop (*Sweet Tooth*) is part of. Some people are included, and others are not. In this sense, the Abbey is a very British institution because in its modern Anglican image it places the well-known lay person, indeed even the famous nonbeliever, in a prime position. The size of the buildings also projects a sense of awe and power that in smaller cathedral cities is, as Susan Hill noted (above), almost impossible to consider removed. To Bennett, people visit the Abbey on a daily basis and pay money to be close to greatness that, on some level, they feel that they can admire and, in the modern vernacular, 'relate to'. But at the same time Bennett also opens the door to the realities of life at the Abbey, including the lay clerks (men of the choir) playing darts before a choir rehearsal or the senior

---

[89] Richard Hurrell Froude, *Remains of The Late Reverend Richard Hurrell Froude, M.A.* (London, 1839), vol. 2, p. 31.

An Atheist's Portrayal of the Church of England   55

clergy immersed in a meeting about future administrative plans, both of which are far removed from the sublimity of liturgy. Bennett concludes the final (third) episode with a statement that borrows from the nineteenth-century Dean of the Abbey, Arthur Stanley. Stanley was a Broad churchman, of whom a caricature even appeared in *Vanity Fair* in 1872, who regarded the Abbey as a 'mirror of England', although this can now be seen in a different vein in line with Steve Bruce's comments (above) about the public expectation of clergy and therefore the church.[90] It can be seen as the institution the British want it to be. The overarching impression that Bennett leaves is of a church for which the role of being a national monument is an unavoidable daily concern rather than a necessary blessing or solace. Although it is near inconceivable that a member of the Abbey clergy would express that view, these frustrations were expressed in a 1999 interview with the celebrated former Abbey organist, Simon Preston, who commented that '... of course it's not entirely a church either, although of course it is a church, the great church in England, although it is very much a museum and [during my tenure there] I felt that I was being sidelined away from music and [instead] becoming the curator of a museum'.[91] There is little affection in Preston's comments for the Abbey and his ultimate resignation was regretted by many in the field of church music as the considerable loss of someone who had demanded the highest standards at both the Abbey and his former employ, Christ Church, Oxford. However, his comments further illumine the sense of a major church being perceived as part of the cultural and societal fabric in the first instance and only secondly as a place of worship, even though that is actually its prime function. This might be easily understood by assessing the thousands of tourists who walk around the Abbey on a weekly basis and then leave before a service begins or only attend concerts. Indeed, the relative dependency on music in cathedrals is observed by Humphrey Clucas, a singer, composer, and poet, in relaying the views expressed by the former Dean of Guildford Cathedral, Tony Bridge, when the cathedral accountant observed that a deficit was the same amount as the music budget: 'We can't do without the music', said Tony. 'What would we have here? Just four old clerics stuck on a hill'.[92] It is this measure of select otherness with beautiful music, vestments, and solemnity, that McEwan brings forward favourably for the prisoner who attends evensong after release in *Machines Like Me* but highlights in a socially constricted way in *Sweet Tooth* with the 'idyllic' residence of the bishop, and the degree that clergy are out of touch with social and ethical concerns in *or Shall we die*? But as a popular author he is also drawing on not only a public perception but, as this section noted, also a professional one. The 'mirror of

---

90   Steve Bruce, 'Serious Religion in Secular Culture', p. 133.

91   'Simon Says', Simon Preston interviewed by Michael Barone for *Pipedreams* (1999), online at <https://pipedreams.publicradio.org/listings/1999/9916/> [accessed 17 December 2020].

92   Humphrey Clucas, *Taking Stock – The First Sixty Years* (Sutton, 2005), pp. 121–122.

56　　*Music and Religion in the Writings of Ian McEwan*

England' aspect that Dean Stanley noted of the Abbey is reflected in McEwan's own picture of the church.

The Populism of Hymns – McEwan and Bennett

In his 2018 play, *Allelujah!*, Bennett draws on the use of a well-known hymn in the Anglican church, *All Creatures of Our God and King*. The text was originally written by Francis of Assisi but remained unpublished for four hundred years. William H. Draper's translation of the original text into English for a Whitsuntide festival in Leeds (Bennett's birthplace) brought the hymn to wider attention, especially after its inclusion within the *Public School Hymn Book* (1919). Bennett selects the first part of the concluding stanza as a recurring musical trope throughout the play that also bears the name of the final 'Alleluia'.

> And thou most kind and gentle death,
> Waiting to hush our latest breath,
> O praise Him! Alleluia![93]

The hymn is not referred to in the published preface *Musical Numbers* nor in Bennett's own Introduction, perhaps because it was simply too well known. However, that it is sung by everyone on the hospital ward of elderly patients that is the location for the play and in a style of easy familiarity demonstrates the perceived acquaintance and accessibility of a sacred work in the larger secular world, not just to the fictional setting of the play but before a contemporary audience. It is the same easy recognition that McEwan alludes to in *The Cockroach*, when the cabinet sings 'Walking Back to Happiness' in 'solemn unison' as 'they might a hymn by Hubert Parry'[94] such as 'Dear Lord and Father of Mankind' or 'Jerusalem'. The sacred appears in the secular world. The use of a well-known hymn is also a reminder of the genuine affection many have for hymns irrespective of belief and McEwan's inference that an awareness of Parry might be as natural as a popular song is significant, especially given the declining attendance at church services. The music and text of the church extend far beyond its walls and this is something that McEwan effectively acknowledges. The comment of Maslama, an Indian from Guyana, in Salman Rushdie's *The Satanic Verses*, speaks of the sense of belonging that hymnody sung in England can provide, even for someone from abroad: 'by the grace of God Almighty. I am a regular Sunday man, sir; I confess to a weakness for the English Hymnal, and I sing to raise the roof'.[95]

As McEwan notes earlier in the text, the Reversalist movement in *The Cockroach* (that is at the centre of the narrative and which the government is trying

---

[93]　Alan Bennett, *Allelujah!* (London, 2018).

[94]　McEwan, *The Cockroach*, p. 43.

[95]　Salman Rushdie, *The Satanic Verses* (New York, 2007), p. 197.

An Atheist's Portrayal of the Church of England 57

to respond to in a vein akin to the British government after the 2016 Brexit vote) is 'impelled towards a goal that lifted beyond mere reason to embrace a mystical sense of nation, of an understanding as simple and as simply good and true as religious faith'.[96] However, it is the 'simple' element of faith that McEwan questions, especially in *The Children Act*, and he approaches this with two overarching questions that relate to his public commentaries on religion as discussed in the Introduction. Firstly, do simplicity and relative subservience suggest a lack of enquiry and natural self-doubt that is (to McEwan) essential for a rational person? Secondly, does the church espouse simplicity to promote its own ends? The comparative simplicity of the hymn in *or Shall we die?* mocks the greater moral question of war. This is a fascinating cross-cultural moment because the overall approach of the oratorio is recognizably Anglican and questioning but yet the style in this section is comparatively naïve. The indication on the score that a section should sound 'sanctimoniously cheerful' as a bomb is delivered is a biting criticism of the church. As hymns remain one of the church's strongest emotional tools for evangelism this is an especially important consideration in terms of the measure of gravitas being considered and realized; thus the two-edged sword of a familiar hymn style. McEwan and Berkeley are using a church style and aesthetic for an argument against the church itself and this brings forward the marked hypocrisy that McEwan sees in the relationship between the church and the state. When the writer and politician Lucille Iremonger commented that 'whether he [the Prime Minister] is a believer or not, he will have a deeply committed interest in religion',[97] McEwan's narrative questions whether the senior clergy are, in turn, too interested in politics.

Continuing Doubt

An inherent dilemma in the public perception of the church comes from the very nature of doubt and questioning that Henry VIII effectively put into practice. In doubting the supremacy of Rome he also set in motion a gradual culture to question other matters, even if that could not include a basic doubting of faith for some time. When the Defender of (the) Faith – the exact translation itself remains a source of debate – is not a priest or even necessarily a regular communicant, the question of leadership by example becomes a source of debate. 'Living a Christian life' does not in any sense demand regular church attendance in the broad Anglican psyche.

However, the idea of presenting challenging questions regarding various aspects of faith is central to the English identity and the perception of the Anglican church of the twentieth century. In this respect there is a distinct Angli-

---

[96] McEwan, *The Cockroach*, pp. 21–22.
[97] Jeremy Paxman, *The Political Animal* (London, 2002), p. 39.

58 *Music and Religion in the Writings of Ian McEwan*

canism to McEwan's arguments, especially when bolstered by the comments of a senior Anglican bishop. The sense of individualism was brought to the fore with the ordination of Dr David Jenkins as Bishop of Durham in 1984. Jenkins had previously commented that he did not believe in the virgin birth and the resurrection was a 'conjuring trick with bones'.[98] Days after his consecration in York Minster the building was struck by lightning in what was to become the worst English church fire seen since the end of World War II. On Jenkins's death in 2016 the former Dean of Durham, Michael Sadgrove, noted that the moniker for Jenkins as the 'unbelieving bishop' was unfair: 'You only had to have half an hour's conversation with him to realise that he was a man of passionate Christian belief and conviction and what is more he believed entirely in the incarnation, that God comes among us fully in the person of Jesus, and he believed entirely in the resurrection. He was simply asking the question "how do we express ourselves in the twentieth century in ways that communicate with people living in the modern world, and a very secular world?"'.[99] Jenkins though was a powerful voice throughout the country and a strong critic of the Prime Minister, Margaret Thatcher, on both issues of social justice and the burgeoning arms race. County Durham had suffered terrible hardships with the closure of collieries during his time as bishop and he was outspoken in his opinions about the government that had left thousands of former miners unemployed with little hope of new jobs. However, McEwan's commentary below in relation to *or Shall we die?* on the role of the clergy as being at some remove from societal engagement is measured because there have been few clergy that have garnered the attention of Jenkins since his retirement and none whose comments have been the source of sustained debate. The campaigning of the then Canon Chancellor of St Paul's Cathedral, Giles Fraser, on behalf of the homeless camped outside the cathedral in 2011 as part of the Occupy London movement brought a rare image of the clergy at the forefront of media attention. Fraser has continued to be a regular contributor to many political programmes on British television.

There remains a social stature related to church attendance that was noted by George Orwell in *A Clergyman's Daughter* (1935) and which in many respects has changed very little since its publication. In the novel the headmistress who is keen to keep attendance high at her problematic school attends church in order to be seen by the parents of her pupils and also by the parents of prospective applicants.[100] Over time, the novel's protagonist, Dorothy,

---

[98] 'Anglican sets off a theology storm', *New York Times* (28 October 1984), online at <https://www.nytimes.com/1984/10/28/world/anglican-sets-off-a-theology-storm.html> [accessed 17 December 2020].

[99] Aaron James, '"Unbelieving bishop" title "unfair" says former dean', online at <https://premierchristian.news/en/news/article/unbelieving-bishop-title-unfair-says-former-dean> (5 September 2016) [accessed 17 December 2020].

[100] George Orwell, *A Clergyman's Daughter* (London, 1990), p. 217.

An Atheist's Portrayal of the Church of England 59

simply loses faith after witnessing the horrors of poverty at first hand. Jenkins's commentaries decades later and then McEwan's blunt criticism sit comfortably together with Orwell's narrative. In a typically subdued English fashion there is no climactic event or Damascene transformation that leads Dorothy to this loss of faith but rather that on returning to her father's parish she comes to the realization that things are not as they once were. Near the conclusion of the novel Orwell writes:

> Your life and death, it may be, are a single note in the eternal orchestra that plays for His diversion. And suppose you don't like the tune? She thought of that dreadful unfrocked clergyman in Trafalgar Square [who was freely changing the words to prayers and scripture]. Had she dreamed the things he said, or had he really said them? 'Therefore with Demons and Archdemons and with all the company of Hell' [as opposed to Therefore with angels and archangels and all the company of heaven]. But that was silly, really. For your not liking the tune was also part of the tune.[101]

or Shall we die?

The final sentence of the Orwell quote above, 'For your not liking the tune was also part of the tune',[102] has a particular relevance to the writings of McEwan because to doubt religion is not necessarily to doubt the existence and role of the church and clergy as a continuing necessary presence (and a potentially positive one) in society, especially if you consider a degree of discomfort with the institution to be natural. In relation to this and also the troubled role of politicians and clergy in society – noting that senior clergy have to be deft politicians in their own sphere – McEwan offers a blistering commentary in the preface to his published lyrics for the opera composed by Michael Berkeley, *or Shall we die?*, that focuses on the contemporary concern of nuclear war in the 1970s and 1980s:

> Before the slaughter [of war] there never seems to be a priest lacking to bless the executioners. The chorus's lines in section three [see below] reflect my conviction that whatever moral or spiritual resources are necessary for us to avoid destroying ourselves they are unlikely to be provided by the world-weary bureaucracies of the established churches, nor by any religious sect that claims that it alone has the ear of God. If, for example, the Church of England comes to accept, as it is likely, the idea that within women as well as men there is a spiritual dimension that could enable them to become priests, it will be far less from conviction than from tired capitulation to changes in the secular world. In the same way, the Church may follow the opposition to militarism but never – as an institution – lead it. This is not to deny, of course,

[101] Ibid.
[102] Ibid.

60   *Music and Religion in the Writings of Ian McEwan*

that many exceptional individuals work within that and other churches. But centuries of mind-numbing dogma, professionalization and enmeshment in privilege have all but annihilated the mystical and spiritual experience that is said to be at the heart of Christianity.[103]

[In the score it is noted that the first section should be sung in the manner of a Victorian hymn followed by a 'sanctimoniously cheerful' style.]

Three
Chorus: The aircrew kneels before the priest.
With God's blessing we deliver his bomb.

———

Chorus: Our God is manly! ... In war he refuses us nothing? ... Refuses us nothing. ... Nothing. Nothing.[104]

In the first text, McEwan raises many of the topical issues surrounding the church in the late 1970s and 1980s, including the ordination of women, the degree of privilege associated with the church that is discussed earlier in this chapter in relation to the residence of the bishop in *Sweet Tooth*, and then a criticism of the church as being close to the state. The final point is discussed at the beginning of this chapter in relation to the long history of the relationship between the church, state, and public, and then later in this chapter with specific reference to the government of Margaret Thatcher. However, this in itself is an important counterpoint to the Chorus's line 'Our God is manly', which superimposes the issues of women's ordination onto the general criticism of the church. It also questions whether Thatcher's approach to war was in some respect a perceived necessity on her part as the first Prime Minister who was a woman. Moreover, the nature of complaint and agitation regarding the church that McEwan speaks of in the preface text to *or Shall we die?* illuminates the nature of the role of the church in society which he consistently approaches separately to his commentaries on the nature of theology, as discussed in the Introduction with regard to *Science*. It could be argued that if he doesn't believe in the role of faith, there is no need to be concerned with the clergy. Surely, if there is no belief then all other matters relating to the church are flawed as well. But in doing so, McEwan creates a questioning narrative that in many respects is more familiar to the churchgoer than the atheist. The points he raises are the very points that the Church of England argues about within its own walls. In a similar fashion to his characterizations about composers in *Amsterdam* and *For You* there is an insider understanding, despite his atheism. In this respect, similar to Stephen Fry, whose Tweet is quoted above, and who encountered the church at a younger age and then moved away from it, there is more than an acknowledgement of the church. There is a

[103]   McEwan, *or Shall we die? A Move Abroad*, pp. 10–11.
[104]   Ibid., p. 19.

An Atheist's Portrayal of the Church of England   61

considered understanding of it. As a consequence, this makes the criticism all the more biting because it is precise and nuanced.

Blake and McEwan

McEwan decided to use texts of William Blake in _or Shall we die?_ after the rest of the libretto had been written and this especially pleased Michael Berkeley whose composition, _The Wild Winds_, was a setting of Blake's _Mad Song_. McEwan writes that 'Blake was a powerful opponent of Newtonian science, and his poetry returns again and again to the perils of divorcing reason from feeling',[105] a point that draws on McEwan's suspicion of religion given his view of people as 'essentially moral beings'.[106] However, as Dominic Head notes, the overall style of writing within the oratorio is 'blunt [as] befits the urgency of the topic but is quite opposed to the non-partisan spirit that McEwan sees as the vital ingredient of the aesthetic of the novel'. He succinctly notes that 'the piece is an assault upon unfettered scientific rationality, and a lament for the ravaged natural world – the nuclear threat being one aspect of this'.[107] In this respect, _or Shall we die?_ offers a rare criticism of both science and faith in one narrative.

The questioning of a Christian deity is brought into stark terms in the chorus texts of the oratorio at the end of scene five. Following the Woman's lament while searching for her daughter at the conclusion of the oratorio there is a dualism with science as both the creator and the destroyer of human life. The text in scene five is taken from Blake's _The Tyger_ and this has especial resonance because it brings to mind the well-known opening of the poem: 'Tyger Tyger, burning bright,/In the forests of the night;/What immortal hand or eye,/ Could frame thy fearful symmetry?'

The fearful symmetry in this context can allude to the nature of weaponry, the symmetry of war, as well as the bitter and fateful symmetry of cause and effect in war. The symmetry too is also McEwan's in the use of Blake's text alongside his own questioning in scene Seven: 'Are we too late to love ourselves? Shall we change, or shall we die?' Here the use of 'love', rather than the Divine 'Love' is brought into deeper consideration. Do we love ourselves or do we trust in the 'human form divine'?

The symmetry can also relate to the contrasts between Blake's _Songs of Experience_ and _The Divine Image_. As Nicholas Shrimpton notes: 'Seen through the eyes of innocence, God is a lovely shepherd who protects his sheep (_The Lamb_). Seen through the eyes of experience (_The Tyger_), God is a sadist who deliberately created carnivores.'[108] McEwan writes that since he could 'never aspire to

---

[105]   Ibid., p. 12.

[106]   Richard Dawkins and Ian McEwan interview.

[107]   Head, _Ian McEwan_, p. 72; McEwan, _Preface. A Move Abroad_, pp. xxi, xxiii.

[108]   Nicholas Shrimpton (ed.), _William Blake, Selected Poems_ (Oxford, 2019), pp. xxvii.

62   *Music and Religion in the Writings of Ian McEwan*

Blake's density of meaning or the simplicity and beauty of his expression, [he] decided to draw on his strength by quotation and to think of him as the presiding spirit of the piece'.[109] Moreover, Blake's poetry 'returns again and again to the perils of divorcing reason from feeling'.[110]

Five	
Chorus:	When the stars threw down their spears,
	And water'd heaven with their tears,
	Did He smile His work to see?
	Did He who made the Lamb make thee? *(Songs of Experience*, Blake)
Seven	
Man and Woman:	The planet does not turn for us alone.
	Science is a form of wonder, knowledge a form of love.
	Are we too late to love ourselves?
	Shall we change, or shall we die? (McEwan)
Woman	The moon lifts higher and brightens.
	Only shadows point the way. (McEwan)
Chorus	For Mercy has a human heart,
	Pity a human face,
	And Love, the human form divine,
	And Peace, the human dress. (*The Divine Image*, Blake)
	Then every man, of every clime,
	That prays in his distress,
	Prays to the human form divine,
	Love, Mercy, Pity, Peace. (*The Divine Image*, Blake)

The use of Blake's *The Divine Image* at the end of the oratorio is an equally poignant juxtaposition because of the suspended knowledge created by the unsung final stanza of the poem, which counters both arguments as Blake and likewise McEwan (above) question whether the believer is in fact undeniably wed to the Creator and if not through belief then, in societal terms – via the church which McEwan has criticized – through association. A reference to Blake is also found in *Amsterdam* where the chief inspector is working towards a degree at the Open University and has an enthusiasm for Blake.[111] Blake's *Jerusalem* cast an unavoidably English identity to Christ on earth. Hubert Parry's setting of it as a hymn created a vision for an English church that many could freely and conveniently associate with. Its popularity as a hymn continues, and, as observed earlier in this chapter, surpasses religious or political concerns.

---

[109] McEwan, *or Shall we die? A Move Abroad*, p. 13.

[110] Ibid., p. 12.

[111] McEwan, *Amsterdam*, p. 151.

Contemporary Politics

For McEwan the writing of the libretto was 'more of an inevitability than a choice'[112] during the years of the Margaret Thatcher premiership and also relates to his sustained presence in the media as a commentator on political matters. As he notes in the preface to *or Shall we die?* 'moral revulsion, openly or tacitly expressed was not sufficient'.[113] He also came to realize that the degree of public awareness of the literary and musical worlds was not as close as he first thought, and so when *The Child in Time* was subsequently published, people assumed he had not been writing at all, whereas he had been writing the oratorio libretto.[114] McEwan's and Berkeley's approach to the topic of nuclear disarmament through an oratorio followed a well-established stance of the artistic community towards pacifism in general. In *On Chesil Beach*, Florence is a member of CND and also, perhaps coincidentally, performs the music of well-known pacifists, including Benjamin Britten and Frank Bridge. McEwan notes:

> Throughout 1980, along with many others, I found myself disturbed and obsessed by the prospect of a new and madly vigorous arms race. Russia had recently invaded Afghanistan and later in the year there was the possibility of intervention in Poland.
>
> The language of nuclear apologists had taken a fresh turn: there was open talk of a limited and winnable nuclear war in which Europe would serve as a battleground for the two major powers. Weapons had been devised accordingly. The fragile concept of deterrence had been shaken by the determination on both sides to find ever more accurate missiles that could hit enemy silos – weapons that were only of use in a first strike, before the enemy could empty its silos.[115]

In a 2018 interview,[116] Berkeley was clear that not only did McEwan take a keen interest in the scientific aspect of the scientists' work but he also had a significant concern about the US government's attitude and actions during the Cold War. In this respect, the oratorio was an opportunity to express a critical view in an artistic light. Even though some people felt it was a piece allied to the ongoing work of CND, that was not the intention of either Berkeley or McEwan. Rather it was a work that followed in the tradition of Michael Tippett's *A Child of Our Time* (1939/41/44) and Benjamin Britten's *War Requiem* (1961/62). The purpose was not to give a polemic argument a musical voice but rather, in a spirit akin to many of McEwan's novels, to give the audience a

---

[112] McEwan, *or Shall we die? A Move Abroad*, p. 3.

[113] Ibid., p. xx.

[114] Ibid., p. xxvi.

[115] Ibid.

[116] Iain Quinn, 'Interview with Michael Berkeley' (2018).

64   *Music and Religion in the Writings of Ian McEwan*

perspective on the degree of loss that a nuclear war would create and the sense of responsibility of governments, the church, and the general public. As a result of the performance of the oratorio Berkeley and McEwan suffered a degree of criticism that they were participating in a political argument but their purpose was to heighten awareness of the potential threat of nuclear conflict.[117] This was a sentiment echoed by Tippett, who related his concerns directly to the artistic world:

> We are all threatened by the suicidal lunacy of nuclear warfare and everyone carries a concern for this over into his own sphere of work. I think that, in so far as the artist is interested in the inner nature of human beings, one might say he suffers from living in a society in which external things are so prominent. The artist may feel, therefore, that he has less social backing, that his work is not as highly prioritized as it was.[118]

As noted above, McEwan's libretto for *or Shall we die?* had a pronounced scepticism of the church and this is buttressed by his criticism of the Thatcher government, which he freely admitted left a 'nasty taste'[119] any time he later thought of it. Margaret Thatcher had employed scripture at various turns in speeches and this can be viewed as a double negative for McEwan, who opposed both her social policies and her role in the arms race. In Graeme Smith's article 'Margaret Thatcher's Christian Faith – A Case Study in Political Theology', Smith notes how in her Iain Macleod Memorial Lecture of July 1977, she reinforced a belief that to her 'no other ideology or party could claim a closer connection with the Christian faith'[120] than the Conservatives, a point that, as discussed in the Introduction in relation to McEwan's *Science*, brought her closer still to the thinking of Ronald Reagan. Thatcher stated:

> The Tories began as a Church party. Concerned with the Church and state, and in that order, before our concern extended to the economy, and many other fields which politics now touches. Religion gives us not only our values – a scheme of things in which economic, social, penal policy have their place – but also our historical roots.[121]

Robin Harris's research also draws attention to the work of George Lindbeck, who in his study of postliberal theology, argues that religious belief can be appreciated as a 'cultural-linguistic system' that shapes 'the entirety of life

---

[117] Ibid.

[118] Murray Schafer, 'Michael Tippett', *British Composers in Interview* (London, 1963), p. 100.

[119] John Haffenden, *Novelists in Interview* (London, 1985), p. 87.

[120] Graeme Smith, 'Margaret Thatcher's Christian Faith – A Case Study in Political Ideology', *Journal of Religious Ethics*, 35:2 (June, 2007), 234.

[121] Robin Harris, *Margaret Thatcher: The Collected Speeches* (London, 1997), pp. 58–59. The Ian Macleod Memorial Lecture.

An Atheist's Portrayal of the Church of England 65

and thought'.[122] This is a critical statement when considered alongside McEwan's writings because McEwan readily places the church in a cultural context and through references to hymns, also in a literary context. However, he is opposed to the idea of religion shaping 'the entirety of life and thought' for the reasons Harris goes on to describe. This approach 'diminishes the place of voluntarist or cognitive assent to propositional truth claims; these follow induction into the religious system. It also displaces the notion of personal religious experience seeking theological expression; for an experience to be religious, a religious language with which to have the experience is required'.[123] In this sense Harris's analysis of Lindbeck's work heightens the possibility of studying Thatcher's commentaries from a discrete theological perspective. But more obviously we see Thatcher's use of language in often blatant terms, not least in quoting the prayer of St Francis after she returned from her meeting with the Queen on 4 May 1979 following her election victory. Standing outside 10 Downing Street she remarked:

> I know full well the responsibilities that await me as I enter the door of No. 10 and I'll strive unceasingly to try to fulfil the trust and confidence that the British people have placed in me and the things in which I believe. And I would just like to remember some words of St Francis of Assisi which I think are really just particularly apt at the moment. 'Where there is discord, may we bring harmony. Where there is error, may we bring truth. Where there is doubt, may we bring faith. And where there is despair, may we bring hope'.[124]

For an atheist like McEwan, the adoption of this text by a representative of the larger public is a considerable liberty. As Thatcher took liberties with the adoption of religious text, so too did Berkeley and McEwan take a relative liberty with the use of a familiar church style in the oratorio. In both cases, an argument is strengthened and seen anew. But the nature of these specific criticisms of church and state has to be considered in the context of the church of the time. McEwan's libretto of 1983 appears at the beginning of a decade of significant re-evaluation by the Church of England of its role in society, made light of in *Yes, Minister* earlier in this chapter, but relevant in the context of *or Shall we die?* because it highlights the nature of displacement many were starting to feel from the church and its positions that were increasingly difficult to discern.

In 1985 the Church of England published its now famous *Faith in the City* report, in which the authors argued that 'no "theology" was required to moti-

---

[122] George Lindbeck, *The Nature of Doctrine. Religion and Theology in a Postliberal Age* (Philadephia, 1984), p. 33.

[123] Smith, 'Margaret Thatcher's Christian Faith – A Case Study in Political Ideology', pp. 237–238.

[124] 'Remarks on becoming a Prime Minister' (4 May, 1979), online at <https://www.margaretthatcher.org/document/104078> [accessed 17 December 2020].

66   *Music and Religion in the Writings of Ian McEwan*

vate Christians to the plight of the poorest in Britain's inner-city areas'.[125] But, as Graeme Smith notes, what was required was 'a recognition that the Thatcher government's policies had led to a situation in which the social and economic conditions of the poorest were worse and so the values underpinning those policies contradicted Christian norms'.[126] As McEwan bluntly censures: 'there never seems to be a priest lacking to bless the executioners'.[127] In this sense, both the government and the church were out of touch with greater moral and ethical priorities and consequently the 'inevitability' (McEwan) of writing the libretto and the ultimate oratorio draws attention to the dual hypocrisy of the time. As Raymond Plant observes in 'The Anglican Church and the Secular State':

> It is not clear what the Church is adding, for example, to a theory of redistributive justice of its own, and one is left with the despair of feeling that one is looking for the odd bit of theological backing for one's political preferences which are held on quite other grounds.[128]

John Vincent believed that 'for a time in the 1970s [Thatcher] seemed to have some sort of "public Christianity" in mind ... but either she lacked the words, or there were too few Christians for it to matter'.[129] Arguably, Thatcher realized that religion could have a different sort of leverage even if churches were seeing their congregations diminish. However, it is this sort of casual application of, or worse, intentional misuse of religion for political gain that causes suspicion at best and ire at worst in the perception of the church in modern Britain. The declining numbers in congregations have further magnified the points made by Rowan Williams at the beginning of this chapter[130] because to many the archbishop represents a steadily declining constituency. With Thatcher's nonconformist upbringing and her own doubts about the nature of the male-dominated Establishment she also saw and seized upon a vacuum of influence that the church had fallen into. As such, the question of national spiritual renewal was something that she saw herself as influencing through deeds, while the Church of England muddled along with still more reports and liturgical reinvention. The public watched it seemingly drift away to such an

---

[125]   Smith, 'Margaret Thatcher's Christian Faith – A Case Study in Political Ideology', p. 239.

[126]   Ibid.

[127]   McEwan, *or Shall we die? A Move Abroad*, pp. 10–11.

[128]   Raymond Plant, 'The Anglican Church and the Secular State', in *G. Moyser (ed.), Church and Politics Today. Essays on the Role of the Church of England in Contemporary Politics* (Edinburgh, 1985), p. 329.

[129]   John Vincent, 'The Thatcher Governments, 1979–1987', in Peter Hennessy and Anthony Seldon (eds), *Ruling Performance – British Governments from Attlee to Thatcher* (Oxford, 1987), p. 283.

[130]   Williams, *Faith in the Public Square*, p. 1.

extent that clergy could become regularly mocked in television comedies. McEwan's libretto and comments[131] in the preface to the work seize on the impression of a church that has lost its way. The spirit Thatcher sought to renew or at least embolden in Britain was the Christian spirit as she believed it to be. With an absence of hope and clear direction from the church, she instead sought to convince people that they could be renewed by a faith she had in them while tracing her own nonconformist identity in resisting established practice. The approach was obviously more palatable if you were gainfully employed and not directly disadvantaged by her many social policies. As Harris noted, to 'revitalize the "spirit" of the past'[132] was to recapture a Christian spirit that to Thatcher was being eroded in British society and she believed that the same society had a fundamentally Christian identity that needed replenishing.[133] In a 1981 commentary at the church of St Lawrence Jewry in the City of London, Thatcher again employed a narrative where she comfortably spoke of her own perception of British faith:

> These characteristics of our nation – the acknowledgement of the Almighty, a sense of tolerance, an acknowledgement of moral absolutes and a positive view of work – have sustained us in the past. Today they are being challenged. Although we are still able to live on the spiritual capital passed down to us, it is self-deceiving to think we can do so for ever. Each generation must renew its spiritual assets if the integrity of the nation is to survive.[134]

As Smith notes, Thatcher's concern was 'not to fill churches, but to ensure economic growth and prosperity'[135] but, largely through design, her voice was the only one consistently heard. Doubtless aware that a discussion about the church and religion was not an illimitable resource for advancing political policies when the numbers of congregants were consistently declining, Thatcher instead turned on the broader and more easily intelligible 'moral' argument whereby choice was the only natural determiner of right and wrong in society. This is a point that speaks to McEwan's understanding of people as being 'essentially moral beings'[136], but in the oratorio text and its preface it is clear that he considers the role of the contemporary government and the contemporary church as falling short of winning a moral argument. The seemingly contrary stance of being an atheist and yet being critical of the church not doing enough

---

[131] McEwan, *or Shall we die? A Move Abroad*, pp. 10–11.

[132] Smith, 'Margaret Thatcher's Christian Faith – A Case Study in Political Ideology', p. 250.

[133] Ibid.

[134] Margaret Thatcher, 'St. Lawrence Jewry, 1981', in Robin Harris (ed.), *Margaret Thatcher. The Collected Speeches* (London, 1987), pp. 121–30.

[135] Smith, 'Margaret Thatcher's Christian Faith – A Case Study in Political Ideology', p. 251.

[136] Richard Dawkins and Ian McEwan interview.

68 *Music and Religion in the Writings of Ian McEwan*

brings the argument back to the central point of seeing the church in a primarily cultural role which, as a popular writer, McEwan is further reinforcing. I would argue that the reason that a seemingly impossible dichotomy exists is because McEwan fundamentally observes there are values within the church, whether they are the promotion of music, culture, architecture, or moderate debate which inevitably align with rationalist thinking in Britain. This begs the question of whether the Church of England influences society or vice versa and in trying to appear 'relevant' (as comedically discussed in the *Yes, Prime Minster* scene above) is in fact codependent.

Criticism from the Pulpit

Earlier in this chapter, I discussed the nature of McEwan's presentation of the church through a very specific lens that favours traditional liturgy and indeed public impressions surrounding the life of senior clergy, together with the place and also the value of evensong as a liturgy that consistently finds a congregation of believers and nonbelievers and is 'open to all'. These perceptions of McEwan are not inaccurate, even if they represent a singular view of the Church of England in a contemporary setting within the novels. However, in terms of the presentation of clergy willing to 'bless the executioners', there were many exceptions and the most well known was the Bishop of Durham, David Jenkins. To consider the role of the church in the 1980s amid liturgical upheavals, new church designs, the *Faith and the City* report, and most significantly, the ordination of women, is to engage in a complex web of issues that ultimately started to fracture congregations within the Church of England. These issues are not raised in McEwan's narratives and nor do they need to be. But to consider the national landscape in which *or Shall we die?* is set without observing the powerful public voice of David Jenkins would be an omission, because the resulting impression of the church as presented by McEwan is limited to a niche identity. As one of the Church of England's most senior bishops and with a seat in the House of Lords, his comments clarify that the church cannot be portrayed in one light. Indeed, in the often-simplistic nature of new atheism someone like Jenkins is a problematic figure because he argued strongly and provokingly against many within the church.

When Jenkins became Bishop of Durham in September 1984, the opening words of his sermon, following a text from Romans, summed up the feelings of many of the forgotten in Thatcher's Britain.

> May the God of hope fill you with all joy and peace by your faith in him until, by the power of the Holy Spirit, you overflow with hope. (Romans 15.13)

> We could do with some help from this 'God of hope' here in the North East. Unemployment is at thirty-five to fifty per cent. They [the government] propose to dump radioactive waste on us as if we were the scrap-yard of Britain. The miners strike highlights how divided and distressed society is,

An Atheist's Portrayal of the Church of England   69

to the point of violence. Christians seems absorbed in bad-tempered arguments about belief, marriage, or politics. The organized churches find financial problems looming larger and larger. We all wonder if the old men in the Kremlin or in the White House will overreach themselves and actually use nuclear weapons which are unthinkable but real. If you stop and think, hope does not come easily.[137]

The last two sentences of this text strongly mirror McEwan's comments in *Science*,[138] as discussed in the Introduction in relation to McEwan's perception of the overreaching US dominance in the Cold War and Reagan's comments on Armageddon. The earlier references to the North East of Britain as being a 'scrapyard' for radioactive waste relate not just to the libretto and preface for *or Shall we die?* but also Florence's association with CND in *On Chesil Beach*, and CND's sustained work in trying to remove weapons from American airbases in Britain. In all of these points, there is an obvious accord in the views of Jenkins and McEwan despite their respective positions as believer and atheist. The broad nature of the Church of England is often confounding to new atheists because at its core and in its history, there has been strong argument and dissent. However, McEwan's commentaries on the church can also be seen as part of a sustained twentieth-century criticism of the Established Church. Although McEwan points to a perceived willingness of clergy to support government actions in *or Shall we die?*, the actions of individual clergy do not necessarily align with the wishes of either the larger church or the government of the time. Indeed, Jenkins's arguments are in line with McEwan's own anti-nuclear stance.

Russell to McEwan

The measure of English apathy towards established religion discussed by Scruton, and yet the relative acceptance of the Church of England as central to the Establishment and thus the identity of Britain, is dealt with in eviscerating terms by an earlier English philosopher, Bertrand Russell. His comments find a parallel with those of McEwan almost sixty years later when the subject of war was again a topic on which the church's role was, to both writers, unacceptably vague. Russell's later-published speech to the South London Branch of the National Secular Society titled 'Why I am not a Christian' was delivered on 6 March 1927 and speaks to the same topics as McEwan's commentaries. Whereas the speech is designed to challenge the notion of faith over fact, the most powerful areas of discussion are Russell's criticisms of 1) the actions of the modern church (which McEwan portrays as unethical and inconsistent with its own teachings) 2) the interpretation of scripture to further the church as an institutional body (which Thatcher readily employed and which is parodied

---

[137]   David Jenkins, *God, Politics and the Future* (Wilton, 1988), p. 3.

[138]   McEwan, *Science*, pp. 90–91.

70   *Music and Religion in the Writings of Ian McEwan*

with the pseudo-Victorian hymn style in *or Shall we die?*) and 3) the use of force in the place of peace (which McEwan observes in *Science*[139] and *or Shall we die?*).[140] It is for these reasons that the cynicism through the oratorio hymn with its 'sanctimonious' air is so potent. Doubting the church and especially the role of moral authority for an Established Church during the Cold War is deliberately provoking and Berkeley was clear that attention needed to be drawn not just to the horror of a nuclear holocaust but also to the too easy acceptance of an establishment, including the church, towards that end.[141]

Russell's arguments in the wake of The Great War and his continued commentaries on television in subsequent decades provided a sustained challenge to the image of the Established Church as a cornerstone in a moderate society. His commentaries find a significant alignment with McEwan's systematic disassembling of the absence of criticism by church leaders during the Cold War. The 'folly of testing bombs'[142](*On Chesil Beach*) and potential nuclear holocaust is the central focus of the oratorio *or Shall we die?* and in *On Chesil Beach*, set in 1962, a nuclear holocaust is referred to as the modern equivalent of the apocalypse,[143] albeit with CND being likened to a millenarian sect.[144] Russell's commentaries align with new atheism and the notion that religion is based on a system of fear. In this respect, his comments speak to McEwan's concerns in *Science* regarding Reagan[145] and his close association with the agenda of the more fundamentalist views of conservative evangelicals. But in the preface to *or Shall we die?* McEwan also notes that the idea of writing on the topic of the Cold War was also 'promising [as it included] public policy [and] private fear – the kind of opposition I like'.[146] This comment on 'fear' is interesting to juxtapose alongside Russell's text below where he notes that the church, too, uses fear.

> Religion is based, I think, primarily and mainly upon fear. It is partly the terror of the unknown and partly, as I have said, the wish to feel you have a kind of elder brother who will stand by you in all your troubles and disputes. Fear is the basis of the whole thing – fear of the mysterious, fear of defeat, fear of death. Fear is the parent of cruelty, and therefore it is no wonder if cruelty and religion have gone hand in hand. It is because fear is at the basis of the two things. In this world we can now begin a little to understand things, and a little to master them by the help of science, which has forced its way step by

---

[139] Ibid., pp. 92–98.

[140] McEwan, *or Shall we die? A Move Abroad*, pp. 10–11.

[141] Iain Quinn, 'Interview with Michael Berkeley'.

[142] McEwan, *On Chesil Beach*, p. 30.

[143] Ibid., p. 143.

[144] Ibid., p. 144.

[145] McEwan, *Science*, p. 73.

[146] McEwan, *Preface. A Move Abroad*, p. xviii.

An Atheist's Portrayal of the Church of England   71

step against the Christian religion, against the churches, and against the opposition of the old precepts. Science can help us to get over this craven fear in
which mankind has lived for so many generations. Science can teach us, and
I think our own hearts can teach us, no longer to look around for imaginary
supports, no longer to invent allies in the sky, but rather to look to our own
efforts here below to make this world a fit place to live in, instead of the sort
of place that the churches in all these centuries have made it.[147]

When Russell discusses the emotional aspect of religion, he essentially talks of
guilt and the social notion and acceptance that a Christian is by default a good
person, although not necessarily in the nature of clergy 'niceness' as earlier
discussed in the research of Steve Bruce.[148] He emphasizes this idea while also
referring to the brutality of the Spanish Inquisition, the burning of witches,
racism, the mitigation of slavery and stating that 'every moral progress that
there has been in the world has been consistently opposed by the organized
churches of the world'.[149] This is a criticism that relates to McEwan's observations in the preface for *or Shall we die?*[150] and the dubious moral position of
clergy willing to 'bless the executioners'. It is a criticism centred on clergy being
on the wrong side of moral and ethical arguments and unwilling to stand up
against the state which, in the case of the Church of England, is arguably in
part because it is central to the same Establishment framework. Russell's inference that 'self-respecting human beings' do not need the church is mirrored
later in McEwan's conversation with Dawkins and his comment that humans
do not need 'a God to ordain our moral priorities for us ...'[151] For both Russell and McEwan there is a belief that extends beyond the scientific arguments
of new atheism and towards specific criticism of the church as an institution.
Although McEwan's most critical comments in *Science*[152] are related to the USA
and the close association of conservative evangelicals to the levers of power,
his criticism of the Church of England and state in Britain in *or Shall we die?* is
extremely clear when it comes to political matters.

Whether reading Russell's statements in 1927, in the immediate aftermath
of World War II, during the Cold War or alongside McEwan's arguments in
the preface to *or Shall we die?*, there is a fundamental flaw in an argument that
the church holds sufficient sway to influence the larger trajectory of society,
although it can certainly be a critical voice. However successful a voice it can be
is limited, as discussed earlier, by the degree of freedom the press and the larger
public will enable. If clergy are solely expected to be 'nice' and generally com-

---

[147] Bertrand Russell, *Why I am not a Christian* (London, 1957), p. 22.

[148] Bruce, 'Serious Religion in Secular Culture', in *Scottish Gods*, p. 133.

[149] Russell, *Why I am not a Christian*, p. 22.

[150] McEwan, *or Shall we die? A Move Abroad*, pp. 10–11.

[151] Richard Dawkins and Ian McEwan interview.

[152] McEwan, *Science*, pp. 72–74.

Music and Religion in the Writings of Ian McEwan

forting but unable to engage in debates that are perceived to be overly political, then their voices are undeniably muted to a 'still small voice of calm'.[153] A statement from Rowan Williams[154] that I refer to earlier in this chapter concerning the difficult position an archbishop finds himself in when making public comments stops short of a consequential reality. If the clergy are criticized for making comments because they are expected to stay out of politics and instead quietly represent a declining constituency within the population, how can they also be criticized, most often by new atheists, for making comments where they do speak to public concerns?

Of course, there is potential influence from the church, but being the 'principal enemy', as Russell wrote, suggests a cohesion between denominations that does not exist beyond ecumenical endeavours either at the publication of his text or today. In this respect, Russell does not draw a line between different denominations, and although McEwan's references in his fictional writing clearly refer to the Church of England, he also does not set one denomination apart from another. In *The Children Act* both Jehovah's Witnesses and members of the Church of England are considered as possible followers of a cult.[155] However, this expansive approach finds traction with the spirit of new atheism that Richard Dawkins, Christopher Hitchens, and Sam Harris fixated on because, to quote Karen Armstrong, 'it has focused exclusively on the God developed by the fundamentalists, and all three insist that fundamentalism constitutes the essence and core of all religion' and that 'they refuse, on principle, to dialogue with theologians who are more representative of mainstream tradition'.[156] McEwan's approach is undeniably influenced by new atheism but it is much more nuanced, beginning with the fact that he understands the cultural, societal, and emotional attachment people can have with the church, irrespective of whether they are believers or not. In this respect his commentaries and depictions are also more nuanced than Russell's because they lean towards the image of the church most commonly portrayed in literature and indeed the media, as discussed earlier.

In considering not only McEwan's doubt but that of a sceptical culture and society in Britain, the question of how this translates into his writings is therefore not simply one of science first and religion never, although there is a discrediting of the church in favour of science in *Solid Geometry*[157] and more bluntly in *Solar* where, in relation to advanced science, there is the comment that 'God was nowhere near this clever'.[158] Rather, McEwan's approach is of a

---

[153] Text taken from part of John Greenleaf Whittier's *The Brewing of Soma*, which was extracted to form the hymn 'Dear Lord and Father of mankind'.

[154] Williams, *Faith in the Public Square*, p. 1.

[155] McEwan, *The Children Act*, pp. 68–69.

[156] Armstrong, *Religion*, pp. 13–14.

[157] Ian McEwan, *Solid Geometry* in *First Love, Last Rites* (London, 1997), p. 53.

[158] Ian McEwan, *Solar* (New York, 2010), p. 22.

An Atheist's Portrayal of the Church of England   73

questioner and thinker with a scientific approach who also understands the nuances of British culture and society and the interaction between the church, the Establishment, and the public perception and expectation.

The overarching enquiring aspect of McEwan's approach relates to the nature of *logos* and *mythos* discussed earlier in this chapter. For Max Planck, the relationship between religion and science was one of compatibility because, as Armstrong notes, 'science dealt with the objective, material world and religion with values and ethics'.[159] In this spirit of enquiry, McEwan draws the reader towards a critical perspective that, as Roger Scruton observes in his review of *Enduring Love*, makes even the believer ask questions:

> *Enduring Love* situates the conflict between science and religion in a context so original and startling, and at the same time so believable, as to force you to recognize that the conflict lies in you.[160]

As McEwan observes in *Sweet Tooth*, there is a certain appeal to the 'clever, amoral, inventive, destructive, single-minded, selfish, emotionally cool, coolly attractive' men who could be preferred to 'the love of Jesus'.[161] In five near-comical pages of *Sweet Tooth*,[162] McEwan captures a scene of distinctly British believability. The comedic portrayal of the church in films and television programmes referred to earlier in this chapter is brought to the fore in a literary narrative. Two brothers, one an atheist and the other a priest, face a dilemma when the brother who is the priest is laid low with influenza on the Sunday of a visit by a bishop, when there is also an unusually large congregation. The atheist brother preaches in his place with a sermon that refers to the idea of love as viewed by a modern Christian.

> Jesus's idea is irresistible and irreversible. Even unbelievers must live within it. For love doesn't stand alone, nor can it, *but trails like a blazing comet, bringing with it other shining goods – forgiveness, kindness, tolerance, fairness, companionability and friendship, all bound to the love which is at the heart of Jesus's message.*[163]

The reception of the sermon is extremely positive, with applause which is 'not done' in an Anglican church in West Sussex.[164] 'Shakespeare, Herrick, Christina Rossetti, Wilfred Owen and Auden'[165] have all been quoted and 'when the bishop straightens, purplish from the effort of leaning forward, he's beaming and everyone else, the retired colonels and horse breeders and the ex-captain

---

[159] Armstrong, *Religion*, p. 37.

[160] Roger Scruton, 'Review of Enduring Love', *Sunday Telegraph*, 16 September 2001.

[161] McEwan, *Sweet Tooth*, p. 98.

[162] Ibid., pp. 94–99.

[163] Ibid., p. 96.

[164] Ibid., p. 97.

[165] Ibid.

74   *Music and Religion in the Writings of Ian McEwan*

of the polo team and all their wives beam too, and beam again as they file out through the porch.'[166] It is, of course, intentionally comic to imagine this mistaken identity, especially with a bishop's visitation included in the narrative, but McEwan understands the nature of the dramatically engaged sermon, as well as the common use of secular texts within sermons, as discussed earlier in relation to services of *Lessons and Carols*. The image of the church is clichéd with the description of personalities in the congregation but only insofar as not describing ordinary parishioners as well. In this respect, the portrayal builds on the comments about the bishop's life earlier in the novel, including the 'idyllic'[167] (*Sweet Tooth*) quality of the cathedral precinct and the world of privilege that also defines the church as different from the everyday world.

However, it is the comments of the bishop's daughter, Serena, that bring McEwan towards the world of Bennett, Betjeman, Larkin, and Scruton in the degree of affection for a church that can hold both the head and the heart, albeit in a sentimental, romantic vein.

> In fact, the ecclesiastical trappings [of the story] entranced me – the Norman church, the smells of brass polish, lavender wax, old stone and dust that [the brother] evoked [in his/Edmund's sermon], the black, white and red bell ropes behind the font with the wonky oak lid held together by iron rivets and ties across a massive split, and above all a vicarage…[168]

With an ability to easily communicate a recognizable character and intuit the sentiment and aesthetic of Anglican identity, McEwan captures central believable points of reference. When contextualising these characters within the larger world of the church as a pillar of the British Establishment and indeed readily identifiable British culture, McEwan sheds light not only on the received perceptions of the age but also the character of the same. His understanding of the alliance between church and state, whether of sovereign or Prime Minister, shows the nuanced nature of institutional structure and relative impediment that is as distinctly British as the mannerisms of so many of his characters. As such, his atheism is allied to the historical questioning and debating nature of the British, including, in David Jenkins's case, a senior bishop. In McEwan's case, narratives are developed that also show the cultural legacy of the church that both fictional writers and public commentators have similarly seized upon. A consequence of this balance between doubt, faith, and attributable tradition is the reality of a church that continues to be one part of the national identity, even though how that identity is defined varies within the population. As Durham Cathedral stands tall above the River Wear and holds numerous civic services each year, including the first part of the annual Miners' Gala, so too is there a relative understanding of a cultural and recognizable

---

[166] Ibid.

[167] McEwan, *Sweet Tooth*, pp. 2–3.

[168] Ibid.

institution even among those who question its role. Betjeman's reference to Stanford in A is consonant with McEwan's observations of Serena's father being part of a clericus that is untroubled by a small congregation. The service of evensong referred to in *Machines Like Us* may be attended by very few, but it is nonetheless a part of the English cultural landscape and sufficiently so that the BBC currently broadcasts a service of choral evensong not once but twice each week. McEwan's perceptions about the strengths and weaknesses of the Church of England are both perceptive and precise while demonstrating an awareness of the subtleties of the modern church that suggests that, even to an atheist, the cultural and societal relevance of the Established Church is also inevitable rather than a choice.[169]

---

[169] Paraphrased from McEwan, *or Shall we die? A Move Abroad*, p. 3.

2

THE VALUE OF SUBLIMITY: SOLITUDE, VOYEURISM, AND THE TRANSCENDENTAL

This chapter examines the nature of sublimity in relation to the performing musician and the specific musical references found in McEwan's writings. Beginning with the value of solitude and individualism, I focus on key moments that illuminate why understanding McEwan's choices is critical to understanding those of his characters that encounter music each day. To understand their interpretation of a musical language is to better understand their own language, behaviour, and decisions. The nature of response to music is personal and not necessarily related to whether someone is a professional musician or not. This is a point that McEwan is clear about as he portrays both amateur and professional musicians. Consequently, the nature of emotional engagement with music in McEwan's writings ranges from the detached appreciation of a partner's commitment to performance to a contrasting world of otherness that borders on an enveloping secret world and understanding that is remote to those around them. It is this latter world that bears special contextualisation.

Public and Private Solitude

Since the 1980s there has been a rising complaint against the addition of unnecessary noise in public spaces in Britain. Background music in lifts, shops, shopping centres, commercial aircraft, restaurants, and pubs has become typical throughout the country in recent decades. It is a point that McEwan has discussed personally,[1] but it also relates to the nature of quiet, the use of background music in his novels, and the role of sublimity, specifically when music can be chosen by a character rather than imposed upon them. This chapter examines the role of musical encounters in McEwan's novels and how certain pieces of music can have specific relevance to a particular character. In order to consider this topic, it is important to initially examine McEwan's approach to silence and solitude as this has a direct bearing on how music is ultimately

---

[1] Iain Quinn, 'Interview with Ian McEwan' (2018).

Music and Religion in the Writings of Ian McEwan

heard by his characters. Music in his novels does not serve as a background but rather fills a particular role in understanding the context of the narrative.

The relative place of silence has been replaced with an energy of sustained noise, the only difference being which noise is considered the most effective in terms of the commercial outcome it is supposed to generate. For some people, it is constant sensory overload as well as the removal of a freedom to encounter the world on individual terms. It is a removal of personal freedom to which the Sony Walkman, released in 1979, had been something of an antidote and its popularity owed as much to convenience as the appeal of individual choice, with the default exclusion of imposed circumstances. In the same decade that the public were given the ultimate choice to listen to whatever music, radio play or oration they chose, or even the sound of their own recorded voice, they were also to experience the obligatory environment of background music in many areas of life. Initially, this was met with sustained opposition, and restaurants and pubs would sometimes post a sign near their entrance that indicated no music would be played inside.

One of the most outspoken musical critics has been the organist Gillian Weir. In an interview with Jonathan Rennert, she explained the problem from a musician's perspective. Her analysis of the issue relates to McEwan's frustrations in his own life and the nature and value of silence and solitude in his novels. The text of her response, related to the Muzak Corporation, is followed by a complementary commentary from the neurologist Oliver Sacks, who examines the challenge from a clinical perspective and as a doctor with a deep sympathy for music.

> If you wanted to hurry people along through Waterloo station in the morning you played marches, which was busy music and got them going. Why not? You wanted people to stay longer in the supermarkets because the longer they stayed the more they were likely to pick up [you have] quiet, soothing music. But, [now] people simply turn on the nearest radio station and that will virtually always be ... some form of rock because [it is] fitted to almost everything automatically. The reason for this is that it is hypnotic and addictive.

> It's particularly bad news for musicians because every single minute of our training is in awareness to the most tiny nuances and subtleties of sound. The more subtle we are, the more service we are giving to the music, but people are hardly able to determine those subtleties any more.[2] (Gillian Weir)

> Half of us are plugged into iPods, immersed in the daylong concerts of our own choosing, virtually oblivious to the environment – and for those who are not plugged in, there is nonstop music, unavoidable and often of deafening

---

[2]   Gillian Weir and Jonathan Rennert, 'Interview on Music, Muzak, Noise, Silence and Thought', online at <http://gillianweir.com/articles/en/muzak.shtml> [accessed 20 December 2020], *Organ Club Journal*, 4 (1993) [London].

Solitude, Voyeurism, and the Transcendental   79

intensity, in restaurants, bars, shops, and gyms. This barrage of music puts a certain strain on our exquisitely sensitive auditory systems, which cannot be overloaded without dire consequences. One such consequence is the ever-increasing prevalence of serious hearing loss, even among young people, and particularly among musicians. Another is the omnipresence of annoyingly catchy tunes, the brainworms that arrive unbidden and leave only in their own time – catchy tunes – that may, in fact, be nothing more than advertisements for toothpaste but are, neurologically, completely irresistible.[3] (Oliver Sacks)

Weir's comments address not only the commercial relationship of music to the public at large but also the musician's concern about the nature of nuance which is central to the life of the classical musician as someone interpreting the works of others. This point is reinforced by Sacks who notes that there is a consequence to the 'overload' of information. For Weir, the 'hypnotic' aspect is similar to Sacks's 'irresistible' description but, most crucially, Sacks draws attention to the fact that the 'omnipresence' of certain 'unbidden' tunes can relate to hearing loss for musicians.

McEwan has personally asked the staff or manager of a restaurant to turn the music being piped in not 'down' but to turn it off completely,[4] frequently to the gratitude of other diners sitting nearby.

McEwan's description[5] of the decorum at the Wigmore Hall in *On Chesil Beach* relates to the expectation of many in audiences for a degree of quiet, if not silence, as they listen to concerts. In a 2006 letter to John Updike, he discussed the possibility of including a noisy cougher in the cast of his opera libretto, *For You*, which although it did not come to pass, is nonetheless consonant with perceptions of the modern concert experience:

> I thought too of having a chronic cougher planted in the audience. At last! My composer will stop his concert to have a furious, sung exchange with this person.[6]

In *The Child in Time*, the music in a toy shop from 'speakers hung high above the hooded lights [providing] music for children – a bouncy clarinet, a glockenspiel, a snare drum'[7] is designed to entrance the young customer and because the music is recorded and not live, it fulfils a sustained ambient aesthetic quality from which there is no escape, as Sacks notes above. Although that setting is one where music is heard in the background, the frustration of not being able to experience satisfying broadcast music is paralleled in the

---

[3]   Oliver Sacks, *Musicophilia* (New York, 2007), p. 48.

[4]   Quinn, 'Interview with Ian McEwan'.

[5]   Ian McEwan, *On Chesil Beach* (New York, 2007), pp. 49–50.

[6]   Letter from Ian McEwan to John Updike (21 February 2006).

[7]   Ian McEwan, *The Child in Time* (London, 1992), p. 138.

80   *Music and Religion in the Writings of Ian McEwan*

same novel with the irritation of 'searching for tolerable music on the radio'.[8] If music is going to be heard at all then it must be to the liking of the character. It is a point of anxiety when, trying to find comfort in a situation, an individual seeks control of their environment. McEwan's narrative clarifies this still further with a description of train travellers and a desire for quiet and solitude:

> A ride on the crowded underground brought him to Victoria. From here the train rumbled out across the river's broad white sky. He walked the length of every carriage looking for the most secluded seat. A disruptive minority of humankind regarded journeys, even short ones, as the occasion for pleasant encounters. There were people ready to inflict intimacies on strangers. Such travellers were to be avoided if you belonged to the majority for whom a journey was the occasion for silence, reflection, daydream.[9]

The question McEwan raises relates to the management of sound, where only silence or particular music is appreciated. As discussed later in this chapter, he takes this further to consider not just particular pieces of music but specific performers of those pieces. This is a heightened sense of individualism and knowledge that relies on the 'sophistication' of the reader that Head describes[10] and is discussed in the Introduction. In the extract above, the desire for silence is considerable as the character walks the length of the train looking for a seat apart from other passengers. But the extent of required seclusion is also important and the use of the words 'disruptive' and 'inflict intimacies' is an example of McEwan pointing out, quite bluntly, that there is a frustration to this approach by some. The passenger does not seek any small talk from other passengers and the narrative clarifies that the 'majority' seek to be left alone. The description of the 'majority' is powerfully portrayed as an unquestionable fact which reinforces the point. Inasmuch as McEwan challenges readers to consider different points of view, he portrays an image where it is shown that conversation and external interruptions can be seen as intrusive to a way of life. Part of the experience of travel is portrayed as being in solitude, untroubled by others, and here McEwan's reference to the 'modern plague of tourism',[11] with all its attendant frustrations, in his early story *The Comfort of Strangers*, resonates not only with the narrative above in *The Child in Time* but also his personal views. Further, by referring to the 'majority' he suggests that the nature of individual pleasure comes from a communal understanding, and that by removing a communal setting of quiet the individual is directly affected. As Scott Burnham notes of listening to Mozart, it is the ability to 'quiet the noise of local time, so that we

---

[8]   Ibid., p. 99.

[9]   Ibid., pp. 50–51.

[10]   Dominic Head, *The State of the Novel – Britain and Beyond* (Oxford, 2008), pp. 8, 6.

[11]   David Howard, 'Ian McEwan – The first editions of this young novelist are already collectible', *Book and Magazine Collector*, 84 (1991), 33–34.

Solitude, Voyeurism, and the Transcendental   81

can hear the passing of global time'.[12] The train journey in *The Child in Time* described above is an example of the multiple needs for individual time in this regard, as is the walking of Fiona in *The Children Act* while she listens to Bach.[13] The experience allows the individual to suppress temporary concerns in a controllable environment.

The nature of the controlled environment for a listener who can detect and appreciate differences in performances of the same repertoire, which as Weir notes is now possible for some but not others, relates to McEwan's observations on different performances of the same pieces and the inference that his characters, most especially Henry Perowne in *Saturday*, are discerning listeners. Like McEwan, Henry is not a professional musician, but he is someone with highly specific tastes from a musician's perspective, as will be discussed in detail later. In this instance, when McEwan[14] refers to different recordings of Bach's *Goldberg Variations*, he does so in a manner that denotes a particular understanding of performance practice to musicians reading his texts, while drawing a reader who is unfamiliar with the subtleties of performance into the field of performance practice. In *Black Dogs* the *Goldberg Variations* are mentioned in a role that is similar to a coming-of-age experience when encountering other parents who provide different experiences to one's own: 'At the Langley's I learned of the sacrificial practices in the Arabian desert, improved my Latin and French and first heard the *Goldberg Variations*.'[15]

In the late twentieth century and early twenty-first centuries it is not enough for the public to have access to only one recorded interpretation of a masterwork of Bach, Mozart or Beethoven to listen to. Rather it is the expectation – and commercial sales support this – that a masterwork can be interpreted with numerous different approaches towards the score. The long-term success of Glenn Gould's two recordings of Bach's *Goldberg Variations* – a piece that has particular importance to McEwan – is significant in this regard. Not only was the first recording (1955) seen as offering a revolutionary interpretation to many but so was the second recording (1981) Gould issued. One artist alone had created a supportive audience for two different recordings of the same piece beyond the several dozen additional recordings by other artists.

The cellist Pablo Casals was also a pianist and composer. In his nineties, he commented to an interviewer that he had played one of each of Bach's *Forty-Eight Preludes and Fugues* each morning for the previous eighty-five years. When the interviewer asked if there wasn't a certain tedium to this, he responded that each playing was a new experience, an act of discovery.[16] Many listeners develop an affection for a particular interpretation of a work. How-

---

[12] Scott Burnham, *Mozart's Grace* (Princeton, 2012), p. 134.

[13] Ian McEwan, *The Children Act* (London, 2014), p. 119.

[14] Ian McEwan, *Saturday* (London, 2005), p. 22.

[15] Ian McEwan, *Black Dogs* (London, 1998), p. 13.

[16] Quoted in Sacks, *Musicophilia*, fn 212.

82   *Music and Religion in the Writings of Ian McEwan*

ever, their affection may not extend to other performances of different repertoire by the same artist. Just because someone appreciates Gould's recordings of Bach does not automatically suggest they will be captivated by his approach to Alban Berg's piano sonata or even his interpretation of other works by Bach. One of the reasons that McEwan's literary approach to Western art music is important is because to a musician he writes with an authority that understands and indeed appreciates this degree of specific listening.

The Interpretations of Glenn Gould

McEwan's understanding of music and performance has been developed not only through listening to many recordings but by attending concerts for several decades, especially at the Wigmore Hall, London, and becoming friends with many musicians, including the composer Michael Berkeley and the pianist Angela Hewitt. Hewitt is a noted interpreter of the works of Bach that McEwan offers comments on. In *Saturday*, the surgeon Henry Perowne listens to Bach's *Goldberg Variations* while he works and 'favours Angela Hewitt, Martha Argerich, sometimes Gustav Leonhardt [and] in a really good mood he'll go for the looser interpretations of Glenn Gould'.[17] To a musician reading this text these are not random choices but markedly different interpretations that can elicit different responses from the listener. The suggestion that when Henry is in a better mood he can listen to the 'looser interpretations' of the Gould recording implies that the particular performance relates to a specific emotional state that, when listening, he can anticipate and attune to.

Gould's interpretations have often been described as highly personal because of the number of interpretative choices he made that were very different from the then-established performance practice. This degree of interpretative freedom regarding the *Goldberg Variations* is described by Gould in the following quote:

> It is, in short, music which observes neither end nor beginning, music with neither real climax nor resolution, music which like Baudelaire's lovers 'rests lightly on the wings of the unchecked wind'. It has, then, unity through intuitive perception, unity born of craft and scrutiny, mellowed by mastery achieved, and revealed to us here, as so rarely in art, in the vision of subconscious design exulting upon a pinnacle of potency.[18]

Gould's description highlights the perception of the musical work being positively set apart from other works, and in a sphere of beauty that is unencumbered by predictable resolutions. Rather, it is a piece that moves the listener

---

[17]   McEwan, *Saturday*, p. 22.

[18]   Glenn Gould, record liner to his first recording of the *Goldberg Variations*, Columbia ML 5060.

Solitude, Voyeurism, and the Transcendental 83

towards a value in the subconscious. As discussed later in this chapter, Oliver Sacks has noted the direct relationship between music chosen by an individual and the music the brain seeks pleasure from. In the case of Henry, the choices are laid out and correspond to particular mental states. However, this does not occur at the primary level of gaining satisfaction from hearing a particular work that he has an affinity with but rather with an elevated understanding and knowledge of particular interpretations.

Not only was Gould's initial recording considered revolutionary by many, but he also saw failings in it over time, which alludes to a certain representation of the human aspect of music as well as the nature of individual response that McEwan highlights through the different interpretations he refers to. In particular, Gould felt the first recording was simply too fast: 'It was very nice, but it was perhaps a little bit like thirty very interesting but somewhat independent-minded pieces going their own way and all making comment on the ground bass on which they are all formed,'[19] which consequently gave the impression of a suite of ideas rather than a cohesive whole. Instead, with the second recording he hoped to find a way of 'making some sort of almost mathematical correspondence between the theme and the subsequent variations so that there would be some sort of temporal relationship.'[20]

While Henry prefers a selection of extremely different interpretations – the Leonhardt recording is played on the harpsichord as Bach had intended rather than the modern piano of the other three recordings – the dualism that makes a contrasting performance and the ability of the listener to discern differences is reinforced. It is Leonhardt's recording of the *Goldberg Variations* on the Vanguard label that McEwan chose in his 1986 appearance on Michael Berkeley's radio programme, *Private Passions*, alongside Glenn Gould's CBS recording of Bach's Three-Part *Invention in C minor*.[21] McEwan's choices support the argument that different pieces bring about different expectations even when written by the same composer and performed by the same person.

Further, there is the particular nature of McEwan's choice of the *Goldberg Variations*. In one sense, there is the musical precision one can hear in the myriad complementary contrapuntal figures of Bach that is akin to the purity of individualism one encounters with the precision of a performer and a surgeon alike. This is a point Dominic Head also notes when he writes that in *Amsterdam* 'McEwan betrays a fascinated respect for the intellectual effort that is involved [in orchestral composition] which anticipates his celebratory descriptions of neurosurgery in *Saturday*.'[22] There is an element of flair and esteem associated with both fields. Both are uncompromising specialists in

---

[19] Glenn Gould, 'The Goldberg Variations', Vol. XIII of The Glenn Gould Collection, Sony Classical SLV 48 424.

[20] Ibid.

[21] Michael Berkeley, *Private Passions* (London, 2005), p. 49.

[22] Dominic Head, *Ian McEwan* (Manchester, 2007), p. 150.

84   *Music and Religion in the Writings of Ian McEwan*

their fields, and both align with McEwan's own specific approach to writing and the exacting nature of performance that makes a listener give value to one performance over another. Ultimately, the reception is a matter of timing, form, space, and individual perception of a work in a performer's hands.

> His taste then is for terse murmurs or silence. If a registrar fumbles with the positioning of a retractor, or the scrub nurse places a pituitary forceps in his hand at an awkward angle, Henry Perowne might on a bad day issue a single staccato 'fuck', more troubling for its rarity and its lack of emphasis, and the silence in the room will tighten. Exploratory musings and anecdotes by senior colleagues, tolerated by most as an occupational hazard, make him impatient; fantasising should be a solitary pursuit. Decisions are all.[23] (*Saturday*)

> I think architecture [in the structure of a novel] really makes for clarity, and it's clarity that I'm most interested in in the sentences too – not principally music, but precision and a strong visual clarity. So as I become clearer about what it is I'm going to do, so I make alterations to the shape of what is going to happen in the future. Then of course there is the delicious moment of having your first draft down finally, and then you can go back and make sure that everything confirms to that architectural sense.[24] (McEwan)

In these two texts, one fictional and the other a commentary on the process of writing, McEwan draws attention to the nature of passing time, silence, and the careful use of available time, all of which are also found in musical interpretations. In the case of Henry and the keyboard music he listens to, it is also an instance of another use of hands towards a precise, exacting conclusion. The 'taste' for silence and the uses of verbal accent are all the more striking because of their rarity. This also correlates to the nature of the unexpected in Gould's interpretations which were far removed from predictable performance practice during his lifetime. The nature of the performance of a large-scale work like the *Goldberg Variations* also corresponds to the value of structure and the 'architecture' of the larger interpretation. Both the surgeon, working over an extended period of time, and the performer he is listening to have to instil a sustained presence of calm for the necessary factors of skill and precision to coalesce.

The nature of precision also has a bearing on an important performance aspect of the *Goldberg Variations*, of which the opening bar of music is a good example. The piece begins with two repeated notes (G) in the right hand. The timing of these two notes is critical, for though a piece of music has a basic tempo, rather like a pulse, it is seldom rigid. For players of the harpsichord and the organ the timing, the spacing, between the notes has an expressive

---

[23]   McEwan, *Saturday*, p. 22.

[24]   Margaret Reynolds and Jonathan Noakes, *Ian McEwan – The Essential Guide to Contemporary Literature* (London, 2012), p. 14.

Solitude, Voyeurism, and the Transcendental   85

quality similar to the opening gesture of a slow courtly dance. Is the second note simply to be played with the approach of subservience to the first note or should it be slightly delayed and thus embody a gesture of its own? Should both notes be held for their true (full) value or should one be shorter? As Henry's work is described, 'decisions are all'.[25] For some keyboard players the note will be played with the same finger of the right hand but for others it is (potentially) more expressive to change fingers (for instance from the central third finger to the second finger to its left). This allows a particularly natural articulation between the two notes almost as if each starts with a gentle consonant. The summit of performance practice on instruments of Bach's time – and this is a consideration that pianists have had to bear in mind when performing Bach's music on their own instrument, which is quite unfamiliar to anything Bach knew – relies on the balance between tempi, touch, articulation and rubato, the fluctuating and highly nuanced expressive approach to the overall speed that can help shape the inner phrase. This subtlety is similar to a great orator who will never recite a Shakespeare soliloquy quite the same way twice. If a performer has a full command of all of these skills, then a piece can success-fully unfold with an approach to its performance that goes at least some way towards matching the mind of the master composer who wrote the score in front of them with the performer's contemporary interpretation(s). The use of the *Goldberg Variations* as a piece that a surgeon listens to in an operating theatre in *Saturday* is therefore extremely meaningful because of the multiple layers of complementary thought. The well-known story about the *Goldberg Variations*' creation centres on the influential Dresden Count Keyserlingk, who employed a young house-musician called Johann Gottlieb Goldberg. The Count was often unwell and had many sleepless nights during which Goldberg would spend the night in the adjoining room so that he could play to the Count during his sleepless episodes. The Count had once remarked in Bach's presence that he would very much like to have keyboard pieces written for Goldberg that were gentle yet merry in character so that he could be cheered up during these difficult nights. Bach believed he could best fulfil this request with a set of variations. The relationship to a soporific state and the still environment of an operating theatre with a patient under anaesthesia in *Saturday* is clear enough, but so too is the intellectual stamina demanded by the composer of himself and the performer with the similarity of craftsmanship required by the hands and the mind of a surgeon. The repetitive nature of variations also has a hypnotic quality that speaks to Gould's 'vision of the subconscious'. In the preface of Ralph Kirkpatrick's 1935 edition of the *Goldberg Variations* there is the inclusion of a quote from Sir Thomas Browne's *Religio medici* of 1642: 'there is something in it of Divinity more than the eare discovers'. As Peter Williams noted, Kirkpatrick 'was looking for a way to signal his own admira-tion and enthusiasm for a unique piece of actual music, to invoke not so much

---

[25]   McEwan, *Saturday*, p. 22.

86   *Music and Religion in the Writings of Ian McEwan*

the cleverness of its strategy and tactics as the kind of spiritual world it seems to occupy and the special feelings it arouses in both player and listener'.[26] It is a piece set apart from others, in some measure because of its length which, depending on the interpretation, can vary considerably and individually. But there is also the relationship between the fictional world of Henry, a neurosurgeon, and the scientific world of neurology in the studies of Oliver Sacks. This bears examination in considering how Henry is portrayed.

Oliver Sacks and the Reception of Music

The 'clinical' aspect of Bach that can calm or at least help align thoughts is discussed by Sacks in relation to the autistic scientist, Temple Grandin, who had Asperger's syndrome and was especially attracted to the music of Bach. She attended a concert of Bach's *Two- and Three-Part Inventions*. When Sacks asked her if she enjoyed them she responded that 'they were very ingenious', adding that she wondered if Bach would have been capable of writing four- or five-part inventions. Sacks persisted and asked again, 'But did you *enjoy them*?', and she gave the same answer regarding finding intellectual pleasure from Bach's *Inventions* but nothing more. He observed her comments that music 'did not "move" her, move her to her depths, as it apparently could (she had observed) with other people' but she could detect a value in their construction as musical works, nonetheless.

Sacks continued that 'there is some evidence, indeed, that those medial parts of the brain involved with experiencing deep emotions – the amygdala, in particular – may be poorly developed in people with Asperger's. It was not only music that failed to move Temple deeply; she seemed to experience a certain flattening of emotion generally'.[27] On occasion, the absence of a musical response can be caused by a major event in an individual's life, thus causing a temporary silence of its own. The psychiatrist Alexander Stein was a patient of Sacks who lived opposite the World Trade Center on 9/11. He saw the whole morning unfold, including being caught up with the terrified crowds fleeing the area, not knowing whether his wife had survived. For the following three months they were homeless.

> My internal world was dominated by a dense and silent pall, as if an entire mode of existence were in an airless vacuum. Music, even the usual internal listening of especially beloved works, had been muted. Paradoxically, life in the auditory sphere was in other respects heightened immeasurably, but calibrated, so it seemed, to a narrow spectrum of sounds; my ears now were attuned more to the roar of fighter jets and the wail of sirens, to my patients, to my wife's breathing at night.

[26]   Peter Williams, *Bach: The Goldberg Variations* (Cambridge, 2001), p. 1.
[27]   Sacks, *Musicophilia*, pp. 290–291.

Music finally returned as a part of life and in me. [The first piece he heard internally was Bach's *Goldberg Variations*].[28]

This clinically diagnosed absence of music in someone's life that Sacks describes is different from the specific absence of the emotive power of music when an individual makes choices because of subconscious need. That is discussed further in the next chapter, which concludes with the subject of what happens when music no longer has the same influence on a professional musician that it once did. However, the importance of silence as an agent of free thought is central to understanding the narratives of McEwan, because they rely heavily on the individual responses of readers for an appreciation beyond the surface narrative. As discussed above, the references within *Saturday* to specific performers of a specific piece are sufficiently detailed to demonstrate McEwan's understanding not only of the nuances of different interpretations but also, from a musician's perspective, performances that are artistically contrasting.

Silence and Solitude

Silence also holds an important role in the longer-term aspects of McEwan's writings, with both the use of time to suspend a story over the longer narrative and also as a means of appreciating music following silence. This is in contrast to the shorter, heart-stopping moments such as the man falling from a balloon (*Enduring Love*) or the sudden absence of a child (*The Child in Time*). In *Nutshell*, the narrator is a fetus commenting on the relationship that brought him into being, and the reader knows that there will be a nine-month period of gestation during which the fetus is silent except to the reader. In *Machines Like Me*, the reader knows that sexual interaction – if a relationship between a machine and a person can be considered this way – will clearly not lead to a child and silence is witnessed in the void within the relationship. However, in *The Child in Time*, it is only at the end of the book that the reader discovers that the timescale of the novel aligns with a time lapse following conception. This is part of a multilayered examination of the idea of time in this particular narrative, and what it means in relation to maturity, with complementary narratives that examine both a man's escape into childhood behaviour – or conversely his escape from adulthood – and the absence of a child from a couple. They each approach the loss differently, first together, then apart and finally together again. The reader is left to interpret time and the silence between them in these presentations, and the response is inherently subjective because the suspension of time, whether through absence or waiting, is individual. By contrast, does a reader see the immediate absence of an abducted child as the greater story or the joy in the newborn at the end of the novel? Can joy truly replace grief? This

---

[28] Ibid., p. 300.

88 *Music and Religion in the Writings of Ian McEwan*

use of time and indeed timing relates closely to music and the aspect of performance that determines a critical emotional response, as noted above with the observation in *Saturday* that 'decisions are all'.[29] Whereas Anthony Burgess's *Napoleon Symphony – A Novel in Four Movements* (1974) deliberately follows the musical structure of Beethoven's third symphony (*Eroica*), McEwan's use of silence in structure has the feature of suspending tension but with an often unknown sense of duration that has particular bearing when it relates to the consequent reception of music.

The abduction of the daughter in *The Child in Time* is followed by the mother leaving the family home and so McEwan's acceleration of emotion is followed by a blunt pause and then the silence of solitude. The need for solitude and silence that allows Julie, the mother, to finally realize that her child was more important than either her marriage or her musical life as a violinist. Music and marriage are commented on with equal weight: 'I came out here to face up to losing Kate. It was my task, my work, if you like, more important to me than our marriage, or my music.'[30] However, Julie also refers to the overpowering sense of music and its ability to, in other ways, distract her from focusing on her emotions. The loss of a child was a point of complete emotional removal from the world, as was her physical relocation to a quieter place to live. The solitude caused by her daughter is further translated by her removal from a musical world. The daughter represents perfection, and her abrupt departure shatters the association with another beautiful aspect of her life. Her relationship to both music and her daughter required an emotional vulnerability. Like Florence (*On Chesil Beach*), it is a quintet that holds a special meaning for her, but whereas Florence always speaks of the Mozart *Quintet in D*, Julie speaks of the Schubert *Quintet in C major*. The 'evasion' that Julie refers to relates to her removal from an aspect of her life that also provided a predictable and intelligible emotional response, unlike the abduction.

> One afternoon the quartet came out. They brought an old friend from college, a cellist, so we played, or tried to play, the Schubert C Major Quintet. When we got to the Adagio, you know how lovely it is, I didn't cry. In fact, I was happy. That was an important step. I started playing again properly. I'd stopped because it had become an evasion.[31]

The nature of the solitude that Julie experiences away from city life and the relative opportunity to meditate on life in general is also found in *Amsterdam*, where the composer Clive Linley needs to escape from London to the Lake District[32] in order to focus on the melody for his *Millennial Symphony*. He believes

---

[29] McEwan, *Saturday*, p. 22.

[30] McEwan, *The Child in Time*, p. 237.

[31] Ibid., p. 238.

[32] The Lake District is especially associated with Percy Bysshe Shelley and William Wordsworth.

Solitude, Voyeurism, and the Transcendental   89

that solitude would be the solution to his creative dilemma: 'As Clive had predicted, the melody was elusive as long as he remained in London, in his studio. Each day he made attempts, little sketches, bold stabs, but he produced nothing but quotations, thinly or well disguised, of his own work. Nothing sprang free in its own idiom, with its own authority, to offer the element of surprise that would be the guarantee of originality.'[33]

In the case of Julie (*The Child in Time*) and Clive (*Amsterdam*), solitude and silence ultimately serve a specific purpose that they know can be achieved through a withdrawal from the daily noise of their urban lives. Clive's difficulty with finding 'original' material in his work is replaced in London with 'quotations' (short excerpts) which, though they might have been successful as earlier compositions or in the public's perception of him as a composer, would not satisfy the critical professional reception he now hopes to achieve with his new piece. For Julie, it is a similar separation and need for silence but equally relates to where and when she can devote her attention and to what musical standard. The longer she is removed from performance, the more significant it becomes and the further removed she is from the standard she once attained when she played regularly.

Musical Exploration, Absence, and the Child

The literary moment that is similar to an everyday surprise which is commonly referred to as the skipping of a heartbeat is something that Michael Berkeley[34] comments on and can also be seen in the use of musical absence in McEwan's writings, not just in Julie's (*The Child in Time*) case, discussed above, but the nature of expectation and consequent absence when music is removed for a child. The predictable patterns of so much children's music are similar to music heard in other settings that are designed to be immediately familiar in style. The hypnotic aspect that Sacks refers to and which Weir notes is part of the larger use of music towards commercial ends is discussed at the beginning of this chapter. However, the use of repetition can also be found in the music of military marches and familiar patriotic songs. McEwan's exploration of this in *Rose Blanche* is notable, not just because he was the child of a military father, but also because of his anti-war stance. A related instance occurs in *The Child in Time* and both involve children.

A particular turn of phrase or a particular harmonic progression can engender an emotional response that is equally similar when heard multiple times, not just because of its ready familiarity but because of the depth of feeling encountered in that particular moment. In *Rose Blanche*, it is the presence and then absence of music that helps depict the contrasting emotions of soldiers

---

[33] Ian McEwan, *Amsterdam* (London, 2005), p. 61.

[34] Iain Quinn, 'Interview with Michael Berkeley' (2018).

90   *Music and Religion in the Writings of Ian McEwan*

going to and returning from conflict. Consequently, music is part of the larger depiction of the actions that the child witnesses. As the relationship between music and children is typically overwhelmingly positive, the addition and sub-traction of music as part of this narrative is significant. The joviality of the first quotation (below) concludes with a warning from the mother, whose reference to the coming winter is not solely related to weather but the impending dif-ficulties of wartime. The second quote is a further observation of the cheeri-ness that buoys the soldiers' spirits, if only to create a distraction from the task at hand. The nature of cheery military music also allows war to be seen in a positive emotional state, especially to a naïve child. Further, the children are engaged in the action by waving to the soldiers. The contrast with the third quote is then especially pronounced because the waving and physical engage-ment have been removed and there is no longer any singing. This use of music in what might be judged a manipulative, emotive fashion is mirrored in Berke-ley's parody of a Victorian hymn, with a text that shames those involved in the nuclear arms race, in *or Shall we die?*.

> A marching band played, everyone cheered, and the fat mayor made a boring speech. There were jokes and songs and old men shouted advice to the young soldiers. Rose Blanche was shivering with excitement. But her mother said it was cold. Winter was coming.

> The soldiers in the lorries sang songs. They smiled and winked at the children as if they were old friends. The children waved back.

> Soldiers, thousands of them, exhausted, wounded, dispirited – poured back through the town and on into the night. There was no singing or waving now.[35]

In *The Child in Time*, the moment of musical discovery, sometimes the same for different children, but sometimes purely individual, is referred to in the use of music, dance, and painting as pedagogical aids for young children. Here, the realization of an artistic experience is considered more beneficial to children than a new approach to early literacy that a parliamentary committee is other-wise considering:

> the sensual exploration of the world, music – for, surprisingly enough, musi-cal symbols are not abstractions so much as precise instructions for physical movements – painting, discovering through manipulation how things work, mathematics which is more logical than abstract, and all forms of intelli-gent play, these are the appropriate, essential activities of the younger child, enabling its mind to remain in harmony with, to flow with, the forces of cre-ation. To inflict literacy at this stage [is] nothing less than a banishment from the Garden, for its effects are lifelong.[36]

---

[35]   Ian McEwan, *Rose Blanche* (London, 2004), pp. 5, 6, 23.

[36]   McEwan, *The Child in Time*, pp. 81–82.

Solitude, Voyeurism, and the Transcendental   91

McEwan draws on the artistic encounter as an essential aspect of early learning that justifies a balance between the factual world and the development of imagination. The text stresses the need to avoid a rules-based system of evaluation. This is later described as a 'harsh isolation'[37] from the potential freedom a child could otherwise experience. But there is also a parallel in the experience of the father attending the meeting who has lost his daughter and a consideration of the loss of innocence in a physical as well as emotional form. In both cases, something has been removed. The text highlights the balance between exclusion from music and the comfort that it can provide.

In Kingsley Amis's *Lucky Jim*, there is a complementary statement where it is observed that 'in children's art, you see, you get what you might call a clarity of vision, a sort of thinking in terms of the world as it appears, you see, not as the adult knows it to be'.[38] This point speaks to the nature of the valued experience of art in childhood education that McEwan's narrative addresses and also that children experience art differently to adults. This is another example of McEwan drawing on a measure of otherness and subtle awareness of the reader. Adam Phillips writes that the 'unforbidden pleasure of childhood for Blake and Wordsworth was the child's capacity to be absorbed', and for musicians this can often signify a place of known comfort that they return to. Music is not merely an entertainment but an embrace that extends beyond the physical and directly towards the emotional. The observation by Karen Armstrong included in chapter 1 regarding the balance in Greek culture between *logos* and *mythos* is reinforced by Milner's belief that society is lacking something if one aspect is missing. As much as mysticism plays a role in the perception of the church for many believers and nonbelievers, it is founded upon the nature and strength of individual imagination. In *A Life of One's Own*, Milner writes of the need for 'a method for discovering one's true likes and dislikes, for finding and setting up a standard of values that is truly one's own and not a borrowed or mass-produced ideal'. This also relates to the nature of the forced listening of muzak as discussed earlier and the addition of unavoidable auditory stimuli in modern Western societies. Milner's objective, Phillips argues, relates to Seamus Heaney's note in *Crediting Poetry* for 'a less binary and altogether less binding vocabulary'[39] in order that the mind can roam freely, especially in this

---

[37] Ibid.

[38] Kingsley Amis, *Lucky Jim* (New York, 1954), pp. 80–81.

[39] Adam Phillips, *Unforbidden Pleasures* (London, 2016), pp. 159–160; Antony Storr, *Music and the Mind* (Toronto, 1992), p. 42; Seamus Heaney, Nobel Lecture: Crediting Poetry (7 December 1995), online at <https://www.nobelprize.org/prizes/literature/1995/heaney/lecture> [accessed 20 December 2020]. This topic can also be examined alongside Plato's comments on the value of a musical education in shaping the whole person and thus the betterment of society at large: '..musical training is a more potent instrument than any other, because rhythm and harmony find their way into the inward places of the soul, on which they mightily fasten, imparting grace, and making the soul of him who is rightly educated graceful, or of him who

92   *Music and Religion in the Writings of Ian McEwan*

case, for children. They can explore its language with inhibition and that in itself allows the language to develop.

The Counterpoint of Life and Music

In *Ian McEwan*, Jack Slay, Jr. writes:

> One element that distinguishes McEwan's fiction is his intense interest in the male-female relations of contemporary society. His study of interpersonal relationships reflects the current condition of our societies and individual lives. He introduces characters who continuously attempt to build alliances, hoping to ward off the encroaching horrors of their societies. The often-desperate need with which these individuals seek comfort through another individual (who, more often than not, is just as lost, just as desperate) is a reflection in itself of the collapsing state of contemporary society. These characters believe that relationships – the acceptance by even a single human being – is a means to escape the pain and lovelessness of their all-consuming worlds.[40]

There is a relative subjectivity to this statement because each novel involves quite different characters and circumstances but the sense of dependency and often tense interaction between characters is certainly magnified when music is an added component. The character does not turn to another friend to discuss their stresses at work but frequently to music and, typically, music experienced in solitude. They are removing themselves from others and towards an experience the other person cannot readily access. In this sense there is no desperation for comfort but a certain reliability to it and, if viewed through a musical lens, an often-reliable outlet, whether the music is being performed or heard.

Fiona Maye (*The Children Act*) is beyond the point in her life of having children but still questions what might have been had her life and choices taken a different course. The purity of Bach's musical language that is a guaranteed panacea for her (as it is for Henry in *Saturday* and indeed McEwan himself) is brought into the context of her professional as well as her personal choices. The counterpoint of life is portrayed as unequal to the counterpoint of Bach's music, and the reader is left with the impression that music and not marriage has been a sustaining factor in her life to date and will probably remain so for

---

> is ill-educated ungraceful; and also because he who has received this true education of the inner being will most shrewdly perceive omissions or faults in art and nature, and with a true taste, while he praises and rejoices over and receives into his soul the good, and becomes noble and good, he will justly blame and hate the bad, now in the days of his youth, even before he is able to know the reason why; and when reason comes he will recognize and salute the friend with whom his education has made him long familiar'.

[40]   Jack Slay Jr., 'Looking Forward', *Ian McEwan* (Twayne's English Authors Series 518) (New York, 1996), p. 146.

Solitude, Voyeurism, and the Transcendental   93

the future. Even if she tires of one work, she can move on to another. Realizing that music provides her with a joy that is beyond what her husband can provide her, her husband buys her a new grand piano as a surprise present. This demonstrates one of the few moments of true joy in the story, even if the piano effectively becomes her stronger and more reliable emotional partner. The following text relates to the anguish felt by Fiona in balancing her personal life with her professional commitments and through it the relative model of Bach. The meaning of music for her provides an inner sublimity, but when she examines Bach's life, she also sees that her own decisions are not so easily justified. She sees Bach not only as a musician who allows her to be removed from her daily concerns but also as a father. In an unusual juxtaposition, McEwan equates the 'demanding' fugue with 'childlessness' and the nature of complexity that can be viewed personally as well as musically. The difficulty she finds in performing the fugue can also be seen in the challenges of life itself. This sentiment is superimposed on her initial reception of the piece that brings to the fore her own doubt at getting older. She is in the 'infancy of old age' and the 'carefree' aspect of the *andante* she is listening to not only demands a learned understanding from her but symbolizes how she is 'learning to crawl' within both her life and her abilities as a musician. She has a deep appreciation for the art of music but knows that she falls short in her performances. Thus, McEwan draws a line between the innocence of decision-making and the innocence of interpretation and then the maturity in both the musical form of the fugue and her decisions. The fugue and indeed the impression of Bach represent the substantial and the constant in her life.

> An abandoned fifty-nine-year-old woman, in the infancy of old age, just learning to crawl. Over the drumming of raindrops on her umbrella, she heard the lilting andante, walking pace, a rare marking in Bach, a beautiful carefree air over a strolling bass ... The notes strained at some clear human meaning, but they meant nothing at all. Just loveliness, purified ... Johann Sebastian had twenty [children] by two marriages. He didn't let his work prevent him loving and teaching, caring and composing for those who survived ... The inevitable thought recurred as she moved on to the demanding fugue ... her childlessness was a fugue in itself, a flight ... her failure to become a woman, as her mother understood the term.[41]

Music also fulfils a role beyond the narrative surrounding the first violinist of a string quartet in *On Chesil Beach*. The title of the book relates to a conversation that takes place on the beach after a failed consummation on a wedding night. A young woman (Florence) has formed a string quartet and has great hopes and aspirations for a future career with the quartet, while her husband plans to write history books on lesser-known figures of the past. Anthony Storr argued that there is a special intimacy between the members of a string quartet and that the experience of performing in a quartet is a better performing

---

[41] McEwan, *The Children Act*, p. 215.

94   *Music and Religion in the Writings of Ian McEwan*

experience than any other form of music making[42] because of the necessary balance and the need for collective responsibility, understanding, and cohesion. Despite an intellectual attraction between the couple, especially in their student years, her boyfriend and later husband (Edward) has never quite been able to grasp the language and emotion that music gives her, despite his earnest efforts. When Florence plays, she is described with a measure of poise and confidence that belies her youth, and this in itself impresses Edward, even if the repertoire she performs remains largely distant from his understanding.

> She held herself gracefully, with back straight and head lifted proudly, and read the music with a commanding, almost haughty expression that stirred him. That look had such certitude, such knowledge of the path to pleasure.[43]

Much about Florence's character is exacting and precise in nature. She commands a strong presence in rehearsals and has an astute approach to the music profession with her long-term plans for repertoire. However, it is a world of comfortable isolation from which she derives an emotional range all her own, while also being naïve to the larger world around her. Music provides her with a rich language with which to converse without speaking, and when she has reason to speak with the rest of the quartet in rehearsals, she issues commands rather than seeking consensus.[44] All attention is drawn to the nuances of the musical language, first and foremost. Whereas her first husband is ambitious about publishing research on lesser-known historical figures and speaks of his passions relatively freely, her second husband who is the cellist in the quartet is, from the outset, seen in a quite contrasting submissive role. He has always taken directions from Florence and she readily provides them. Her life before divorce is a musician's life, with the many hours of private practice.[45]

T. S. Eliot's commentary in *The Perfect Critic* (below) regarding the nature of emotional substitution discusses a life that Florence easily associates with. In relation to Florence, Eliot's text highlights the complexity of the known and unknown that exists between individuals and segments of society that simply do not understand the thinking of another, as Florence does not fully comprehend Edward or the nature of communication within a relationship. Rather than understanding the relationship – and the same could be said of Edward's inability to comprehend Florence – she substitutes a different emotional aspect which for her rests largely with her musical life.

> When there is so much to be known, where there are so many fields of knowledge in which the same words are used with different meanings, when everyone knows a little about a great many things, it becomes increasingly difficult for anyone to know whether he knows what he is talking about or

---

[42] Storr, *Music and the Mind*, pp. 108, 124.

[43] McEwan, *On Chesil Beach*, p. 18.

[44] Ibid., pp. 18–19.

[45] Ibid., pp. 49–51.

Solitude, Voyeurism, and the Transcendental   95

not. And when we do not know, or when we do not know enough, we tend always to substitute emotions for thoughts.[46]

Storr argues that to 'appreciate art, the observer must adopt a special attitude of mind; the same attitude required by Plato, of detachment from personal concerns, so that the work of art can be appreciated in contemplative fashion uncontaminated by personal needs or preoccupations.'[47] This observation relates both to the musician's (whether amateur or professional) lack of interest in unnecessary noise and also unnecessary music which causes irritation. By this argument, music is a separate force in life that can only be emotionally and intellectually valued with a measure of distance. In Florence's world, and also Fiona's (*The Children Act*), it is a matter of providing calm for the self in the first instance, amidst an environment where far from bringing the relationship closer, music is unavoidably empowering one character and distancing another. McEwan's approach is one that highlights the emotional value of music over a simple, relatively superficial entertainment. In Florence's case, the self-sacrificing nature of the art illuminates the personal introspection, with hours of practice undertaken in solitude followed by performances with a small number of colleagues who, in the case of a professional string quartet, are very largely the same colleagues throughout a working year. As Florence leads the quartet, she effectively self-selects her other family with herself in a matriarchal role.

It is an inner passion that drives Florence to such a point of distraction that, because her (musical) heart and soul are engaged in a pursuit, her personal relationship becomes secondary. One can argue that the strident approach of her interactions with the rest of the quartet is far from conducive to a healthy relationship either, any more than Julie mourning the loss of her daughter in *The Child in Time* being alone in her cottage practising Bach partitas with 'notebooks and sharpened pencils, writing [her ex-husband] slowly out of her existence.'[48] Music is seen as a reliable and comforting alternative to the difficulties of personal relationships. In a different vein, Clive, the composer in *Amsterdam*, notes how he was able to focus far more on his composition the moment he was out of a relationship and was all the more content as a result: 'for when she went he was happier than ever to be alone and wrote the *Three Autumn Songs* in less than a month.'[49] The inner passion of a musical life is often hard to understand even for those, like a partner, who are close to it on a daily basis. The composer Michael Tippett captured much of the sense of submission that musicians easily and very happily acquiesce to in comments that relate to Joshua Reynolds's writings of the sister arts at the end of the eighteenth century:

---

[46]   T. S. Eliot, 'The Perfect Critic', in *The Sacred Wood* (London, 1920), p. 9.

[47]   Storr, *Music and the Mind*, p. 136.

[48]   McEwan, *The Child in Time*, p. 140.

[49]   McEwan, *Amsterdam*, pp. 7–8.

96   *Music and Religion in the Writings of Ian McEwan*

> Symphonic music in the hands of the great masters truly and fully embodies the otherwise unperceived, unsavoured inner flow of life. In listening to such music we are though entire again, despite all the insecurity, incoherence, incompleteness and relativity of our everyday life. The miracle is achieved by submitting to the power of its organized flow; a submission which gives us a special pleasure and finally enriches us. The pleasure and the enrichment arise from the fact that the flow is not merely the flow of the music itself, but a significant image of the inner flow of life. Artifice of all kinds is necessary to the musical composition in order that it shall become such an image. Yet when the perfect performance and occasion allow us a truly immediate apprehension of the inner flow 'behind' the music, the artifice is momentarily of no consequence; we are no longer aware of it.[50] (Michael Tippett)

> Whatever is familiar, or in any way reminds us of what we see and hear every day perhaps does not belong to the higher provinces of art, either in poetry or writing. Art cuts itself free from any servitude in order to raise itself to the truth which it fulfils independently and conformable with its own ends alone. In this freedom is fine art truly art.[51] (Joshua Reynolds)

Both Reynolds and Tippett analyse the nature of submission to art that, when complete, removes the sense of servitude to allow the inner flow of life – an impression that resonates with the 'forces of creation'[52] described in *The Child in Time* – to appear more fully. Their arguments further resonate with the complementary sentiments expressed in *The Child in Time* and the nature of art being essential to well-being and balance for the individual, especially children, as discussed above. However, the dilemma faced in Florence's case is whether the degree of artistic submission that allows for a total understanding of art – a point Fiona (*The Children Act*) observes she will never quite achieve because of the limits of her piano technique[53] – allows for an 'inner flow of life' that can also enable relationships with others that she is not in some way dominating. Although emotionally complex, the artistic side of life is, to the musician, often the most easily comprehensible because of its enveloping emotional attraction and influence.

Musical Taste and Perception

One of the consequences of a seemingly fulfilled life through the rich repertoire available to musicians is the illusion of complete fulfilment. This, too, can change with time, giving a sense of the maturing self when in fact other areas

---

[50]   Tippett, Michael. 'Art, Judgement and Belief: Towards the Condition of Music', in Peter Abbs (ed.), *The Symbolic Order: A Contemporary Reader on the Arts Debate* (London, 1989), p. 47.

[51]   Joshua Reynolds, *Discourses on Art* (New York, 1961).

[52]   McEwan, *The Child in Time*, pp. 81–82.

[53]   McEwan, *The Children Act*, p. 119.

Solitude, Voyeurism, and the Transcendental 97

of life, whether romantic, familial, financial or medical, can be unknowingly or relatively easily put to one side. Musical tastes frequently change with age as can sexual proclivities or even basic interest in the physical aspects of life with another person.

Children are often introduced to the music of Bach or Mozart in the womb and children's programmes like *Little Einsteins* expand this musical vocabulary further. If a child takes up an instrument, their awareness of musical languages quickly becomes broader. Most children do not develop an easy affinity to atonal music, although the younger they are, the less concerned they are with dissonant harmonies. But as they mature into young adults and eventually older adults, their tastes shift and generally expand. However, as Daniel Levitin has noted,[54] different people can tolerate different levels of dissonance and children are noticeably more open to new experiences, including musical ones. McEwan's narrative in *The Child in Time* (below) raises the discussion of musical reception and the formation of musical tastes in children. Critically, he raises the question of the abstract work that is nonetheless intelligible to a child. The text (below) is a commentary on pedagogy intended for children and the observation that children are naturally without the studied judgement of most adults, but also able to analyse a musical language without difficulty. The argument stresses the need for children to be allowed to engage with art without prescriptive categorizations. In this respect, the childlike aspect that takes hold of the former government minister (Charles) is seen in the context of the value that childhood can teach society as a whole.

> You could describe writing in much the same way as you're describing musical symbols – in this case a set of instructions on what to do with lips, tongue, throat and voice. It's only later that children learn to read quietly by themselves. But I'm not sure that either description, of music notation or writing, is correct. Both activities seem highly abstract, and perhaps abstraction of a certain kind is precisely what we're good at from our earliest days. The problems come when we try to reflect on the process and define it. A tune has a kind of meaning. It's hard to say what it is, but a child has no difficulty understanding it. [55]

Although there is no precise point when musical tastes seem to be fully formed, most people have developed their own tastes by the age of eighteen or twenty.[56] The expansion of taste does not necessarily mean an expansion of repertoire of different centuries or different composers. Someone with a deep interest in the works of Byrd or Palestrina might choose to spend many years becoming better acquainted with every work they can find of those composers and, in turn, find the activity of self-pursuit completely engrossing and

---

[54] Daniel J. Levitin, *This is your brain on music* (New York, 2016), p. 227.

[55] McEwan, *The Child in Time*, p. 83.

[56] Levitin, *This is your brain on music*, p. 232.

98   *Music and Religion in the Writings of Ian McEwan*

highly rewarding. They might equally develop a strong interest in a particular period of music. In general terms, the tastes of most musicians modify and expand over time, even to the extent that certain pieces serve particular ends as they do for characters in McEwan's writings. The nature of the role of specific repertoires in society is heard especially in radio broadcasting. Morning music is typically drawn from buoyant works of the Baroque or Classical eras whereas Romantic symphonies (when heard in their entirety) are often only broadcast in the afternoon or evening. The world of atonal or experimental music is often relegated to the early hours of the morning. Although it is now possible to hear almost any music at any time of day, these perceptions and indeed programming trends still apply. However, in a complementary field, the self-selective nature of the professional musician who chooses to plan certain works for certain points of their career, as Florence (*On Chesil Beach*)[57] does, is typical. Florence plans her future repertoire in a manner that is similar to someone determining other aspects of their life far in advance. Fiona (*The Children Act*) and Cathy (*The Imitation Game*) also plan ahead but on a smaller scale, especially Cathy who has been working on one piece of Mozart for some time. All three characters assert their own individual decisions, not just on the interpretation of repertoire, but when they feel they will be emotionally able to approach it.

Perspectives of a Profession

Florence's view of music as a future profession and also her perception of how the public sees the world of classical music is imbued with a romantic air, especially as she sees both circumstances in relation to the Wigmore Hall, which for many, whether young or old, is an almost sacred setting for vocal and chamber music concerts in central London. It is a place where the great names of the past have performed, and many young artists make their debuts.

> Florence practiced five hours a day and went to concerts with her girlfriends. She preferred above all the chamber recitals at the Wigmore Hall.
>
> She loved the seriousness of the place, the faded, peeling walls backstage, the gleaming woodwork and deep red carpet of the entrance hall, the auditorium like a gilded tunnel, the famous cupola over the stage depicting, so she was told, mankind's hunger for the magnificent abstraction of music.
>
> She revered the ancient types, who took minutes to emerge from their taxis, the last of the Victorians, hobbling on their canes to their seats, to listen in alert critical silence, sometimes with the tartan rug they had brought draped across their knees.[58]

---

[57]   McEwan, *On Chesil Beach*, pp. 50–51.
[58]   Ibid., pp. 49–50.

Solitude, Voyeurism, and the Transcendental   99

McEwan's description has a romantic sentimentality that is familiar to his portrayal of the Church of England, as discussed in chapter 1. The reference to the hours of necessary practice is mirrored in *Lessons*, as Roland notes that had he been a concert pianist 'he would have been bound to five hours of practice a day for the rest of his life'.[59] As Lynn Wells notes, the novel can have a measure of 'historical distance'[60] to it. Not only does the reader of *On Chesil Beach* look at a slightly earlier age in this case but also at a concert hall that is older still and repertoire of centuries before. There is an attention to detail that the non-practising musician notices – in this case an amateur musician (McEwan) writing about a professional musician's perspective – that many contemporary professional musicians would take for granted. The ambience of the Wigmore Hall as a physical space is described both from the audience's perspective as well as its appeal to Florence as a young musician, well aware of the history of the hall in the profession she seeks to enter. The 'seriousness' of the place echoes Larkin's 'Church Going' and the consequent image is of a physical space that embodies more than the functional aspect. The description of the cupola and the nature of abstraction in music and the enabling of the imagination, as previously discussed in relation to *The Children Act*, is brought to the fore. The 'revered' older patrons being described as Victorian in nature further captures the romantic and somewhat clichéd impression of the hall that is similar to McEwan's portrayal of the church. It is a fictional description that, like the impression he creates of the church, is nonetheless recognizable.

* * *

It is notable that McEwan includes a reference[61] in *On Chesil Beach* to Britain's most famous cellist of the twentieth century, Jacqueline du Pré, who was a child prodigy and died at only forty-two from multiple sclerosis. The novel begins in 1962 and du Pré had made her formal debut at the Wigmore Hall in March 1961 at the age of sixteen with a programme that included a solo cello suite of Bach. In 1962, she made her concerto debut at the Royal Festival Hall playing the Elgar concerto with the BBC Symphony Orchestra with Rudolf Schwarz conducting. At this point she was Britain's most celebrated young musician and also perceived to be a deeply serious musician, so much so that the senior figure of Yehudi Menuhin – who had recorded the Elgar *Violin Concerto* with the composer conducting – took a special interest in her career and invited her to play trios with him as a violinist and his sister, Hephzibah Menuhin, as the pianist. Musicians reading the text would instantly recognize du Pré's name, although the timing of her early career success may not instantly come to mind. Aside from being an interesting point of detail in McEwan's research for the

---

[59] McEwan, *Lessons*, p. 390.

[60] Lynn Wells, *Ian McEwan* (London, 2010), p. 93.

[61] McEwan, *On Chesil Beach*, p. 50.

Emotional Arousal and Communication

The philosopher, Susanne K. Langer, explains that music can not only put us in touch with emotions which we have felt previously, but can also 'present emotions and moods we have not felt, passions we did not know before. Its subject-matter is the same as that of "self-expression," and its symbols may even be borrowed, upon occasion, from the realm of expressive symptoms yet the borrowed suggestive elements are *formalized*, and the subject-matter "distanced" in an artistic perspective.'[62] In relation to this argument Storr notes that 'although painting and architecture and sculpture make statements about relationships between space, objects, and colours, these relationships are static. Music more aptly represents human emotional processes because music, like life, appears to be in constant motion.'[63]

The breakdown of communication between Edward and Florence during their unconsummated wedding night draws on the question of what Florence, in particular, sought from music that was in itself fulfilling to her. As Storr notes, there appears to be a closer relationship between the *hearing* and emotional arousal than there is between the *seeing* and emotional arousal,[64] which in this case further distances the respective worlds of Florence and Edward. The remoteness of the conversational counterpoint on the beach continues to question what exactly the nature of their relationship is and even whether, beyond the question of their sexual life, the relationship would have been sustainable for the rest of their lives. When considering the question of communication and understanding between individuals, McEwan's comments on *The Child in Time* and *Enduring Love* have particular bearing:

> Clearly misunderstandings occur in life all the time. Not only between people who are very close, but between people who are not close, simply because they don't understand each other. What I think is exceptional about the novel as a form – and here it exerts superiority over movies, over theatre – is its particular ability to get inside minds and to show us the mechanics of misunderstanding, so you can be on both sides of the dispute.[65]

---

[62]   Susanne K. Langer, *Philosophy in a New Key* (Cambridge, Mass., 1960), p. 222.

[63]   Storr, *Music and the Mind*, p. 79.

[64]   Ibid., p. 26.

[65]   Reynolds and Noakes, *Ian McEwan*, p. 18.

Solitude, Voyeurism, and the Transcendental   101

The failure to complete intercourse was something that Florence took as a personal inadequacy largely, if not wholly, through her inexperience of the physical side of the relationship. This is something Edward does not contradict but rather draws a parallel to in the musical side of her life.

How typical, her overconfident meddling in matters of awesome complexity; she should have known well enough that her attitude in rehearsals for the string quartet had no relevance here.[66]

Edward's comment is designed to cut to the core of Florence's personality and character. The 'typical' overconfidence regarding complex matters infers that her leadership of the quartet has an air of arrogance that is similarly naïve. It is a double insult. First, that her approach to leading the quartet is flawed, and second that she does not understand what Edward perceived to be the basics of sexual interaction. The 'awesome complexity' had no 'relevance' in the bedroom from Edward's perspective. In a cruel irony, the fingers that could produce beautiful music when sensitively placed on the string of a violin were the same fingers that had brought about his early sexual response. Following her 'cry of revulsion'[67] that demonstrated the 'contempt she showed for him',[68] he was in turn contemptuous towards her.

and she wanted to punish him, to leave him alone to contemplate his inadequacies without any thought for her own part. Surely it was the movement of her hands, her fingers, that brought him on.

he had suffered in passive torment wanting her till he ached,

what pleasures she had denied them both.[69]

The 'pleasures she had denied them both' are only commented on by Edward. Florence does not hint at a sense of loss, let alone 'aching'. The 'punishment' of Edward relates to her perception of him knowing his own role. She had little thought for her place in the situation beyond her presence. Thus, Edward quickly falls into a subservient role similar to a member of her quartet who makes a mistake. Moreover, like a musician, it was the perceived misuse of the hands and fingers that had been responsible. In every respect, Florence approaches the matter from a practical perspective that mirrors her musical relationships. Edward is humiliated because he too lacks the mastery of technique.

---

[66]   McEwan, *On Chesil Beach*, p. 130.

[67]   Ibid., p. 162.

[68]   Ibid.

[69]   Ibid., pp. 162–163.

102   *Music and Religion in the Writings of Ian McEwan*

Performance as Voyeurism

In the national press of the same era as *On Chesil Beach* there had been sustained coverage of scandals involving high-profile figures and the government of Harold Macmillan. In *Lessons* McEwan writes that 'In that time, moral standards were high in public life and so, therefore, was hypocrisy. Delicious outrage was the general tone. Scandals became part of the anecdotage of their sex education.'[70]

In 1962, news broke of the Admiralty clerk John Vassall, who had been blackmailed by the Soviet Union which had threatened to expose his homosexuality, together with the fact that he had been potentially shielded by his minister, Tam Galbraith. The Minister for War, John Profumo, had begun an affair with the model Christine Keeler after meeting her at Cliveden in July 1961. This affair had particular interest because of Keeler's coincidental relationship with Yevgeny Ivanov, a naval attaché and intelligence officer at the Soviet embassy. As Jeremy Paxman notes, 'Discretion began to die in the 1960s. Until then, the popular mindset had tended to accept at face value the Conservatives' self-proclaimed association with old-fashioned values based on the teachings of the Church,'[71] as later noted by Margaret Thatcher and discussed in chapter 1.

The narrative of *On Chesil Beach*, centres on a young man and woman who have both achieved university degrees. Family relationships are strained for both of them and in the case of Florence the isolation of life as a young musician has become second nature. However, part of the allure of Florence to the equally naïve Edward is the image of her authority. She is commanding when leading a rehearsal and the music itself provides her with a voice more powerful than either of them. Germaine Greer's seminal text, *The Female Eunuch*, evaluates the impression of women in society just a few years after the setting of McEwan's novel and this relates to the circumstances of this particular text. Dominic Head has commented on how Greer's writing was an important early encounter for McEwan, and in other respects it can also be shown to have been an influence in *The Imitation Game, The Comfort of Strangers, or Shall we die?*, and *The Child in Time*.[72] McEwan described his own reading of *The Female Eunuch* in 1971 as a 'revelation' that 'spoke directly to a knot of problems at the heart [of his own] family's life'. He added that his 'female characters became a repository of all the goodness that men fell short of'.[73]

> As long as she is young and personable, every woman may cherish the dream that she may leap up the social ladder and dim the sheen of luxury by sheer natural loveliness.

---

[70]   McEwan, *Lessons*, p. 108.

[71]   Jeremy Paxman, *The Political Animal* (London, 2007), p. 253.

[72]   Head, *Ian McEwan*, p. 5.

[73]   Zachary Leader (ed.), *On Modern British Fiction* (Oxford, 2003), p. 42.

Her value is solely attested by the demand she excites in others. All she must contribute is her existence. She need achieve nothing, for she is the reward of achievement. She need never give positive evidence of her moral character because virtue is assumed from her loveliness, and her passivity. If any man who has no right to her be found with her she will not be punished, for she is morally neuter. The matter is solely one of male rivalry. Innocently she may drive men to madness and war. The more trouble she can cause, the more her stocks go up, for possession of her means more than the demand she excites. Nobody wants a girl whose beauty is imperceptible to all but him; and so men welcome the stereotype because it directs their taste into the most commonly recognized areas of value, although they may protest because some aspects of it do not tally with their fetishes.[74]

The text of Greer contextualises Florence's character, for the 'loveliness' she exudes is a musical one. Florence's own 'moral character' cannot be questioned because she is 'morally neuter'. Further, the more difficult she becomes, the more she 'excites' as can be seen in Edward's year-long wait and aching. The last sentence of the Greer extract is especially significant because the beauty of Florence through her role as a musician is perceptible to many, and yet this persona is difficult to understand because it does not align with Edward's own views of her and, arguably, women more generally. Of McEwan's description of Florence and Edward, John Updike wrote:

> Your descent into a woman's sensibility – the claustrophobia of being sexually desired, the intrusiveness of the whole physical experience, her deep distaste and yet the flickers of some faint sexual interest that alas go undeveloped – is a virtuoso feat that doesn't feel like one, it spins out so naturally. Poor Edward's epic premature ejaculation is a masterpiece of its type.[75]

The 'morally neuter' aspect returns when Florence suggests that in place of a sexual relationship within the marriage, Edward could pursue other women for his sexual needs. In a moment of intentional liberalism, Florence endeavours to show her worldliness by commenting that 'mummy knows two homosexuals, they live in a flat together, like man and wife. Two men. In Oxford, in Beaumont Street. They're very quiet about it. They both teach at Christ Church. No one bothers them. And we can make our own rules too.'[76] Her proposal is for Edward to sleep with other women, and this could perhaps shock him given her own uninterest in sexual matters. But critically, her comment that one day she would play 'something beautiful' for him 'like the Mozart, at the Wigmore Hall'[77] demonstrates the difference she sees between music and physical attraction or need. Edward's sexual needs are seen as a practical matter whereas music is

---

[74] Germaine Greer, *The Female Eunuch* (New York, 1970), pp. 50–51.

[75] Letter from John Updike to Ian McEwan (30 April 2007).

[76] McEwan, *On Chesil Beach*, pp. 188–189.

[77] Ibid., p. 189.

104 *Music and Religion in the Writings of Ian McEwan*

something of beauty. Although the impression Florence wants to create is of a liberated young woman who is the opposite of the person Edward describes as 'frigid', her actions are a distraction and an alternative course from the reality he wishes. The separation of reality and art was addressed by Freud in the following statement. In this context Florence's relative liberalism is part of a larger emotional freedom that she considers as an artist.

> An artist is originally a man who turns away from reality because he cannot come to terms with the renunciation of instinctual satisfaction which it at first demands, and who allows his erotic and ambitious wishes full play in the life of the phantasy.[78]

By this statement the fantasy would not be for Edward to engage in activities with other women, but for Florence to have knowledge of these adventures. It would be her fantasy, and thus she engages with Edward sexually in a role of near-complete domination. In assessing Freud's statement, Storr notes that 'artists are burdened with the same elements of arrested sexual development as neurotics, but, because of their gifts, are able to sublimate their impulses in their creations'.[79] Freud goes further by describing the 'artist's joy in creating' – in this instance on the level of Florence's own performances and her hope for orchestrating Edward's own performances. Storr notes Freud's observation that 'the artist's joy ... has a special quality [and its] satisfactions seem "finer and higher," but "do not convulse the physical being" '.[80] In this sense the 'oceanic' experience that Freud speaks of can be 'triggered by the actual performance of music [but it is] not comparable with either orgasm or with union with another person',[81] even though musicians can describe the feeling of being 'taken over' or 'possessed' during a performance, which can be interpreted as a type of ecstasy.[82]

McEwan writes that 'When Einstein found that his general theory made correct predictions for the shift in Mercury's orbit, he felt so thrilled he had palpitations, "as if something had snapped inside". "I was beside myself with joyous excitement". This is the excitement any artist can recognize. This is the joy, not of simple description, but of creation.' (Einstein)[83] The argument regarding Florence's liberal stance is bolstered by her own sexual inexperience. The fantasy is the idea of sexual relations as she presumes them to be, but in fact she has no experience. As such, the circumstances she describes for Edward are

---

[78]   Sigmund Freud, *Formulations on the Two Principles of Mental Function*, trans. and ed. by James Strachey et al., Standard Edition, Volume XII (London, 1961), p. 224.

[79]   Storr, *Music and the Mind*, p. 91.

[80]   Sigmund Freud, *Civilization and its Discontents*, trans. and ed. by James Strachey et al., Standard Edition, Volume XXI (London, 1961), pp. 79–80.

[81]   Storr, *Music and the Mind*, p. 95.

[82]   Ibid., p. 96.

[83]   McEwan, *Science*, pp. 52–53.

Solitude, Voyeurism, and the Transcendental   105

doubly removed from reality. The imagination she can imbue her performances with has an alternative use in her relationship.

With her statement on the beach to Edward, Florence not only clarifies her true feelings, which she believed to be a mistake as soon as she had uttered them, but illuminates the true role that music holds in her life. She reiterates her love for Edward but in a psyche of her own devising. Further, as much as he is welcome to be with other women, she most wants him to watch her perform (but only) in a musical sense. The summation of this would be a musical voyeurism as she controls not one other person, including ultimately her second husband (the cellist), but the other members of the quartet, too. Storr writes of the pleasure to be gained from 'seeing the coordinated bowing of various string sections, just as there is from seeing other examples of group coordination, like gymnastic displays', and that those who engage in music professionally can produce a performance where the physicality of the musical moment is itself increased.[84] Debussy's quote on the nature of professional performance is apposite: 'The attraction of the virtuoso for the public is very like that of the circus for the crowd. There is always a hope that something dangerous may happen.'[85] Florence effectively plays Edward and others, too, in this special style of voyeurism. Edward wants the image of Florence but 'some aspects' 'do not tally' with her 'fetishes' (Greer). In the text below there is an interesting overlap in a speech of McEwan's and the nature of fantasy discussed above:

> I got on to incredibly dangerous ground when I suggested that many women probably have masochistic fantasies and that many men probably have sadistic fantasies, which are acted out in private but never spoken about in any kind of public debate. And then I said that it would be far better in a relationship to embrace this than to deny it, and that true freedom would be for such women to recognize their masochism and to understand how it had become related to sexual pleasure. The same was not less true for male masochists. I was talking here of sexual fantasy. The whole room exploded, and I came away feeling terribly bruised because I had been very inarticulate, as one is when speaking against such hostility. But I was attacked for providing a 'rapist's charter' and for poaching on forbidden territory – women's experience.[86]

The nature of the relationship between Florence and Edward does not extend into a realm of fantasy beyond Florence's suggestion, unexpected as it is. However, the balance between McEwan's reading of *The Female Eunuch* and his intention that female characters would represent the 'goodness that men fell

---

[84] Storr, *Music and the Mind*, pp. 31–32.

[85] Claude Debussy, 'Monsieur Croche the Dilettante Hater', in B. N. Langdon Davies (trans.), *Three Classics in the Aesthetics of Music* (New York, 1962), p. 22.

[86] Haffenden, *Novelists in Interview*, p. 175.

106   *Music and Religion in the Writings of Ian McEwan*

short of'[87] is complicated in the case of Florence, whose suggestion to Edward is not a matter of embracing an idea rather than denying it, but one of lowering the perception of other women in Edward's eyes. Florence assumes that the behaviour she encourages for Edward will be acceptable to other women and that casual relationships are reasonable. To him this is anathema. owever,

Florence is in her own way liberated and ultimately in control. Even when Edward declines her offer, she does not retract it. The question therefore becomes whether Edward is inhibited and parochial in his view of marriage in an otherwise increasingly liberated time. Years later the question of his response to her continues to haunt him. At the time he had lashed out at her and his comments clarify the suggestive nature of the arrangement. In calling Florence a 'fraud' as a wife who had tricked him, the reader sees Florence as someone who wants a husband on her terms so that she will not be troubled by other suitors in the future. Whether she later marries and has children through latent guilt over Edward, or simply because she now feels with the eventual success of the quartet that her personal life can now develop, is a subjective matter that each reader will interpret individually. However, Florence's sense of resolve is clear and the fact that she sees no reason to modify her suggestion, despite Edward's uninterest, confirms this.

Pacifism

Florence's choice of Bridge, Bartók, and Britten quartets for her last year of college[88] is interesting as they were all pacifists, as she is similarly portrayed with her membership of CND. Further, Ralph Vaughan Williams, who serves as a figure of inspiration for Clive Linley in *Amsterdam*, was deeply affected by his role in The Great War. Considering McEwan's own anti-nuclear stance and the mention of CND and the oratorio *or Shall we die?*, in addition to his respect for the women of Greenham Common,[89] this choice in *On Chesil Beach* presents a curious alliance of otherwise quite contrasting composers under one heading. Florence's choices (and arguably McEwan's) support her anti-nuclear interests[90] while portraying the musical world of the 1960s in a particular image that balances high art, anxiety about the Cold War, and also the role of women.

Florence was a member of CND when she met Edward and the role of women in the nuclear disarmament movement cannot be underestimated. In 1960, Eleanor Roosevelt was one of the first signers of Sane Nuclear Policy's (SANE) first advertisement. Although the role of feminism as it is seen later in

---

[87]   Leader (ed.), *On Modern British Fiction*, p. 42.

[88]   McEwan, *On Chesil Beach*, pp. 50–51.

[89]   Haffenden, *Novelists in Interview*, p. 184.

[90]   For further reading see Haffenden, *Novelists in Interview*, pp. 184, 186 and Iain Quinn, 'Interview with Michael Berkeley'.

Solitude, Voyeurism, and the Transcendental   107

the decade was not a primary concern to the women in CND, childcare was, not least because it remained of little concern to men. As Lawrence S. Wittner notes:

> In Great Britain, CND – much like its Women's Group, churning out litera- ture warning mothers about the hazards of strontium-90 – proclaimed 'the right of our children to live, uncrippled by nuclear poisons.'[91]

> [An advertisement concluded] The time has come for mothers and fathers to speak up in no uncertain terms ... Demand a stop to nuclear tests. Raise hell; it's time you did.[92]

In McEwan's interview with John Haffenden, he notes that in *or Shall we die?* the libretto draws on the notion of war as a protector for future genera- tions, while failing to acknowledge that children are, in McEwan's words, the world's 'major resource.'[93] In *Lessons* it is noted that 'The bomb was a threat to humanity, to life on earth, a moral abomination, a tragic waste of resources.'[94]

Aside from Florence's views on the options for Edward to enjoy sexual relations with other women, the prevailing climate and conversation within the peace movement that Florence was part of placed the decisions of women squarely in a role of superior responsibility. Through the well-known speeches of Henry Kissinger and later President Kennedy, the masculinity of a just war had been emphasized and re-emphasized. The role of women to potentially respond independently in compelling terms is seen in the adver- tisement text above.

The year 1962 also saw the publication of CND's pamphlet titled 'Women ask Why', which included the text of three speeches from its recent Women's Meeting. As Wittner notes, 'The chorus for one of the most popular songs among British activists – "The H-Bomb's Thunder" – composed (by a man) for the first Aldermaston march, put the movement's gender assumptions and hopes clearly enough':

> Men and women, stand together!
> Do not heed the men of war.
> Make your minds up now or never.
> Ban the bomb forever more.[95]

There is a significant confluence of views between the media coverage of CND, Florence's participation in CND, McEwan's own anti-war stance in rela-

---

[91] Lawrence S. Wittner, 'Gender Roles and Nuclear Disarmament Activism, 1954– 1965', *Gender and History*, 12:1 (April 2000), 207.

[92] Ibid.

[93] Haffenden, *Novelists in Interview*, p. 182.

[94] McEwan, *Lessons*, p. 104.

[95] Wittner, 'Gender Roles and Nuclear Disarmament Activism, 1954–1965', pp. 210–211.

108　　*Music and Religion in the Writings of Ian McEwan*

tion to the women of Greenham Common, and the oratorio *or Shall we die?*. Florence is consistently portrayed as a conscientious, principled presence in the novel's narrative, albeit with progressive views on the sexual life of her marriage. Politically, she is far from 'morally neuter' (Greer). This is in contrast to the muddled, or arguably brutish, responses of Edward, whose approach throughout the earlier part of the novel borders on either insensitivity or simple immaturity. Further, Florence's moral and ethical approach to the world is, like her approach to classical music in an era with an increasing public enthusiasm towards popular music, a small voice of calm against the multitude. The generation of Edward and Florence were convinced that the country would be 'transformed for the better' and in their first decade of adult life it 'surely belonged to them'.[96]

In *On Chesil Beach* the reader is left to ponder whether Florence or Edward or both are possessed of guilt or regret by the end. However, in the film version the ending leaves no doubt about conviction. Edward is a broken, or at least a lesser, man for his life having stopped in part at their separation. Florence has the confidence of the largely unrepentant, and a life in music has reassured her of her own identity and her sense of right, if not a certain self-righteousness. Taken further, not only does Edward have to witness the musical marriage in front of him when he attends a later concert at the Wigmore Hall, but Florence sees her first husband in a seat (physically) beneath her and her new husband across from her as she leads the quartet. In performing, Florence is in command of every nuance and every aspect of the relationships around her and she appears entirely comfortable with that. It is ultimate control of both the personal and professional aspects of her life.

With the passing of years following their divorce, Florence and Edward had no reason to stay in contact, but occasionally Edward would look at the arts section of newspapers even though his interest in classical music was sporadic. He had been unaware of the Ennismore Quartet's debut at the Wigmore Hall. The programme for the later concert included the Mozart *Quintet in D* that Florence had said she wanted to play for him many years before. Curiously, it is a quintet not a quartet that she had always wanted him to hear. The extra person is perhaps a subtle symbolism of McEwan to the somewhat extraneous nature of the other in their relationship or her willingness towards considering other people in relationships, which in the case of a guest musician with a quartet, can be seen with a relative parallelism to her suggestion to Edward. In the student rehearsal that she oversaw many years before, she drafted in a second violist without consulting the other members of the quartet in advance. The usual members had 'preferred to avoid complications',[97] and a new person creates a very different dynamic. After a musically awkward beginning of that part of the rehearsal, 'Florence's resolve in the face of opposition, one against

---

[96]　McEwan, *On Chesil Beach*, p. 31.

[97]　Ibid., p. 99.

Solitude, Voyeurism, and the Transcendental   109

three, and her tough-minded sense of her own good taste,'[98] dictated the out-come. The choice of another woman for the quartet was arguably calculated on Florence's part, for not only did she assert still greater feminine authority over her (later) second husband, Charles, the cellist, but she also created an inten-tional unease among the others present.[99] Thus, she doubly asserts her own power both over Charles and also in a voyeuristic sense towards Edward, who was observing this unfold. Florence was the woman in this situation with the greatest authority, including an authority over another woman.

On reading the review of the quartet's July 1968 concert at the Wigmore Hall, Edward is finally seeing Florence through the eyes of the profession she has committed to, indeed, that she committed to instead of to him. He reads of her natural poise and expressivity that had been so lacking when they were last together, whether in the bedroom or in their discussion on the beach. The final statement lances his own hope for what might have been when Florence's great love was not Edward, Charles or herself, but the higher calling of music that would continue to fill her life.

> Miss Ponting [Florence], in the lilting tenderness of her tone and the lyrical delicacy of her phrasing, played, if I may put it this way, like a woman in love, not only with Mozart, or with music, but with life itself.[100]

The book and screenplay end quite differently. In the book, Edward decides that he will never again seek an association with Florence. 'He would never attend the concerts, or buy, or even look at the boxed sets of Beethoven or Schubert [quartets].'[101] However, in the film adaptation by McEwan, Edward attends the concert at the Wigmore Hall, sitting in the seat near the stage that he had once sat in years before, when Florence had taken him on a tour of the hall. She notices him in the audience and pauses, much as her life had paused many years before with him. As McEwan has commented, the ending of the film was received with different views, but the alternative ending in which Edward reappears and sees Florence was necessary to McEwan because of the different medium.[102] Once more, McEwan creates a moment, if not several consecutive ones, where time stands still in the manner Michael Berkeley refers to in his comments on McEwan's writing style.[103] It is all the more poignant because it is a silence before the opening of a work that had long been promised for Edward's pleasure, as Florence interpreted it. The long-promised aspect can also be seen in the maturity of thinking that surrounds this later encounter. Claudia Schemberg writes of the 'mature artistic conception, evident in the

---

[98] Ibid.

[99] Edward's presence at the rehearsal occurs in McEwan's screenplay of the novel.

[100] McEwan, *On Chesil Beach*, p. 198.

[101] Ibid., p. 202.

[102] Quinn, 'Interview with Ian McEwan'.

[103] Quinn, 'Interview with Michael Berkeley'.

110   *Music and Religion in the Writings of Ian McEwan*

sections of [*Atonement* as] Briony has learned how to imaginatively put herself in the position of other people'.[104] This can also be seen when considering Florence in a concert setting with the past coming to the fore and all in relation to the same piece of music. She returns to the same quintet and the promise made years before and sees a person who was very close to her in the past and is now only a short distance away.

Fantasia and Fantasy

The approach to pleasure, or the absence of it, is encountered differently in *The Imitation Game*, where sexual control is observed within the male-dominated environment of the World War II British intelligence service operations at Bletchley Park. The patriarchal attitudes of condescension, patronage, and sexual injustice are portrayed in a relationship between Cathy, an intelligent girl from a middle-class family, and Turner, a Cambridge mathematician who takes an interest in her while she is playing the piano one day.[105] He invites her to his rooms but clumsily begins to make love, which he is unable to do satisfactorily. Like Edward with Florence, Turner sees this as a humiliation and storms out. McEwan notes that women were perceived as essential to the war effort as moral arbiters, and the closer someone moved to the nucleus of the intelligence world, the more women they encountered.[106] This situation is reversed in the relationship between Cathy and Turner, as the closer Turner gets to Cathy, the less she is under his patriarchal control. As McEwan comments, this related to:

> his [Turner's] sense of total competence in the outer world, and therefore his fear of failure in the inner world. There is among men a fear of women and of their power. What is meant to be in the scene is that once Cathy is sexually excited she becomes very demanding, which is very frightening for Turner, and so his anger seemed to be dramatically in order. Once she had made the journey to the centre of official secrets, the other secret – the secret in the private world – creates the same response: she meets the masculine defensiveness that won't admit weakness: I see this defensiveness as a burden for

---

[104] Claudia Schemberg, 'Achieving "At-one-ment": Storytelling and the Concept of the Self in Ian McEwan's *The Child in Time, Black Dogs, Enduring Love*, and *Atonement*' *(thesis)* (Frankfurt, 2004), p. 85.

[105] Ian McEwan, *The Imitation Game* (London, 1982), p. 129.

[106] In an interview with John Haffenden McEwan observes how 'going to Greenham Common, for example, was to visit people who had a very clear sense of value and attitude. I had to measure the extent to which I had ideas and the extent to which I would love them out, and I felt great admiration for the women at Greenham Common. I thought of the Greenham Common women as a kind of measure of moral certainty'. Haffenden, *Novelists in Interview*, pp. 184, 186.

Solitude, Voyeurism, and the Transcendental   111

men, and not just as the thing men do to women. I would not like to say who is unhappier in that scene, but it is quite clear who is the more powerful.[107]

Cathy, like Florence, is the commanding presence, but music provides the surety of response that she seeks through the sublimity and relative 'fantasy' (Greer) of playing the Mozart *Fantasia* in her non-working hours. However, the nature of sexual powerplay that McEwan mentions in his public comments earlier in this chapter is seen to play out in this narrative, with the emphasis on 'masculine defensiveness that won't admit weakness' which also relates to his comments on the 'goodness'[108] of women. The 'secret' world is also the world of fantasy, and McEwan's inference at the end of the quote that Cathy is the more powerful of the two resonates with his intention to portray women in a particular light, that by holding greater moral authority they are also by nature superior decision makers.

Absolute Sublimity and the Programmatic

The references to music in McEwan's novels centre around chamber music, song and lieder literature, and very occasional references to Mozart's *The Magic Flute* in *The Comfort of Strangers*,[109] *For You*,[110] and *Amsterdam*.[111] Although the composers portrayed in both the opera *For You* and the novel *Amsterdam* work on orchestral compositions – and McEwan's narratives show a keen understanding of the nature of both the craftsmanship of composition and the composer in the musical profession – there are no other references to strictly symphonic works in his writing. His collaborator for the opera *For You* and the oratorio *or Shall we die?*, Michael Berkeley, speaks of his understanding of McEwan's tastes over many years of acquaintance. To Berkeley, McEwan sees art as a central element towards points of inspiration and also higher aspirations. McEwan's knowledge of the field is one grounded in learning and personal experience, but it is also the abstract nature of music as an art form that he believes appeals to McEwan because of the inner-mind's emotional response, especially when it concerns chamber works. In Berkeley's[112] understanding of McEwan's appreciation of the genre there is an informed interest in the intricate interplay that exists in the chamber repertoire that is a critical focus in *On Chesil Beach*.

---

[107]   Haffenden, *Novelists in Interview*, pp. 176–177.

[108]   Leader, *On Modern British Fiction*, p. 42.

[109]   Ian McEwan, *The Comfort of Strangers* (London, 2006), p. 2.

[110]   Ian McEwan, *For You* (London, 2008), pp. 40–41.

[111]   McEwan, *Amsterdam*, p. 95.

[112]   Quinn, 'Interview with Michael Berkeley'.

112   *Music and Religion in the Writings of Ian McEwan*

An Absence of Commentary

During the late twentieth century to the present, there has been an increasing trend for performers to speak with audiences and share their views on a piece of music they are about to perform, especially if it is a new piece being heard for the first time. There are strong arguments against this practice, particularly if some of the piece is played in a demonstration, because the element of immediate musical surprise on first hearing is removed from the complete performance. However, this layering of a narrative on a given piece is not limited to pieces that have an intended narrative quality, such as a song or impressionistic or character works. What might be helpful and entertaining or even meaningful to one member of the audience is misleading and obtrusive to another because the potential natural musical flow of the concert is interrupted by an external interpretation. McEwan's performers do not offer extended commentaries from the concert stage about the pieces they play, even in the more informal setting of a Christmas concert with legal colleagues in *The Children Act*. Neither are the performers that McEwan is especially familiar with and refers to in his writings (Shura Cherkassky, Angela Hewitt, John Ogdon, Gustav Leonhardt, András Schiff) known for speaking at length with audiences about works in advance of performing them. Indeed, Glenn Gould, who McEwan refers to in *Saturday*,[113] retired from the concert stage early in his career and was principally recognized for his recordings. The pieces of instrumental music that McEwan's characters perform are also not programmatic. Florence (*On Chesil Beach*) does not, for instance, discuss her future repertoire with options to include singers and thus incorporate significant chamber pieces like Ralph Vaughan Williams's *On Wenlock Edge* (with texts of A. E. Housman) or Samuel Barber's *Dover Beach* (with texts of Matthew Arnold). Rather, she discusses other pieces of absolute music (quartets of Bridge, Bartók, and Britten).[114]

McEwan's approach is consistently towards instrumental where the music itself is allowed to communicate its own language and without subjective commentary. As such, there is no programmatic narrative within McEwan's novels concerning instrumental music. Moreover, it is the references to Bach that Fiona (*The Children Act*) finds especially affecting, rather than the song literature she is accompanying. This view coalesces with her own playing and musical development. However, the presentation of a view that leans towards absolute music is not universal, even if it is coincidental that the repertoire McEwan refers to in his novels is consistently in line with his personal tastes. It also aligns with the 'what if?' aspect of Head's[115] view on McEwan's questioning nature and whether a reader who knows the scores being discussed then interprets them independently while reading the narrative too. Without a narrative

---

[113]   McEwan, *Saturday*, p. 22.

[114]   McEwan, *On Chesil Beach*, p. 51.

[115]   Head, *The State of the Novel – Britain and Beyond*, pp. 8, 6.

Solitude, Voyeurism, and the Transcendental   113

the listener (and reader who knows the scores) is by nature able to interpret the piece and performance on their own terms. This explains the sometimes-bewildering contrary reviews of the same concert by two critics.

The composer James MacMillan believes a balance between the abstract element of music and the contemporary age needs to be borne in mind and this is important to consider because it is not a view that is fostered in McEwan's portrayal of performance.

> Like all musicians, I take pride in the fact that music is an abstract form. It's *the* most abstract of arts, probably. And it has self-sufficiency: it seems to communicate its completeness according to its own designs, without the need to be explained through words. [However] we live in a society that's dominated by the visual and the verbal, and people can sometimes be baffled when they confront something that can't be explained in visual or verbal ways.[116]

Considering this commentary in the context of McEwan's writings and in particular his approach to the world of classical music as an accessible, indeed appealing, other world, it is possible to see how McEwan's portrayals are not clichéd but show a definable interest towards a specific nature of performance. This aligns with the approach to silence and a controlled environment that is discussed at the beginning of this chapter, as well as Florence's approach to the Wigmore Hall as a hallowed space. To insert commentary is to insert control over a medium that is itself sufficiently enabled to allow for free communication. It can also be seen to lessen the artistic experience because a casual commentary before a serious work is by nature a different aesthetic encounter. When there is applause between movements of a work and some in the audience frown on those who did not realize the presumed protocol for waiting until the end of the piece, it is in part a frustration with the fracturing of the gradually emerging artistic moment. The poise and control that Florence is noted for in her work relate to the sense of timing of both the music and the silence that surrounds it. No words are necessary for her.

The Individual Response

The possibility for music to convey the unspeakable is also seen at the very end of Anaïs Nin's *A Spy in the House of Love*, which similarly relates to a string ensemble. It also depicts the nature of emotional and psychological departure that musicians like Florence encounter with an experience that is enveloping, rewarding, and beyond a normal life. The language and narrative of music is seen in both cases as something that is intelligible as well as untranslatable.

---

[116] Andrew Palmer, 'James MacMillan', *Encounters with British Composers* (Woodbridge, 2015), pp. 289–290.

114   *Music and Religion in the Writings of Ian McEwan*

But no words came as one of Beethoven's Quartets began to tell Sabina as Djuana could not, of what they both knew for absolute certainty: the continuity of existence and of the chain of summits, of elevations by which continuity is reached. By elevation the consciousness reached a perpetual movement, transcending death, and in the same manner attained the continuity of love by seizing upon its impersonal essence, which was a summation of all the alchemies producing life and birth, a child, a work of art, a work of science, a heroic act, an act of love. The identity of the human couple was not eternal but interchangeable, to protect this exchange of spirits, transmissions of character, all the fecundations of new selves being born, and faithfulness only to the continuity, the extensions and expansions of love achieving their crystallizations into high moments and summits equal to the high moments and summits of art or religion.[117]

The 'crystallization' and 'summits' relate importantly to Florence as a professional musician who devotes her life to the art, but equally to Cathy (*The Imitation Game*) and Fiona (*The Children Act*) who have a love of music but do not have the opportunity to be engaged with music for large parts of each day. It is the inner voice and language that musicians strive to communicate through their performances, and it is this aspect that drives Florence's critiques in rehearsals and which compels Cathy and Fiona to continue to practise, because in seeking the inner language of the piece, they also gain a deeper meaning of the work in relation to themselves. The piece becomes an emotional puzzle but one that cannot injure the player emotionally and one that the player can halt. For this reason, when Fiona senses a barrier between herself and her performance at the Christmas party with colleagues, she stops and leaves the stage. The mysticism that envelops her appreciation of the music has been removed and so too must she depart. The response of the partners in both *The Children Act* and *The Imitation Game* is encapsulated in a comment from Tony in *The Imitation Game*:

> Cathy plays a stormy passage from [the Mozart *Fantasia*] K. 475 – a series of wild runs.
>
> Tony reads The Times.
>
> Tony: I get the impression you are more interested in practising the piano than in anything else. I mean, you've hardly spoken a word to me all afternoon. You don't seem to be taking the war very seriously, Cathy.[118]

The potential technical challenges for Cathy in the Mozart that might be the reason for her extensive practising are not discussed but rather the significance of a world peace in the life of a musician. Only war is offered as a parallel to her engagement with music. This may seem an extreme parallel. However, the

---

[117]   Anaïs Nin, *A Spy in the House of Love* (London, 2001), p. 123.

[118]   McEwan, *The Imitation Game*, p. 89.

Solitude, Voyeurism, and the Transcendental   115

nature of this often-beguiling individualism and intense focus in musical study can be contextualised with Laurence Dreyfus's writings in *Bach and the Patterns of Invention*. Dreyfus speaks with the knowledge of both a scholar and a performer and his commentary examines the nature of trying to understand the puzzle of 'miracles' that composers leave for performers to understand. Critically, to encounter a composer as a 'thinking' person and a formidable mind that is not simply understood.

> Rather than conceiving musical structure as unconscious growth – an aesthetic model that presumes a spontaneous invention beyond the grasp of intentional human actions – I prefer to highlight the predictable and historically determined ways in which music was 'worked out' by the composer. The intention to speculate on Bach's willfulness invites us to imagine a piece of music not as *inevitably* the way it was, but rather as a result of a musicality that devises and revises thoughts against a resilient backdrop of conventions and constraints ... while it is true that parts and whole in Bach cohere in a way that is often just short of miraculous ... I find it more profitable to chip away at musical 'miracles', pursuing instead Bach's inclination to regard certain laws as binding and others as breakable, to accept certain techniques as productive and others fruitless, and to admire some ideas as venerable while regarding others as outmoded. In brief, I favor analyses that capture Bach as a thinking composer.[119]

Dreyfus addresses the questioning that applies to performance and how music presents a dialogue for performers to observe as they study and then, in performance, reengage with. Through their emotional and practical encounters it is possible to recognize the nature of dialogue that exists for a performer that is set apart from their outward conversations. Seen through this lens, Cathy, Fiona, and Florence are experiencing another world that is both private and rewarding, while discovering 'miracles' along the way. They are already in conversations when they are playing.

Towards the Transcendental

The interpretative aspects of Bach and the ability to achieve nuance within performances was discussed earlier in this chapter in relation to Henry's (*Saturday*) choice of one performer over another when listening to recordings as he works. However, it is perhaps no coincidence that McEwan selects a neurosurgeon as the character who has a special affinity with Bach and, in particular, the *Goldberg Variations*, as this is a piece we have come to believe relates to a mental state of relaxation, rest, and sleep. The sense of peace and a higher calling are all the more embracing bearing in mind McEwan's atheist position.

---

[119] Laurence Dreyfus, *Bach and the Patterns of Invention* (Cambridge, 2004), p. 27.

116   *Music and Religion in the Writings of Ian McEwan*

To listen to the *Goldberg Variations* is for many people an intense experience as the pieces unfold in ever-increasing developments of the material. When Ralph Kirkpatrick borrowed a quote from Sir Thomas Browne's *Religio medici* that 'there is something in it of Divinity more than the eare discovers' he raised the question of a piece of secular music surpassing earthly concerns. There is nothing specifically religious about the pieces and yet the superiority of the writing engenders a response that it is removed from the norm. This measure of perfection can be translated into a believable transcendence for an atheist like McEwan, who is deeply interested in the arts because a tangible artwork can evoke a different sense of awe. As nineteenth-century composers considered Bach a god and simply above others, the noted Bach exponent and Holocaust survivor Zuzana Růžičková explains how his music could be seen to emanate a transcendental quality.

> For me, it is Bach that teaches me faith. He was a sort of mystic. He didn't adhere to any single church when he composed. He wrote his music in protest and passion. That spirit, the spirit of Bach, was always with me and it kept me alive. It has been my one constant since childhood. I have developed my spirituality through his music, which is transcendent. Bach is of the highest order, God is everywhere with him – making children, drinking wine, singing, being desperate, being sad. With Bach there is always solace. He gives us something eternal that surmounts being human.

> Bach has sustained me through every trial of my life and remained with me as a comfort in old age. I owe him my life. When people ask me what he means to me, I tell them: Bach's music is order in chaos. It is beauty in ugliness. I have seen enough of both in my life to know what I am talking about.[120]

For many musicians who begin their studies early in life, music can be viewed as the longest relationship they experience beyond their family. It is a constant and one that they can largely control. A violinist who plays in chamber and orchestra settings where they do not necessarily choose the repertoire they are playing can nonetheless still perform a solo Bach partita in the confines of their own home or indeed in a solo concert. It is an expressive language that they can summon and respond to. In this sense, it is a relationship of near equals as the performer is dependent on the composer as much as the composer is dependent on the performer, even if they happen to be the same person. The skills are complementary but nonetheless independent, and a good composer is not necessarily a good performer and *vice versa*. The element of musical communication found a higher meaning for the Russian composer Igor Stravinsky.

---

[120] Zuzana Růžičková and Wendy Holden, *One Hundred Miracles – A Memorial of Music and Survival* (London, 2019), p. 316.

Solitude, Voyeurism, and the Transcendental 117

the profound meaning of music and its essential aim ... is to promote a communion, a union of man with his fellow man with the Supreme Being.[121]

The nature of communion with a higher power does not relate to theological belief in the case of McEwan's writings any more than it arguably does in the lives of most musicians, including some church musicians. No theological argument is advanced in his novels but rather a sense of questioning and a value of liturgical experience, as discussed in chapter 1. Rather, the critical element is found in the transformation of a musical language into an emotional dialogue that the performer creates, and the listener responds to. In *The Child in Time*, McEwan further relates the nature of art in general to flowing with the 'forces of creation'[122] and as such, unavoidably natural and necessary.

* * *

When the late Russian pianist Sviatoslav Richter insisted that his performances be conducted in a darkened hall with not even the panes of glass in the exit doors visible and with a floor lamp next to the piano while he played from a score and not from memory, it was to allow him to be in near solitude with the musical score in front of him. The audiences were mere observers and, one might suggest, somewhat irrelevant to the proceedings beyond the purchase of their tickets that allowed the event to take place. In this sense, the element of intimacy was brought to a palpable moment as the performance began with the heavy expectation of hearing a master musician perform in his later years. The concert would begin with a long pause between his entrance onto the platform and the first notes of the concert. The silence was as powerful as the moment of musical awakening that followed. For the audience, though, it was a moment where they were able to respond individually after a working day of conformity, much as the audiences attending concerts at the Wigmore Hall do in *On Chesil Beach*. As Storr notes, 'people need to recapture what has been excluded during their working hours: their subjectivity.'[123] McEwan's narratives in *The Children Act*, *For You*, *The Imitation Game*, and *On Chesil Beach* are attuned to the nature of professional and amateur responses to music on an equal level when the amateur is well-versed in the repertoire. Although the technical aspects of performing music can hinder McEwan's characters – Fiona in *The Children Act*, Cathy in *The Imitation Game* – the nature of the musical response of the amateur performer is no different from how McEwan approaches the professional – Florence in *On Chesil Beach*, Charles in *For You*. It is part of the cultural democracy that, though audience members might be frustrated by comments they overhear in the audience from someone less knowledgeable, it is unavoidably

---

[121] Igor Stravinsky, *Poetics of Music* (New York, 1947), p. 21.

[122] McEwan, *The Child in Time*, pp. 81–82.

[123] Storr, *Music and the Mind*, p. 122.

118   *Music and Religion in the Writings of Ian McEwan*

part of the greater public discourse of emotions. Both the person with and without deeper knowledge is able to respond, as will be shown later in this chapter with Edward (*On Chesil Beach*) and his response to the opening of the *Haffner Symphony*. Susan Sontag commented that 'photography is the only major art in which professional training and years of experience do not confer an insuperable advantage over the untrained and inexperienced'.[124] This comment assumes a degree of sophistication in responding to art which in itself is subjective. However, the question of professional training is certainly not an issue when it concerns the appreciation of the arts, including music. Her observation that 'People want to weep. Pathos, in the form of a narrative, does not wear out'[125] relates to music and the role of an inner narrative, as discussed above. The combination of weeping, albeit initially inside and then outwardly, coupled with a musical moment, is found near the end of *The Children Act* when Fiona joins a barrister colleague who is a singer for their annual performance. As previously discussed, she leaves the stage, and the singer receives a standing ovation alone. However, there is also the question of the audience response. 'It was generally assumed that the whole experience must have been unusually intense for her, and the benchers and their friends were sympathetic and clapped all the harder as she passed in front of them'.[126] As such, the non-musicians had appreciated what the nature of art could achieve emotionally, whether they had experienced it to the same degree or not. Of an earlier rehearsal,[127] her concentration on the repertoire, as opposed to her judicial life, had effectively 'protected her from her thoughts, and she had no sense of passing time'.[128] Here is the direct comparison, for in public, where her performance and thus her emotions are subject to the reception of others, her engagement with music is ultimately compromised. The relative austerity of her professional position is replaced with a personal fragility that is exposed, as her private musical world is placed on display. Music had provided her with the outlet her personal relationships and professional life had not allowed her, but in large part because it was a separate, other world. The sense of otherness that McEwan illuminates is seen in relation to her self-criticism earlier in the novel.

> Her hope was that she didn't look too much like a woman in crisis. She kept her mind off the situation by playing to her inner ear a piece she had learned by heart. Above the rush-hour din it was her ideal self she heard, the pianist she could never become, performing faultlessly Bach's second partita.[129]

---

[124] Susan Sontag, *Regarding the Pain of Others* (London, 2005), p. 25.

[125] Ibid., p. 74.

[126] McEwan, *The Children Act*, p. 119.

[127] Ibid., pp. 190–191.

[128] Ibid., p. 62.

[129] Ibid., p. 45.

Solitude, Voyeurism, and the Transcendental   119

The 'ideal self' observation crystallizes McEwan's descriptions of the higher calling of music for an individual. It is notable that the central topic of *The Children Act*, an ethical legal matter, is not presented through the judge's lens beyond an analysis of the law. Further, despite her disagreement with the family, she shares a common language with the child through music. Consequently, music represents an ideal that surpasses a religious ideology, and the otherworldly transformative aspect of music is shown to relate to the individual and their own choice rather than any societal or religious conformity. It is set apart and without censure at a time when all other topics, personal and professional, are the source of discontent. Moreover, the use of music within the novel speaks to the transcendental aspect that Růžičková discusses (above). It is the source of reliable sublimity that transports the characters through both the individual moment and life.

Understanding the Musician

The nature of the closeness of the relationship between music and the musician is often difficult to translate, even for those who are emotionally close to a musician. Not all musicians come from 'musical families' and for this reason it is not unusual for musicians to enter personal relationships with other musicians because there are so many mutual points of understanding. McEwan's characters who are musical are typically in a relationship with someone who is not a musician, the exception being Florence's (*On Chesil Beach*) second husband. Music that to some might be a distraction is to others a supreme language, and this can either be understood or simply observed in a detached sense. Related to this, Storr has observed the feelings of distinct frustration for the amateur musician, who is nonetheless committed to the art of performance, and that these 'musical enthusiasts often confess [that] their lack of musical talent is their greatest disappointment'.[130] In this sense, it is possible to see both Cathy and Fiona in a frustrated light because for the joy that music brings them and the influence it can have on others, they know enough of the practical side of performance to analyse their own musical shortcomings.

McEwan's descriptions in his novels offer some clarity on this to a reader who is unfamiliar with the world of Western classical music. But he also extends the nature of descriptions with specific details, and consequently highlights the careful subtleties that are part of this personal balancing act. In *The Children Act*, Fiona's husband, Jack, typically uses recordings of Keith Jarrett as part of his seduction techniques. Although it is the playing she admires for its 'technical facility, the effortless outpouring of lyrical invention as copious as Mozart's',[131] it brings her closer to her husband with the memories of hearing

---

[130] Storr, *Music and the Mind*, p. 38.
[131] McEwan, *The Children* Act, p. 200.

120   *Music and Religion in the Writings of Ian McEwan*

Jarrett play at the Colosseum in Rome. The music has a direct connection to her husband and also their intimate life, but she does not customarily choose to listen to Jarrett's recording at other points in her life. There is an interesting comparison of the mention of Jarrett in *Lessons* when Roland is 'moodily improvising at the piano in a Keith Jarrett style'[132] with the more relaxed environment removed from a positive contextualisation.

However, it is Jack's comments after the Christmas concert performance that brought her close to tears. The comments betray the language of the spectator listener rather than Leonard Bernstein's description of 'a real music listener' who can understand and appreciate music and performance. Although the comments are intended to be supportive, they are insufficient.

Jack: You were brilliant! Everyone loved it. And so moving![133]

The first sentence becomes a near irrelevance to an amateur (or indeed professional) musician aspiring for perfection and knowing they will always fall short, as Fiona notes in her comment (above). The challenge is not that the comment is spoken by a non-musician but that it lacks a true understanding of the essential craft at work and therefore has a crass simplicity. Further, it suggests a 'performance' rather than a 'moment'. 'You' were brilliant immediately removes the composer from the equation that, for the performer, has been central to the experience. The nature of the performance requires the performer to engage with the artwork and interpret it. It is not to self-glorify. The second sentence is one that the musician knows to be subjective, as well as impossible to prove or rely upon. The nature of superior works and performances is that they bear an imprint of perfection that has to be analysed and evaluated by critics or scholars who have determined its relative value. The comment that Jack 'loved it' belittles the work as well as the performer because it lacks specificity. The third sentence is also problematic given the variety of repertoire that has been heard (Berlioz, Schubert, Mahler) in different musical styles. Is it 'moving' because it was unexpected or 'moving' because it suggests an emotional outlet that has been missing from their marriage in recent times? Further, what is so moving and why? The texts? The musical settings of them? The audience response to the performance? In the maelstrom of emotions between the two characters in a disintegrating marriage and then Fiona's engagement with music which Jack does not fully understand, the narrative highlights the distance between the lover of music and the partner who observes with a detached sensibility. The comments are intended as supportive but are received as shallow.

A similar inability to understand the emotional response of a musician can be seen in the intentionally well-meaning, but equally superficial, comments from Tony to Cathy in *The Imitation Game*. These comments mirror those of her mother later in the play when she is horrified to learn of her daughter's

---

[132] McEwan, *Lessons*, p. 401.

[133] McEwan, *The Children Act*, p. 212.

Solitude, Voyeurism, and the Transcendental — 121

wish to be in active service in the war. In the first instance, Tony does not understand the value of music to Cathy. In the second instance, her mother interprets the value of music as a societal one for a young woman, rather than holding a personal or indeed societal value in its own right. Tony's comments are parallel with Jack's (*The Children Act*) regarding music and are similarly unspecific. Music is referred to as 'it', just as the audience in Jack's perception 'loved it'. Tony's reference to 'that' shows his detached understanding of Cathy's world and her sense of personal accomplishment in returning to practice. Her response suggests that only a serious listener can be taken seriously when they comment. As such, her impression of him might have been improved if he had said nothing at all.

Tony (without conviction) That was terribly good.

Cathy You weren't even listening.

Tony Yes I was. It's coming on very well.[134]

———

Mrs Raine You've had a good home and a decent education.

… you're a respectable girl, Cathy.[135]

The marriage to Edward helped keep other suitors at a distance. The children with Charles proved her ability to bear children to Edward and others, but Florence otherwise continues in her solitary role. Given the place of music in her life and her early absorption in music, in tandem with her ability to remove herself from the emotions of others, this begs the question of whether any lover could replace what she feels for music, which the concert review[136] also infers. Interestingly, even though many young string quartets work with contemporary composers who are naturally free to offer their own opinion of the performance of their works in rehearsals, Florence is portrayed as a musician only concerned with the masterworks of the canon.

The Individual Passion and Focus

Musical passions that focus on particular repertoire come and go as sometimes does the enthusiasm in the art itself, even for professional musicians. Many young musicians who rise to early prominence, for instance playing in a national youth orchestra or serving as an organ scholar to a famous Oxbridge choir, find that in their mid-twenties the typically low pay of the profession of

---

[134] McEwan, *The Imitation Game*, p. 89.

[135] Ibid., p. 94.

[136] McEwan, *On Chesil Beach*, p. 198.

122   *Music and Religion in the Writings of Ian McEwan*

classical music, inconsistent opportunities, and the fact that they have reached a peak early on, makes them look elsewhere for employment, albeit with an affection for what has been a significant part of their life to that point. The financial concerns of the profession, a point unmentioned in *On Chesil Beach*, are often to the fore. The absence of this topic in the novel reveals the purity of thought that encompasses Florence's thinking about musical matters as being paramount but also McEwan's portrayal of a young musician with her own spirit of idealism and focus.

Daniel J. Levitin has written on how such a passion and drive to succeed as a performer can embrace someone, together with the clinical aspect of performance that can satisfy performers while they witness their own progress. By Levitin's study, the responses that Cathy (*The Imitation Game*), Fiona (*The Children Act*), and Florence (*On Chesil Beach*) have while playing music form a therapeutic element to their lives:

> If I'm playing an instrument I like, and whose sound pleases me in and of itself, I'm more likely to pay attention to subtle differences in tone, and the ways in which I can moderate and affect the tonal output of my instrument. It is impossible to overestimate the importance of these factors; caring leads to attention, and together they lead to measurable neurochemical changes.[137]

In *The Imitation Game* and *The Children Act*, the reader sees the balance of this passion in the amateur musician. Both Cathy and Fiona return to music as a tonic or panacea to daily life. Neither is in a satisfying personal relationship, but they each know enough about performance to be able to tell the difference between their own good and bad playing, interestingly both as pianists. Their goal is no less noble than Florence's (*On Chesil Beach*) because each sees music as a higher form of language that provides an inner dialogue as well as a distraction and consolation to the rest of their lives. The dialogue a performer has with the score is one that cannot be truly replicated in any sense in communicating with another person before or after the fact. Rather, it is similar to a conversation between intimates. The title of Michael Berkeley's long-running BBC Radio 3 programme, *Private Passions*, has a double meaning in this sense because not only does the listener learn about the pieces a guest favours, but they learn something about the guest's actual personality in the process. In *The Children Act* the reader witnesses the cruel irony of a husband in a sexless marriage who has purchased a new piano for his wife to play and yet cannot fully understand the language or performance of music that entrances her away from her moments of greatest daily duress. When she rehearses with a colleague ahead of a concert and he wants to discuss his work, there is a disconnect as she is looking to continue with their rehearsal.[138] Work is one world and music is another. It is not simply an entertainment to her or, in this case, a

---

[137]   Levitin, *This is your brain on music*, p. 198.

[138]   McEwan, *The Children Act*, pp. 62, 66.

Solitude, Voyeurism, and the Transcendental   123

moment to demonstrate or show off a talent as is perhaps more obviously the case with the singer colleague. As a judge and an amateur pianist, Fiona commands these same attributes and so does Cathy as someone working in secret at Bletchley Park. Each have found that music can provide what other aspects of their life cannot, a dependable path to inner fulfilment.

The necessary sublimity, whether in someone's own desire for quiet solitude and their intimates' understanding of that need or the central role of sublimity and individualism in music, forms a thread throughout McEwan's writings. As described in *Lessons* 'The music was simply here ... exclusive to him, his private labyrinth of cold sorrow. It would never let him leave.'[139] The author and the protagonist are often only loosely removed from one another, and to many musicians reading McEwan's writings, there is a further, near-perfect symbiotic relationship between fiction and contemporary reality. But McEwan's narratives also portray the nature of self-awareness and the role of music in the lives of many.

> Our ear for harmony was hard-wired. (Furthermore, without a surrounding context of harmony, disharmony was meaningless and uninteresting.) Understanding a line of melody was a complex mental act, but it was one which even an infant could perform; we were born into an inheritance, we were *Homo musicus*; defining beauty in music must therefore entail a definition of human nature...[140] (*Amsterdam*)

McEwan's nuanced portrayal of the greater value of music is centred around an approach that it is accessible to the reader but also seemingly natural in the lives of his characters. The union between 'beauty' and 'human nature' relating to music that has been born 'into an inheritance' is emboldening for a musician to read and potentially eye-opening for non-musicians to comprehend. As such, McEwan does not simply present an image of music, the profession, and the reception of both, but a distinctive argument that suggests that music is part of the greater values of life and inner understanding, while being a form of expression that helps define human sensibilities.

[139] McEwan, *Lessons*, p. 3.
[140] McEwan, *Amsterdam*, p. 23.

3

FROM GILBERT AND SULLIVAN TO MOZART: INFLUENCES AND PERCEPTIONS OF MUSIC IN SOCIETY

The emotional aspect of music and its potential use as a source of intellectual engagement in life is discussed throughout McEwan's writings and is studied in the previous chapter in relation to sublimity. The influence and public perception of the composer in modern British society is discussed in the final chapter. Between these two points of analysis rests the question of how an enveloping 'power' of music as an understandable and translatable force within society, as well as for the individual, can be seen in McEwan's writings. Chapter 2 examined how musicians can seek out particular works and why people are individually drawn to certain repertoire. This chapter moves beyond the point of intellectual engagement with known works and towards the examples McEwan gives of pieces that can powerfully seize the attention of both the music lover and the professional musician. I shall examine complementary points within McEwan's writings that illuminate his particular understanding of this role in performance and reception. The final sections of this chapter examine his particular approach to the music of Mozart.

A Seminal Moment in Life

With respect to his perception of the role of literary reception, the following comments of McEwan are valuable in understanding his overarching approach to the nature of the artistic encounters and individual responses that are a focal point throughout his writings on music.

> From the first sentence, we come into a presence, and we can see for ourselves the quality of a particular mind; in a matter of minutes we may read the fruits of a long forgotten afternoon, an afternoon's work done in isolation, a hundred and fifty years ago. And what was once an unfolding personal secret, is now ours.
>
> we must bring our general understanding of what it means to be a person.[1]

---

[1] Ian McEwan, *Science* (London, 2019), p. 1.

126   *Music and Religion in the Writings of Ian McEwan*

McEwan's statement is taken from a larger lecture delivered at Oxford in 2003. He highlights emotions a reader can relate to even if they are not in a contemporary setting because an author, or a composer, can draw a reader, or performer, into their world. As Lynn Wells notes, there is an 'historical distance'[2] that a reader can be aware of. What it means 'to be a person' is at the core of understanding the place of otherness in McEwan's writings because the nature of character interpretation is subjective. However, the narratives that relate to music are embedded with an especially positive impression of music as both a relatable and a positive presence in the lives of the characters a reader encounters. But the aspect of 'historical distance' (Wells) also has a double meaning for the musicians in his writings and this is an area where his writings are especially persuasive from a musician's perspective. The performer and the listener are by nature trying to draw on another point in history. Consequently, the reader can see both a character in the context of a novel as well as the narrative that character is individually seeking through the language of music. The musicians are seeking to draw their own contemporary setting towards an earlier era. Even when this concerns a contemporary work (Clive in *Amsterdam* and Charles in *For You*), there is an abiding concern with where their work will be situated, both in their own canon and the larger repertoire.

McEwan's early musical background began, as with many of his generation, through the influence of a musical schoolmaster, and then later singing in choirs at university. His schoolteacher at Woolverstone Hall, Michael Channon, had been an encouraging influence early on, and McEwan had two music lessons a week which included singing through the arias of Mozart's *The Magic Flute* in English translations, as well as piano lessons. As noted, there is significant overlap between McEwan's life and some of his narratives and this experience mirrors Roland Baines's in *Lessons*. The combination of being two thousand miles away from his parents in Libya while encountering the music of Mozart remained with him so that years later the sound of the overture to *The Magic Flute* brought back the memory of the homesickness he experienced as a child. McEwan's father had opposed Channon's offer for continuing his piano lessons because of scheduling concerns, and McEwan was also too shy to accept the offer. However, he later saw this as a seminal moment in his life.[3] If McEwan had chosen to continue with his study, what might have become of this opportunity? The aspect of the unknown is explored in *Lessons* but within an abusive relationship. As Miriam Cornell comments, 'You were clearly going to be a superb pianist, right out of my league. You certainly were clearly when I last saw you'[4] but 'hoping that somehow the damage I did might be lessened by your (possible) success (as a pianist). ... And I'm very very sorry for what I

---

2   Lynn Wells, *Ian McEwan* (London, 2010), p. 93.

3   Iain Quinn, 'Interview with Ian McEwan' (2018).

4   Ian McEwan, *Lessons* (New York, 2022), p. 316.

Influences and Perceptions of Music in Society   127

prevented you from having, and the world that loves music from having and for the madness I unleashed on you.'[5]

This question relates to Anthony Storr's observation that one of the greatest regrets of amateur musicians is that they were not able to pursue one of their greatest interests,[6] a point observed in *Lessons*. Roland's father's 'greatest regret was that he never learned to play the piano, never had the opportunity'.[7]

The nature of a critical moment in life where so much of the future hangs in the balance is not unusual in relation to music, nor is it unique to McEwan or indeed to many people who have actually become professional musicians. Many British musicians have pursued study outside their own disciplines. The soprano Emma Kirkby was a Classics student at Oxford and the tenor Ian Bostridge completed his Oxford doctorate on the subject of witchcraft in English public life from 1650 to 1750. The departed friend in McEwan's *Amsterdam* also made a choice: 'She was brilliant. Goldsmith's, then the Guildhall. A fabulous career ahead of her.' He paused for comic effect. 'Then she met me [a man who would ultimately become Foreign Secretary] and chose medicine.'[8] The personal side of life had overtaken the possibility of a professional career as a musician, and this is portrayed as both unfortunate and a joke when a life devoted to art is positioned next to a life in the uneven world of politics. However, in the cultural life of Britain, these transitions are not only characteristic but quite typical. Oxbridge college choirs are frequently comprised of singers from a range of academic disciplines who find the experience of singing with their peers from across the university to be not only musically rewarding but socially valuable. In a similar vein to the choral societies that were to be found in almost every town during the mid-late nineteenth century, music is seen to have a tremendous power to unite communities across numerous social divides. The experience and power of the musical moment can be transformative, but the degree of engagement can also result in tough decisions about whether to pursue a life in music or not, as seen above in *Amsterdam*. Someone who was 'brilliant' and had studied at two leading institutions nonetheless turned away from music as a serious career pursuit. Not taking the decision seriously with the 'pause for comic effect' bluntly conveys a sentiment that the devaluing of music in life was a mistake even by comparison to work in the field of medicine. However, the reception and value of music in Britain have a complex history between the scholarly evaluation of the influence of music and the public acceptance and expectation of music as part of the cultural landscape.

[5]   Ibid., p. 320.

[6]   Anthony Storr, *Music and the Mind* (Toronto, 1992) p. 38.

[7]   McEwan, *Lessons*, p. 46.

[8]   Ian McEwan, *Amsterdam* (London, 2005), p. 14.

The Lineage of Communal Singing

McEwan's appreciation of the value of communal singing and indeed music at an amateur and domestic level came, in the first instance, from his own upbringing. His father, a soldier, had a mouth organ and would play it in social situations around his friends. He believed that if the young McEwan could play the piano, he would have friends. This point forms part of the narrative in *Lessons* and the relationship between Roland and his father.

> The Captain himself played the mouth organ in a clever vamping style. His taste was for songs of the First World War. "It's a Long Way to Tipperary," "Take Me Back to Dear Old Blighty," "Pack up Your Troubles in Your Old Kit Bag". It was his keenest pleasure in life to be drinking beer with his army mates, to play or sing to the company and get them to join in. His greatest regret was that he never learned to play the piano, never had the opportunity.
>
> The chap who could play the piano, he often told his son, would always be popular.[9]

However, this was not a matter of studying an instrument for a possible concert or teaching career but rather being able to lead communal singing. The songbooks that were published following the 1944 Education Act were available in Libya where his family were then based, and through these books McEwan came to know numerous folk songs from which he gained much enjoyment by performing them. He also saw the nature of singing as an art form that could draw people together.[10] As such, music had an influence that extended beyond personal appreciation and could have a unifying impact on others.

Writing of Charles Darwin's *The Descent of Man* (1871), Derek Scott notes that Darwin stated that a single note of music 'could contain a greater intensity of feeling than pages of writing,'[11] while observing Darwin's comment that music 'does not by itself excite in us the more terrible emotions of horror, rage, etc. It awakens the gentler feelings of tenderness and love, which readily pass into devotion'.[12] Music is fundamentally a pleasurable pursuit, and in McEwan's writing the impact of music on the life of a character is always positive. The balance between the social or recreational and the meaningful or rational is something that can be attributed most especially to the nineteenth century and particularly to the sight-singing movement in Britain. Joseph Mainzer, author of *Singing for the Million*, the singing master John Hullah, and John Curwen each offered alternative and consequently competitive approaches to their popular singing classes. Curwen promoted the Tonic Sol-Fa method that

---

[9] McEwan, *Lessons*, pp. 45, 46.

[10] Quinn, 'Interview with Ian McEwan'.

[11] Derek B. Scott, 'The Power of Music', *Musical Style and Social Meaning* (Farnham, *c.*2010), p. 237.

[12] Charles Darwin, *The Descent of Man* (New York, 1902) p. 735.

Influences and Perceptions of Music in Society 129

had been devised by Sarah Glover of Norwich. When the publishing house of Novello was set up in 1811, they took over the publication of Mainzer's *Musical Times and Singing Circular* (1844) while also publishing inexpensive editions of Handel for choral societies.[13] The balance of fine music and community singing provided betterment and civic enhancement. The legacy of this can be found not only in organized choirs that still function on an amateur basis but also in the spontaneous singing that emerges at major sporting events. This is especially the case at football and rugby matches and to a certain extent in pub singing around a piano and family sing-alongs at Christmas. This degree of communal singing is not common in every country. The USA is a notable example of a country with far less informal communal singing. However, when the cabinet sings 'Walking Back to Happiness' in 'solemn unison' as 'they might a hymn by Hubert Parry'[14] in *The Cockroach*, McEwan conveys the image of a social environment that is comfortably established in Britain and which the British, in the case of football and rugby supporters, also take with them when they travel.

As Darwin noted, music does not create ill feelings even though it has been used for ill gains, most especially in World War II. However, the moral power of music as a positive agent was considered all-pervasive in the nineteenth century. As Reverend Haweis noted, 'Let no one say the moral effects of music are small and insignificant',[15] while Arthur Sullivan believed that music could not suggest an improper thought. Rather, the right selection of music in the right setting was considered to act as a 'civilizing influence to which the lower classes were particularly responsive'.[16] This is a point that reflects Matthew Arnold's observation in *Culture and Anarchy* (1869) that culture [beyond the music hall] is required to save society from anarchy.[17] As with McEwan's perceptions and portrayals of other areas of society, not least the church and the concert hall, the references that relate to the influence and thus the power of music are especially precise in their meaning to musicians. As discussed later in this chapter, the nature of class snobbery that could be attributed to Haweis's and Arnold's comments above is present in McEwan's narratives in the late twentieth century, as indeed it is in contemporary society.

Gilbert and Sullivan

The Innocent begins with a quote from John Colville's book *The Fringes of Power: Downing Street Diaries, 1939–1955*, that refers to the music of Gilbert

---

[13] Scott, 'The Power of Music', p. 245.

[14] Ian McEwan, *The Cockroach* (London, 2019), p. 43.

[15] Hugh Reginald Haweis, *Music and Morals* (London, 1871), p. 112.

[16] Scott, 'The Power of Music', p. 246.

[17] Ibid.

130   *Music and Religion in the Writings of Ian McEwan*

and Sullivan's operetta *The Mikado*. It is heard following a dinner with Churchill at Chequers, ten days after the end of the Yalta Conference:

> After dinner we saw an amusing film: Bob Hope in *The Princess and the Pirate*. Then we went in the Great Hall and listened to *The Mikado* [Gilbert and Sullivan] played, much too slowly, on the gramophone. The PM said it brought back 'the Victorian era, eighty years which will rank in our island with the Antonine age.'[18]

The importance of the enduring popularity of Gilbert and Sullivan,[19] not only throughout the first part of the twentieth century but into the twenty-first century, is far-reaching and the reasons are multilayered. Technically, and in a similar vein to the success of oratorios sung during the eighteenth and nineteenth centuries, the majority of vocal parts can be sung with relative competence by amateurs, something which the average opera role would not allow. Over time, many performances of the works of Gilbert and Sullivan have been undertaken with piano accompaniments in church halls, although on a more professional level there has been an International Gilbert and Sullivan Festival since 1994, meeting initially in Harrogate and now in Buxton. The festival includes performances by G&S societies from around the world and has remained extremely popular with capacity audiences and a loyal following. McEwan's reference to Gilbert and Sullivan draws on the nature of British society being able to laugh at itself and characterizations that lampoon national identities. It also represents a bygone era that, like Churchill, seems increasingly distant from modern Britain. Listened to in the presence of Churchill this scene is all the more amusing. The reference to the Victorians is also significant because it illuminates not only the legacy of past musical glories but also a period when communal singing was present throughout the country. Not unlike McEwan's narrative descriptions of the church discussed in chapter 1, there is a noticeable hint of nostalgia and sentimentality in this reference. Despite McEwan's great interest in the advances of science within society, the depiction of cultural spheres is always with an affection for the past.

In considering this reference, there is also the nature of the relationship between music and text and the ability of Gilbert and Sullivan to seemingly break down social barriers with works that many amateurs could sing, while laced with narratives on social topics and people that the performers and audiences rarely experienced on a personal level. In this respect the reach of Gilbert and Sullivan is especially broad, and this is a point that Alan Bennett has also drawn on in two of his plays, *The Habit of Art* and *Alleluia!*. There are several shared points between McEwan's and Bennett's texts that focus on a similar impression and portrayal of society. This is in large part because both have

---

[18]   Ian McEwan, *The Innocent* (London, 1990), p. xii.

[19]   There is a further reference to Gilbert and Sullivan in *Atonement* (London, 2001), p. 108.

Influences and Perceptions of Music in Society 131

a commanding grasp of the subtleties at play in the situations they describe, with references to specific works or circumstances that demonstrate an insider knowledge. This is especially so in the relationship and influence of words and music. In the following example, the work of Gilbert and Sullivan is addressed by Bennett. In a fictional dialogue between Auden and Britten, in Bennett's play *The Habit of Art*, Britten comments on the communicative power of music that, to his mind, surpasses text:

> These magnificent words – I used to think my paltry music just an after-thought, a servant to the words. But it's not. Music melts words … It's the music that matters, even in Gilbert and Sullivan. Music wins.[20]

The British empire was at full strength when Gilbert and Sullivan success-fully and comedically critiqued its leading institutions including the peerage, the judiciary, the armed forces and even the monarchy. Roger Scruton wrote of the national love of nonsense that enabled everyone to laugh at themselves in a way the British have long since understood other countries do not in the same fashion, if at all. Scruton sees a connection between Gilbert and Sullivan and the nonsense poems of Edward Lear and the two 'Alice' books of Lewis Carroll, stories that capture the spirit of Victorian England in a manner that can still resonate with an idealized fairytale perception of Britain in the twentieth and twenty-first century.[21] They normalize the pomp and ceremony that Britain is known for and, as Scruton comments, 'there is no better way to be governed than by a long-standing joke' while 'mocking what was serious [while simulta-neously] affirming it as serious.'[22]

In a contrary spirit the cabinet minister in charge of Social Security, Peter Lilley, invoked Gilbert and Sullivan when he attacked single mothers in a speech he delivered at the 1992 Conservative Party Conference. Although Gilbert and Sullivan can be derided for being politically incorrect on multiple levels and of another age, Lilley's comments were a deliberate misuse of the playful humour their work was supposed to embody. His comments also speak to the nature of government heartlessness that is at the centre of the oratorio *or Shall we die?*. As McEwan noted, 'England under Mrs Thatcher leaves me with a nasty taste.'[23] By changing the text of 'I've got a little list' from *The Mikado*, Lilley commented:

> I've got a little list/I've got a little list of young ladies who get pregnant just to jump the housing list … who will not be missed[24]

---

[20] Alan Bennett, *The Habit of Art* (London, 2010), p. 70.

[21] Roger Scruton, *England: An Elegy* (London, 2006), p. 59.

[22] Ibid.

[23] John Haffenden, *Novelists in Interview* (London, 1985), p. 187.

[24] Also referred to in Owen Jones, *Chavs* (London, 2012), p. 67.

132   *Music and Religion in the Writings of Ian McEwan*

McEwan's reference to G&S draws attention both to the close association of music and humour in considering a national identity as well as the communal role of singing. But it is also the presence of a popular genre with swift entertainment and audience response at its core that is a critical part of the British psyche related to the arts. The comedic element relates to the power of music employed with a brisk agility that also aligns with the British fondness and expectation of free speech, debate, accountability, and wit. Music helps to transcend these issues, and G&S provided an environment where those in power could be derided in a social setting that falls between the pantomime, the music hall, and the opera house. In the context of a popular novel, McEwan's use of G&S illuminates his understanding of the very specific identity their works hold in the twentieth century. Whereas Lilley's comments are intended to draw on the legacy of humour towards critical ends, McEwan's inclusion of the text draws on the sentimental and nostalgic element of England in another age.

The Emotional Power of Hymns

As noted in chapter 1, the reception of hymns and liturgy as portrayed by McEwan manages to capture the points of reference that many believers also value. The lifelong impressions of distinct childhood memories engender a nostalgia for early experiences and in this case a particular image of England. This can also be seen in the writings of Salman Rushdie in his memoir *Joseph Anton*. McEwan observed that while there were hymn tunes he loved hearing at school he could not reconcile the texts with his developing atheism,[25] but his inclusion of hymns within his novels speaks to an understanding of the power of communal singing. Rushdie, born in the previous year and also an atheist, comments on the emotive aspect of hymns that he observed as a child attending chapel services in Rugby School:

> [I didn't] need to *survey the wondrous cross / on which the prince of glory died*; but a lonely boy could not help but be touched when he was asked to sing *The night is dark and I am far from home / Lead Thou me on*. He liked 'Abide with Me' because it was sung by the whole 100,000-strong crowd at Wembley Stadium before the FA Cup Final, and what he thought of as the 'geography hymn', 'The Day Thou Gavest, Lord, Is Ended', made him sweetly homesick.

> The language of unbelief was distinctly poorer than that of belief.[26]

In McEwan's case, the music of hymns was positive by comparison to concerns over the text. The musical moment took precedence. For both writers the singing of hymns also related to homesickness and they both shared an impres-

---

[25]   Quinn, 'Interview with Ian McEwan'.

[26]   Salman Rushdie, *Joseph Anton – A Memoir* (New York, 2012), p. 32.

Influences and Perceptions of Music in Society 133

sion that hymn singing could represent something removed from other daily activities. Hymns had an emotionally transporting quality that was specifically separate. The question of allied unbelief is important to assess though because it demonstrates how music – as Bennett notes in his text for Auden (above) – can remain a powerful emotional agent even when the text is considered 'dishonest'[27] (McEwan). McEwan addressed this personal belief in the fictional world of *Lessons* although, unlike Rushdie, it was the musical text that carried the emotions in a school setting:

> They sat through the compulsory Sunday evening service in contempt of the earnest visiting vicars and their wheedling and beseeching of a non-existent god. It was a point of honour with them never to utter the responses or close their eyes, bow heads or say "amen" or sing the hymn, although they stood to open the hymnal at a random page out of a residual sense of courtesy.
>
> ...he could not bring himself to sing a hymn. However sweet the melodies or the rhythm of the lines he could not get past the embarrassment of their blatant or childish untruths. But the point was not to believe but to join in, to be part of the community. They were starting with "All Things Bright and Beautiful," Rosalind's favourite. Lovely for small children but how could an adult mouth this creationist nonsense?[28]

Belief is not the governing factor in the appreciation of a hymn in this case but rather either the music or the essential alliance of music and text. As Jeremy Paxman writes, 'How many of those joyous, nerdish faces belting out "Land of Hope and Glory" believe a word of it?'[29] In *Middle England*, Jonathan Coe's narrative suggests that Blake's/Parry's hymn 'Jerusalem' is an:

> eccentric hymn to Britain's industrial heritage [and] was the last thing he had been expecting, but there was something hugely affecting and persuasive about it.[30]

In this regard, it cannot be overestimated how the blurred line of choral music in secular and sacred settings has come to inhabit part of the general British perception of classical music, from the hymn and national anthem singing at state weddings and funerals to 'Rule Britannia', 'Jerusalem', and 'Land of Hope and Glory' at the Last Night of the Proms. The latter piece is featured at a Conservative Party Conference in McEwan's play *The Ploughman's Lunch*[31] and signifies a sense of continuity and resolve that the party hopes to inspire. The rise of choral singing in the nineteenth century strongly continues into the twenty-first century with the singing of 'Jerusalem' at meetings of the Wom-

---

[27] Quinn, 'Interview with Ian McEwan'.

[28] McEwan, *Lessons*, pp. 111, 348.

[29] Jeremy Paxman, *The English* (London, 1999), p. 265.

[30] Jonathan Coe, *Middle England* (London, 2018), pp. 131–132.

[31] Ian McEwan, *The Ploughman's Lunch, A Move Abroad* (London, 1989), p. 116.

en's Institute, a significant number of amateur choral societies around Britain, recent television programmes (*The Choir* and *Great British Home Chorus*), the annual broadcasting of Christmas services of readings and music from King's College, Cambridge, the (now) twice weekly broadcasts of *Choral Evensong* on BBC Radio 3, and the sustained presence of professional choral ensembles. The energetic audience participation in songs at annual pantomimes that take place in almost every major city in Britain around Christmas is another example of intergenerational singing as children join with their parents and other family members to sing ever louder while being egged on from the stage.

Although the scholarly and public conversations about the role of classical music in Anglophone countries have many similarities, not least in a unified discussion about the paucity of government funding for the arts, there are particularly strong threads within McEwan's writings with specific associations that mark British society and consequently British identity apart in the reception of the arts. The continuing success of Handel's *Messiah* is the most obvious example of a piece that the British have had a long association with because within British culture it fulfils so many complementary objectives and expectations in the national psyche. Indeed, although other works for soloists, chorus, and orchestra have had a spasmodic appearance in the British repertoire, such as Haydn's *The Creation*, Mendelssohn's *St Paul*, and the once popular, but now largely forgotten, *The Last Judgment* of Spohr, a popular work in the nineteenth century, Handel's seminal oratorio has not left the performing repertoire since its premiere in 1742 and by the standards of popular music in the twentieth or twenty-first centuries this is extraordinary. The vast majority of pieces of popular music are not even performed on an annual basis, even ten years after the life of a composer/performer, let alone hundreds of years later. However, *Messiah* demonstrates the essential formula of later successful British oratorios and larger choral works. Crucially, all of the works are in English, and, in the case of *Messiah*, ennobled with a pastoral tranquillity (Scruton)[32] which curiously aligned itself with national patriotism after the story of George II rising to his feet for the 'Hallelujah Chorus', at which point everyone around him did so as well. The texts have an essential rather than occasional nature and are, therefore, relevant on an annual basis. *Messiah*, which follows the life of Christ, is especially successful as a concert piece in this regard because it can be performed quite suitably in the Advent, Christmas, and Easter seasons. The choral writing is consistently of only modest to medium levels of difficulty by comparison to Bach's *Christmas Oratorio*, which demands highly skilled singers and which is consequently seldom heard in most British cities. There are plenty of opportunities for soloists, which in turn allows for more ambitious vocal writing. But the success is also because Handel knew how to write a melody that could ultimately satisfy the standards of the music profession and appeal to the larger public.

---

[32] Scruton, *England: An Elegy*, p. 224.

Influences and Perceptions of Music in Society 135

Michael Berkeley notes that an important factor to McEwan in considering working with a composer was the ability of a composer to write a good tune.[33] McEwan's relative lack of interest in atonal music[34] and his characters' overwhelming engagement with tonal music reinforces the value he places on well-known music of the Western canon within a popular novel. With a memorable melody comes a natural affinity and connection to an individual piece and, to a certain extent, its composer, and McEwan's preference for referring to very specific pieces highlights the relationship he intuits and then enables between the power of specific music and specific settings. However, McEwan does not mention the most well-known 'classics' of the repertoire, but in assuming the knowledge of the reader – a 'sophisticated' reader (Head) – he includes references to a more select understanding of the canon. Thus, the world of the 'candlelight classics' (Pachelbel, *Canon in D*, Bach, *Air on a G String*, Handel, *Water Music*) does not enter his narratives. Instead, there are references to the *Goldberg Variations* (*Saturday* and *Black Dogs*), the string quartets of twentieth-century British composers (*On Chesil Beach*), and the role of Górecki (*Amsterdam*), the latter discussed in chapter 4. As a consequence, he draws not just on a sophisticated understanding and relative emotional engagement in these works but the value of individual appreciation. Based on his personal preferences (and further noted by Berkeley) and the consistency of repertoire referred to in his writings, it is impossible not to consider that McEwan's fictional world and his own world of preferred repertoire coincide. If a popular novel by definition has a large readership, then McEwan is advancing a personal interest in repertoire he considers worthy of dissemination and doing so with an approach that makes it appear wholly accessible.

The Removal of Inhibition and the Value of Emotional Attachment

There is also the sense of happy personal abandon when music takes hold in private moments as in *The Children Act* and becomes a pleasurable presence as barriers are removed. Singing in the solitude of a house in a fashion seldom dreamed of in public, except more recently in karaoke settings, demonstrates the power of music to overcome inhibition. As Leonard notes in *The Innocent*: 'Beyond the excitement [of the dance floor] Leonard took satisfaction in dancing in a way his parents and their friends did not, and could not, and in liking music they would hate, and in feeling at home in a city where they would never come. He was free.'[35] Music was in every sense a departure and release from his normal life and so much so that he was physically engaged by it.

---

[33] Iain Quinn, 'Interview with Michael Berkeley' (2018).

[34] Ibid.

[35] McEwan, *The Innocent*, p. 124.

136   *Music and Religion in the Writings of Ian McEwan*

It was possible for Leonard to engage in art but on his own terms. This experience can also be found in large choirs where an individual can sing with considerable energy and take part in a large-scale piece but at the same time know that they will not be heard alone. This brings a measure of empowerment, personal pride, and satisfaction. Of private but nonetheless impassioned singing, the story of a man observed from a nearby window in *The Comfort of Strangers* is an example of the performance of a piece that McEwan had sung in his school years,[36] and later came to have a special affinity for. References to *The Magic Flute* appear in *Amsterdam*, *The Comfort of Strangers*, and the libretto for the opera *For You*:

> The moment Colin turned the shower off, the man across the way under his shower began, as on the previous evenings, to sing his duet from *The Magic Flute*. His voice rising above the torrential thunder of water ... the man sang with the total abandon of one who believes himself to be without an audience, cracking and yodelling the higher notes, tral-la-ing the forgotten words, bellowing out the orchestral parts. 'Mann und Weib, und Weib und Mann, Together make a godly span.' When the shower was turned off, the singing subsided to a whistle.[37] (*The Comfort of Strangers*).

> I remember the snowstorm on the bridge when we crossed the river to my first concert at the Festival Hall, as we walked we were singing *Mann und Weib, und Weib und Mann* – my God, how happy we were.[38] (*For You*)

As McEwan writes in *The Child in Time*: 'Some time towards the end of the second bottle they cheered and roared for the hell of it, and for lack of anything else sang "For he's a jolly good fellow".'[39] In all three of these instances music was a force that not only energized a social moment that reinforced an emotional state but was enabled by not being an individual or public (and potentially embarrassing) circumstance.

The degree of personal abandon coupled with idealism can also be seen in Kingsley Amis's *Lucky Jim*, with the informal singing of madrigals. The professor of history remarks 'Of course, this sort of music's not intended for an audience, you see. The fun's all in the singing. Everybody's got a real tune to sing – a real tune. You could say, really, that polyphony got to its highest point, its peak, at that period, and has been on the decline ever since.'[40] Part of this enjoyment comes from the difference of languages – English and the language of music – at play and the fact that though music is itself a language, it can be heard on an individual, personal and even private level. In Adam Phillips's book, *Unforbidden Pleasures*, the author discusses Oscar Wilde's use of language being delib-

---

[36]   Quinn, 'Interview with Ian McEwan'.

[37]   Ian McEwan, *The Comfort of Strangers* (London, 2006), p. 2.

[38]   Ian McEwan, *For You* (London, 2008), pp. 40–41.

[39]   Ian McEwan, *The Child in Time* (London 1992), p. 107.

[40]   Kingsley Amis, *Lucky Jim* (Garden City, 1954), p. 38.

Influences and Perceptions of Music in Society   137

erate and calculated 'in the full knowledge that language is virtually defined by its unintended consequences'.[41] Accepting music as a language of its own, Phillips's commentary on Wilde has particular bearing considering McEwan's use of musical references: 'What we don't know [in language], what we haven't understood, can be the realist thing about us. It can be what happens,' suggesting that it is our response to language that is critical and not just the understanding of it.[42] In this analysis Phillips sees Wilde as encouraging us to 'forge, or to unlearn, certain words and phrases; to forget a vocabulary – words like "seriousness", "duty", "explanation", "fact", and "imitation", and phrases like "living for others", and "making oneself useful".[43] If this approach is applied to the language and to the listening of music with reference to the amateur listener whose world is not largely immersed in the realm of music making, but rather seeing music as a passion that can be adopted whenever possible, then the measure of 'selfishness'[44] that can be viewed through Wilde's commentary encourages the 'laying down of a different kind of law'[45] for the benefit of the response rather than any obligatory intellectual engagement with it. There can be an intellectual engagement, including a raw response, and this is discussed in chapter 2. The law of emotions and the influence of language is paramount because its most important impact is ultimately an individual one. Thus, the personal aspect of the power of music coupled with the unspeakable and, to a certain extent, inexplicable nature of a personal response to music engenders a quiet selfishness to listening. When an architect in Woody Allen's film *Hannah and Her Sisters* (1986) describes attending the Metropolitan Opera and sitting in his private box with a bottle of wine and weeping at the emotional intensity of the drama unfolding, he speaks of his personal response, and also the selfish desire that can overtake his normal life and, in some respects, be a form of release. The individual is able to find their true self, the 'realist' (Phillips) aspect of themselves. As Wilde writes in *The Soul of Man under Socialism*:

> A man is called selfish if he lives in the manner that seems to him most suitable for the full realisation of his own personality; if in fact, the primary aim of his life is self-development ... Selfishness is not living as one wishes to live, it is asking others to live as one wishes to live. And unselfishness is letting other people's lives alone, not interfering with them. Selfishness always aims at creating around it an absolute uniformity to type. Unselfishness recognizes infinite variety of type as a delightful thing ... enjoy it. It is not selfish to think for oneself.[46]

---

[41]   Adam Phillips, *Unforbidden Desires* (London, 2015), p. 22.

[42]   Ibid., p. 25.

[43]   Ibid.

[44]   Ibid., p. 26.

[45]   Ibid.

[46]   Oscar Wilde, *The Soul of Man Under Socialism* (Boston, [1918]), p. 66.

138 *Music and Religion in the Writings of Ian McEwan*

Wilde's concern was that the modern person was being obliged to forget their own thoughts, desires, and development[47] and simply conform to a set of societal expectations. This is no different from the circumstances that surround characters in McEwan's novels, especially Fiona (*The Children Act*), Cathy (*The Imitation Game*), Florence (*On Chesil Beach*) or Clive (*Amsterdam*), each of whom has to conform to societal expectations in some aspect of their work and each of whom consequently finds a release through music. Further, by finally returning to the ways of their earlier lives, when music was fresh and a new source of welcome and invigorating engagement, they find pleasure anew or sustained. In a similar fashion there is the government minister (Charles) in *The Children Act* who, feeling he was denied part of his childhood, decides to return to it. But in the case of a musician, it is not so much a departure from the present but a reminder of the happy past. However, an engagement with the arts and the nature of individual response is inherently personal. A parent might know that their child has heard a particular Mozart symphony because they took them to a public concert where it was performed. They might then be under the impression that in the months following the concert the recording of that work that they purchased for their child has remained unopened. But they will be surprised that years later the very same recording is played endlessly by the same child, now older, with an enthusiasm that once appeared remote, just as McEwan's response to the overture of *The Magic Flute* brought back memories of his homesickness many years before.[48] The piece was known all along, but the response to it was not only personal but temporally significant. Music as an unforbidden pleasure, to adopt the thesis of Phillips's book, allows for this measure of secret response. Phillips writes that 'the tyranny of the forbidden is not that it forbids, but that it tells us what we want – to do the forbidden thing. The unforbidden gives no orders,'[49] and it is in this sense that Phillips asks whether the unforbidden pleasures have more to tell us about pleasure in life than the forbidden ones that are so often discussed.[50] In relation to a consideration of the forbidden and unforbidden, Phillips notes that these expectations have historically been set in place by the church and thus been very sustaining as 'an organizing of desire, as a maintaining of essential meaning and value, as a way of feeling that our lives are worth living. Though each of these religious forms assumes that the pleasure we can take in each other is insufficient and that something transcendent or supernatural is required to really keep us going.'[51] In this respect, the otherworldly nature of music in McEwan's narratives takes on a particular significance. The relative pleasure within Florence's and Edward's relationship in *On Chesil Beach* still requires something that rep-

---

[47]   Phillips, *Unforbidden Desires*, p. 27.

[48]   Quinn, 'Interview with Ian McEwan'.

[49]   Phillips, *Unforbidden Desires*, p. 160.

[50]   Ibid.

[51]   Ibid., p. 162.

Influences and Perceptions of Music in Society

resents the other to be sustained and they struggle to find that middle ground. As music has a transformative emotional quality for many, Phillips's arguments are especially relevant in the context of McEwan's writings, not least because, as an atheist, he is uninterested in the religious aspect but personally, deeply interested in the transformative value of music. This perspective has a fascinating overlap in relation to the many singers who engage with music of a sacred nature in the secular setting of a concert or indeed sing in a church choir but have no strong commitment to the theology of a given congregation and may be a nonbeliever themselves. The transformative aspect is nonetheless present and the positive response to this for both McEwan and Rushdie was discussed earlier in this chapter.

When McEwan discusses the value of evensong for a former prisoner in *Machines Like Me*,[52] he is referring to a service that is often sung by a choir that contains not a few doubters concerning the finer points of theology. The aspect of individual interpretation of language, especially for an atheist like McEwan, allows for the response to the pleasure of music, whether intentionally sacred or not, to have a personally transcendental response. The singers are themselves moved by either the communal experience or the intent of the communal experience that aims for a higher, other, ideal. It is for this reason that what appears to be a perfect unity between a liturgical setting and a musical response can be especially moving as the sacred setting and the music are intentionally interwoven. The conclusion of the funeral of Diana, Princess of Wales, at Westminster Abbey in 1997 was one such moment that for many musicians remained the most powerful musical moment in the service. As the casket was carried down the nave from the chancel of the Abbey to the West door, the choir sang John Tavener's 'Song for Athene'. The serenity of the work with its use of low sustained bass voices and an almost hypnotic repetition of harmonies in a style many equated to the (un-Anglican) world of orthodox liturgy was deeply moving, in part because it was so tautly conceived. The un-Anglican music of Tavener coupled with a slow procession and all perfectly timed. It is in moments like these that the precision of liturgy can capture the emotions. The prisoner's experience draws on this vastly contrasting discovery, which he then continues to experience on release.

Music as Therapy

When the cabinet sings 'Walking Back to Happiness' in *The Cockroach* (published in 2019 amid the Brexit discussions), it is with a sense of optimism that, in the spirit of Brexiteers, a return to the past would be a good thing. In Alan Bennett's play *Allelujah!* of the previous year (2018), there is the recurring use of a hymn ('All creatures of our God and King') which is likewise sung infor-

---

[52] Ian McEwan, *Machines Like Me* (London, 2019), p. 243.

140   *Music and Religion in the Writings of Ian McEwan*

mally and serves to instil a familiar melody for those who sing and hear it, and in turn, the audience who watch the play. In both settings, music has an uplifting role. Bennett's play also captures the harshness that McEwan likewise associates with a government that is seemingly detached from the public. By contrast, music is used to show cohesion and unity. The actions of a political master in *The Cockroach* relate to self-promotion rather than public well-being. This approach is mirrored in Bennett's play, when the senior nurse casts aside the value of individual betterment through a measure of music therapy via singing. It is also a critical contrast to the use of music in the hospital scenes in *The Children Act*, where McEwan emphasizes the therapeutic nature of music as positive. In Bennett's text, the nurse acknowledges that music will give her patients hope but she does not believe that they should have any.

> To my mind having a choir is an admission of failure. Patients shouldn't stick around long enough to make up a choir.[53]

> It encourages them to think that life might still have something to offer.[54]

Music is acknowledged in Bennett's play as providing a solace and a power to experience something hopeful, despite sickness and death being all around. It is the same measure of collective solace that is seen in both *Atonement*[55], with a hymn sung on the bandstand near the Normandy beach when again death is close by, and the playing and singing of 'Down by the Salley Gardens' in *The Children Act*. The moment of transformation through music for those who are sick is central to Oliver Sacks's stories in *Awakenings*. Sacks's early discovery that different patients responded to different music was critical to understanding individual personalities and the power of music to change an emotional state. This is discussed later in this chapter.

The therapeutic nature of music is especially evident in *The Children Act* when Fiona sits at the bedside of Adam and sings while he accompanies her,[56] but it is also discussed with a sense of optimism by the fetus in *Nutshell* as one of the wonderful aspects of life to look forward to that will be comforting and representing the best of life: 'I see the world as golden …Wine by the glass rather than the placenta, books direct by lamplight, music by Bach, walks along the shore, kissing by moonlight. Everything I've learned so far says all these delights are inexpensive, achievable, ahead of me. I have the impression of singing in my head. Choirs of angels!'[57] These are all experiences to cherish and described as known possibilities to encounter.

---

[53]   Ibid., p. 46.

[54]   Ibid., p. 44.

[55]   Ian McEwan, *Atonement* (London, 2001), p. 248.

[56]   McEwan, *The Children Act* (London, 2014), p. 119.

[57]   Ian McEwan, *Nutshell* (London, 2016), p. 162.

Influences and Perceptions of Music in Society   141

Many of McEwan's novels involve children although, with the exception of *The Children Act*, only one child plays an instrument. The relationship of music to a sick child (Adam) provides not only a sense of solace and pride to him, but also the point of speechless communication with the judge (Fiona).[58] The playing of the tune for 'Down by the Salley Gardens' allows the boy to express his personality in a meaningful way, whereas his earlier conversation had been meandering and obtuse. Critically, it provides the setting for near-equitable communication because, through music, they communicate in a language that is set apart from their other concerns. The sense of hope that Fiona considers at the end of the extract is the same hope that Bennett's nurse speaks of. It is a sense that there could be a future despite the odds to the contrary.

> The melancholy tune and the manner in which it was played, so hopeful, so raw, expressed everything she was beginning to understand about the boy ... Hearing Adam play stirred her, even as it baffled her. To take up the violin or any instrument was an act of hope, it implied a future.[59]

The wrong notes in his playing are of little concern given the greater reward and, remembering Ruskin, that 'to banish imperfection is to destroy expression'.[60] Rather, music enables the boy to remove a barrier and experience a moment of otherwise awkward conversation with the judge. Through this he also breaks an emotional barrier with her as her affection for him begins to take shape. Music has moved them beyond one emotional state to another.

The therapeutic nature of music has been known for millennia, but the formal aspect of music therapy on hospital wards only arose with any consistent application during World Wars I and II, when large numbers of wounded soldiers were housed in veterans' hospitals. It was discovered that their pain and misery was reflected in physiological response (pulse rates, blood pressure) that could be improved by hearing music. As a consequence, doctors and nurses started to invite musicians to come and play for their patients. The purpose was not to entertain in one typical aspect of performance, but rather to provide consolation, promote healing, and, to a certain extent, foster measured resolve to an otherwise potentially hopeless situation. In 1977, Yehudi Menuhin and Ian Stoutzker created *Live Music Now*, an organization which continues to provide music in hospitals and care homes throughout the UK, typically performed by young musicians, little older than Adam (*The Children Act*), who are themselves an embodiment of hope and the future.

[58] McEwan, *The Children Act*, p. 119.
[59] Ibid.
[60] John Ruskin, *The Stones of Venice*, Vol. II. (Sunnyside, Orpington, 1886).

Musical Preferences

Oliver Sacks had a strong interest in classical music. The pleasure for the non-musician learning music firsthand is something that Sacks and McEwan shared with complete absorption and commitment, and there were many similarities of musical taste between them. Sacks's iPod list of 2007 included multiple pieces of Bach (*Mass in B minor* and *Chaconne in D minor*), music of Mozart (piano concertos 23–26 and *Don Giovanni*), and Schubert (*Die Schöne Mullerin*). These are all pieces that fall within the canon of taste that coincidentally McEwan subscribes to. In *The Children Act*, Fiona accompanies her colleague in performances of Schubert's *Der Erlkönig* and *Der Leiermann*. The latter was also performed by McEwan and his wife, Annalena McAfee, at a Christmas party.[61] The nature of the powerful influence of music to the non-professional musician was observed by Bill Hayes, the longtime partner of Sacks, who noted how enveloping the musical score could be, even to an amateur musician.

> The last picture I [Bill Hayes] took of him, however, captures something quite different. His eyes do not meet mine, his head rests on a propped hand, and he is completely absorbed in a Bach piece he'd been learning to play.[62]

In 2009, Sacks undertook a study with Columbia University to try and understand the nature of musical preferences in the mind. These are points not just of taste but of physical response and although physical response informs taste, much as individual culinary preferences are initially influenced by parents or those who control our diet, we eventually branch out and discover other possibilities. The same is typically the case with musical tastes. They develop over time even if early tastes remain. This noted, whereas a taste for atonal music often only occurs beyond adolescent years, it is rare to hear of someone who is opposed to Bach or Mozart at a young age, hence the reason for its inclusion in children's games and animations, most especially Mozart's *Eine kleine Nachtmusik*. Sacks's study showed how precise the mind can be in overcoming the preferences an individual believes they have and, in turn, how a degree of self-regulation occurs. The relative power of music over an individual to facilitate healing presents certain works as being not only satisfying to a listener but also potentially necessary to them as part of their lives, hence the response of Adam to playing for Fiona in *The Children Act*. In this respect, the scientific aspect of McEwan's writings overlaps as the nature of the choice of repertoire made by Florence (*On Chesil Beach*), Cathy (*The Imitation Game*), and Fiona (*The Children Act*) cannot be considered merely coincidental but to a large extent self-prescribed. It demonstrates how the music McEwan discusses and writes about in his novels is chosen very specifically for characters and drawn

---

[61] Quinn, 'Interview with Ian McEwan'.

[62] Bill Hayes, 'Oliver Sacks – A Composer and his Last Work', *The New York Times* (24 October 2017), online at <https://www.nytimes.com/2017/10/24/opinion/oliver-sacks-a-composer-and-his-last-work.html> [accessed 17 December 2020].

Influences and Perceptions of Music in Society   143

from a repertoire he sees as personally relating to a character and emotional setting. In his *South Bank Show* interview (2015), he comments on how he saw a certain amount of himself in Henry Perowne, the Bach-loving neurosurgeon in *Saturday*, but in fact the tastes of McEwan, as discussed by Michael Berkeley,[63] personally overlap with his fictional characters very frequently.

In the 2009 study, Sacks was trying to understand why some people are able to decode and respond to musical scores on hearing them and others cannot. But to this study also came the question of whether someone, in this case Sacks himself, was likely to respond in the same fashion to music of different composers. He was played two pieces of music, the first by Bach and the second by Beethoven. The music of Bach had been a lifelong enthusiasm for him. However, unlike some of his patients who responded to certain pieces of music but could not explain why, he was able to offer a commentary after the test. The Bach generated a strong emotional response from Sacks, and he commented on aspects of the musical vocabulary of the piece, whereas the Beethoven had little effect on him. The scans that had been undertaken during the test confirmed this, in addition to the fact that he clearly had a contrasting response to each composer. At another point in the test when Sacks was unable to differentiate between the two composers and he was relatively confused, his brain was nonetheless able to observe the contrasting musical languages. In conclusion, it was noted that Sacks's brain had a higher level of activity when he heard performances of Bach by comparison to Beethoven, even at moments when he was unable to distinguish between them.[64] The nature of preference was being made by the brain even though Sacks was unable to verbalize the same response.

The neurological response that Sacks encountered was paralleled in the responses of many of his patients, several of whom responded to music in ways that were of sufficient substance for him to observe the influence of music in their lives. In understanding the character of Florence (*On Chesil Beach*) and her passion for music, while seemingly little else in life mattered to the same degree, it can be observed through the Columbia study that Sacks undertook and also the writings of Anthony Storr and Daniel J. Levitin, that musical responses are deeper than most, if not all, other sensory responses. The power of music on the mind is considerable, and this has been put into practice through a specific musical study by Peter Hübner, who argued that the laws of harmony could be used to alleviate 'psycho-physiological manifestations of stress'.[65] His argument was that if the right music was played to someone who was ill, then their natural harmonic order could be restored. In this sense, whether it is the use of music in the home to calm the family during the Victo-

---

[63] Quinn, 'Interview with Michael Berkeley'.

[64] NOVA, *A Mind for Music*, online at <https://www.pbs.org/wgbh/nova/video/a-mind-for-music> [accessed 17 December 2020].

[65] Scott, 'The Power of Music', pp. 250–251.

144   *Music and Religion in the Writings of Ian McEwan*

rian era or Florence's (*On Chesil Beach*) focus on music at all costs, the effect of the musical language is not one of entertainment or superficial awareness but rather powerfully induced mental states. Music changes Florence's psycho-physiological state and is therefore a language that serves as a powerful emotional place for her. It can be argued that music is a definitive need for Florence that she self-acknowledges and therefore ensures is sustained at all costs.

* * *

McEwan's narratives draw on the power of music in numerous ways that move beyond the aesthetic pleasure to be gained from a piece, or indeed a performance, and towards a power to alter a state of thinking. In chapter 2, the sublime aspect of this encounter with art is considered with specific reference to a professional performer, Florence (*On Chesil Beach*), as well as the use of music as a relative and reliable escape for Fiona (*The Children Act*) and Cathy (*The Imitation Game*), both of whom value playing the piano as a release from their daily activities. Indeed, it can be fairly argued that it provides them with a considerable point of joy and happiness that they can anticipate each day. In seeking or responding to the sublime there has to be a basic understanding of what music can mean on a higher level rather than a potentially immediate or visceral level. It is for this reason that, among other concerns, so many classical musicians take issue with the pounding volume of so much live popular music with the ubiquitous question, 'Why does it have to be so loud?'. The listening audience is not responding in the first instance to the composed music itself that is being performed but rather to the physical medium of performance, much as they do to the lighting and the dancing. The music itself is simply one aspect of the performance.

The Influence and Portrayal of Setting

However, even in opera, the ultimate visual experience of classical music can have intended or unavoidable distractions, especially with productions that seem at some distance from the aesthetic qualities the composer had set in place and to which audiences have become easily accustomed. Roger Scruton has commented on the failure of some Wagner performances where the 'action is invariably caricatured, wrapped in inverted commas, and reduced to the dimensions of a television sitcom. Sarcasm and satire run riot on the stage, not because they have anything to prove or say in the shadow of this unsurpassably noble music, but because nobility has become intolerable.'[66] Scruton's argument does not only extend to other opera productions but also to the question of the appreciation and value of art in general. His book, *Modern Culture*,

---

[66] Roger Scruton, *Modern Culture* (London, 2005), p. 69.

Influences and Perceptions of Music in Society   145

presents an outline for the withering away of societal values in place of the individual and the growing acceptability of narcissism. McEwan's use of music and the presentation of the concert world, together with the lives of professional musicians, complements the argument that Scruton makes, for there is the perception of a contract with the listener that has perceived boundaries. McEwan's narratives share a particular value in the perception of higher art as a preferable norm, complete with specific points of reference regarding their presentation. If music is to be heard, then the setting of it also matters. In *On Chesil Beach*, the audience does not simply attend a string quartet concert in an unnamed hall, but specifically the Wigmore Hall, and the choice of performing forces and the repertoire is particular, as is the description of the hall's furnishings. In *For You*, the reader is given a specific image of narcissism in the world of conducting, and in *Amsterdam* the difference in perception of conductors in Britain and Europe. All of these points coalesce with Scruton's preference for a profession that abides by the image it has long been associated with. As a consequence, McEwan's narratives offer a subtle initiation into the world of classical music in a society where popular music is the dominant force. This enables a popular author like McEwan to present the supposedly elitist world of classical music in an accessible manner, even though to classical musicians reading his works, it already is. The irony of accessibility is that many people who attend classical music concerts on a regular basis could not afford to attend a concert of pop music in a stadium.

Social Status and Snobbery

In *Sweet Tooth*, McEwan portrays two intelligence officers disguising themselves as cleaning ladies while listening to pop music, as they think it will match their 'cover'.[67] In the same novel Serena is listening to a programme on BBC Radio 1 and relates her former tastes in rock music to a measure of immaturity in her younger years, commenting that 'It no longer moved me ... it had shrunk into mere songs ...'.[68] In both cases, popular music is seen in a lesser light and a social power of association is prevalent. Cleaning ladies are portrayed as people who listen to popular music, and this perception is reinforced by the fact that the decision to use this disguise is made by intelligence officers who are presumably better paid and better educated. Serena also notes how the Watchers (members of the intelligence community who spy on their colleagues) would have listened to a live band 'far closer to the speakers' than she would and that they were the 'easy-listening sort'.[69] This comment is a nuanced point of criticism in relation to the previous one because it suggests that Serena categorizes

---

[67]   Ian McEwan, *Sweet Tooth* (New York, 2012), p. 74.

[68]   Ibid., p 220.

[69]   Ibid., p. 111.

146   *Music and Religion in the Writings of Ian McEwan*

music she has little time for quite precisely. Pop music and easy-listening music (which many would regard as the domains of BBC Radio 1 and BBC Radio 2, or potentially the popular classics on Classic FM, respectively) are both areas she has little interest in. Her sole focus is on (serious) classical music (BBC Radio 3). In the same novel, a similar societal image is created when the former Prime Minister, Edward Heath, leaves Downing Street with his 'piano, sheet music and seascapes'.[70] As a consequence, the use of popular music suggests the transient nature of the field, and, in the case of the cleaning ladies, a social status, rather than the sustained elevated presence of classical music that dominates McEwan's narratives. Popular music is listened to while cleaning rooms whereas classical music is heard in hallowed spaces.

In *The Comfort of Strangers*, McEwan alludes to the nature of music that is in some sense cheapened by its setting and a superficial quality that does not require thinking. It is purely serving as an entertainment. As Colin and Mary walk around Venice their view is:

> enclosed on three sides by dignified arcaded buildings and dominated at its open end by a redbrick clock tower, and beyond that a celebrated cathedral of white domes and glittering façade ... adjacent orchestras ... played simultaneously martial and romantic music, waltzes and extracts from popular operas with thunderous climaxes. Everywhere pigeons banked, strutted and excreted, and each café orchestra paused uncertainly after the earnest, puny applause of its nearest customer.[71]

The environment of the hustle and bustle of the historic square with its 'dignified' buildings and 'celebrated cathedral' is presented as not being conducive to hearing music of substance unlike, for instance, a concert hall. The music has lost a key element of its potential reception and the loss is sorely felt. The frustration of the performing musicians, pausing with 'uncertainty after the earnest, puny applause' portrays the sentiments of musicians who would rather be elsewhere. McEwan has presented a critique of the setting that demonstrates the disappointment of the musicians and the unsatisfactory nature of a setting where serious music is not presented seriously. The balance is upset in their minds. They associate music as having a substantive ability to engage people's emotions and not simply be decorative and a lesser art by comparison to the surrounding architecture.

The notion of the distinctive roles of specific music is also alluded to in *Lessons* when Roland is described as playing the 'dotted notes like a jazz musician' although 'It was a rebuke he took as praise'.[72]

---

[70]   Ibid., p. 252.

[71]   McEwan, *The Comfort of Strangers*, pp. 32–33.

[72]   McEwan, *Lessons*, p. 128.

The Image of the Artist

The power of performance in the classical realm rests heavily with the balance between the composer and the artist. The success of Glenn Gould as a pianist of international distinction provides an example of a musician who for most of his career was nowhere near an audience but only in a recording studio, and consequently removed from external influences, just as his listening audience was from distractions. Much the same could be said of organists performing recitals prior to the early 1990s with organ consoles that were consistently out of sight in churches, not least to avoid being a distraction in a liturgical setting. A member of the audience attending an organ recital would simply hear the repertoire and the execution of it without distraction. This was a point that the organist, harpsichordist, and conductor Karl Richter reputedly felt was preferable, because the organist performing in a concert had so many extra physical movements that did not seem as natural to an audience as those of a pianist or violinist. That McEwan's favourite performers of classical music are known for their unobtrusive performance style, which allows an audience simply to hear the music and judge it for themselves, is unsurprising because his narratives and personal commentaries confirm a knowledge of both the repertoire, the nature of performance, and his value for a particular setting and ambience. The concert hall he frequently attends, the Wigmore Hall in London, which features extensively in *On Chesil Beach*, is known for its intimacy and as a perfect setting for music employing small ensembles or individuals. The intimacy is part of the power of the performing moment because of its very fragility. When listening to an orchestra perform in a concert hall, there is rarely a sense of anxiety on behalf of the performers, but when listening to a singer and pianist or a string trio perform in a small hall, there can be a palpable sense of urgency because the element of risk is simply higher, and the power of the moment is distinctly elevated. In this sense there is another marked difference with most performances in the field of popular music. In a stadium setting there could be over one hundred people involved in the larger production whereas, once the lights are lowered in a concert hall for a pianist, the responsibility for the following sixty to ninety minutes of performance is almost solely on the shoulders of the performer(s). At a certain level, the audience is held in suspense, but more crucially they allow themselves to be captured and enveloped in the mystery of music making as it unfolds. In entering into a communion with the repertoire through the performer, the audience member becomes half of a necessary duality that classical music thrives on. As the performer submits to the composer, so too does the music lover submit to the power of the moment. In this respect, Edward's (*On Chesil Beach*) unwilling submission to Florence's suggestion that he sleep with other women is reflected in his inability to submit to the music that moves her because he does not see it as part of his own character. The nature of that musical submission and corresponding freedom of imagination is discussed in *The Child in Time* with regard to pedagogical approaches to

148   *Music and Religion in the Writings of Ian McEwan*

children[73] and relates to the larger concern of a society that is moving away from the creative impulse and towards the prescribed. Scruton comments that 'subjected to the extreme pressures of a secular and materialistic way of life, art begins to compromise, to lose itself in wishful thinking and in dreams. Ready-made fantasies replace the work of imagination, and firm moral sentiment gives way to vapid sentimentality.'[74] It is this relative vapidity that McEwan agitates against in his presentation of art by illuminating the powerful influence it can have over the individual. He also draws on his own experiences of listening to recordings and attending concerts to portray an image of what this means, even to an amateur musician, when thoughtfully considered. Music is not just an adjunct to the narrative but a central part of a character's portrayal.

When Florence offers Edward a tour of the Wigmore Hall, she comments with pride 'as if she had designed it herself' and asks him 'to imagine the thrill and terror of stepping out to play before a discerning audience'.[75] The hall is a sacred space for her as a *sanctum sanctorum* that is fitting for the highest art. The slight air of snobbery – considering that no musician spends their entire career in one location, with the possible exception of some organists – is seen when she dismisses the idea of a full-time job with a Palm Court-style trio in 'a seedy grand hotel south of London'. Although 'she had no scruples with the kind of music she would have to play – no one would be listening – but some instinct, or mere snobbery, convinced her that she could not live in or near Croydon'.[76] The comment that 'no one would be listening' draws on the same detachment observed (above) in *The Comfort of Strangers* and the dissatisfied musicians who feel unappreciated. The setting of the musical performance matters. It also arises in *Lessons* where Roland had 'been playing piano for six months in the tea room of a second-rank central London hotel – "munch music," the assistant manager called it'.[77] It is 'approachable music'[78] played by the 'soft white fingers of a lounge-lizard pianist'.[79] In an interesting contextualisation McEwan also refers to Peter Sellers's mock-travelogue 'Balham, Gateway to the South' which readers familiar with the recording will know includes a humorous reference to the concerts of a local pianist, Eugene Quills, whose has 'never had a lesson in his life'.[80]

The aloofness also exists in the opera *For You* where a surgeon (who does not have the taste in Bach that Henry Perowne does in *Saturday*) comments

---

[73] McEwan, *The Child in Time*, pp. 81–82.

[74] Scruton, *Modern Culture*, p. 69.

[75] Ian McEwan, *On Chesil Beach* (New York, 2007), p. 152.

[76] Ibid., p. 64.

[77] McEwan, *Lessons*, p. 147.

[78] Ibid., p. 353.

[79] Ibid., p. 344.

[80] Ibid., p. 308.

Influences and Perceptions of Music in Society   149

that he's a 'simple type who prefers Vivaldi,'[81] a point that to many classical musicians would place him in the 'easy-listening'[82] constituency Serena (*Sweet Tooth*) refers to, as opposed to someone with a taste in the contemporary music that is the focus of the opera libretto.

The Pressure of Amateur Performance and the Perception of Amateurs

When Fiona (*The Children Act*) is not thinking of legal matters, including the question of life and death, she is immersed in the world of music that serves as an intellectual complement. By performing for colleagues, she presents an alternative intellectual space to her peers with the implication that what provides stimulation and consolation for her will perhaps also offer similar rewards for them. This is a very different presentation than Florence's in *On Chesil Beach*, where the focus of the music is centred on her in the presence of an audience with various voyeuristic overtones related to Edward, as discussed in chapter 2. Whereas Fiona, an amateur performer, shows an unquestionable vulnerability in her performance that to her is significant because she knows that perfection is not within her grasp. The potential power of the performance escapes her on some level. By contrast, Florence seeks to communicate power from the score itself and it is for others to observe her. At the point that Edward finally has an outburst when listening to the *Haffner Symphony*,[83] something has been achieved for her because the power of the music has resulted in a pronounced response from him.

However, when Fiona (*The Children Act*) expresses her concerns about whether her performance as an amateur pianist performing with an equally amateur tenor, who is a colleague of hers, will satisfy the Wigmore Hall 'faction,'[84] it is not only a partial reference to McEwan himself who regularly attends concerts at the hall, but to many others who have developed a special taste for music in this intimate setting. In anticipating her performance before many legal colleagues, the nature of the fragility of performance is explained:

> A large minority of Gray's Inn benchers spent many evenings a year over in Marylebone, at Wigmore Hall. It was said they knew a bad note before it was played. Here ... standards were punitively high for an amateur affair. She thought she lacked the concentration [and the Mahler] would expose her.[85]

---

[81] McEwan, *For You*, p. 12.

[82] McEwan, *Sweet Tooth*, p. 220.

[83] McEwan, *On Chesil Beach*, p. 203.

[84] Ibid.

[85] Ibid., p. 186.

150   *Music and Religion in the Writings of Ian McEwan*

Within this setting there is an inherent sense of expectation for an amateur performer. In the case of this Christmas concert the anxiety occurs because so many of those in attendance know the repertoire and know the standards of professional performance from attending concerts at the Wigmore Hall. In a similar manner to a club, all have chosen to be there, not simply for a concert of classical music but for a particular concert experience. The concert is an aural snapshot that is either experienced at an expected level of engagement or missed, and so the pressure on the performer is magnified. The relatively select concert hall experience that McEwan describes the benchers being familiar with – 'the Wigmore Hall faction' – is a terrifying parallel for the amateur performer like Fiona. As the performers in a professional concert commune with the composers whose works they play, the audience observes and responds, but the amateur performer like Fiona may not be able to communicate the musical score as successfully. The potentially powerful moment of performance that the audience anticipates can be dashed. The music that she loves to be part of her life and that the benchers love to hear professional musicians perform is something she knows she could ruin in a moment. As a consequence, the pressure of the performance in tandem with her personal thoughts is too much for her to bear and she leaves the stage.

The feeling of escape from a musical situation is also seen in *Psychopolis*, when a flautist attempts a performance of a Bach flute sonata while inebriated. Although initially the approach of the performer has a carefree aspect, the conclusion is that the repertoire is best left to professional performers and the performer, like Fiona, breaks off from the performance.

> I played my Bach sonata no worse than usual, perhaps a little more confidently for being drunk, but my mind ran against the music. For I was weary of this music and of myself for playing it. As the notes transferred themselves from the page to the end of my fingers I thought, Am I still playing *this*?
>
> Leave it to others, to professionals who could evoke the old days of its truth.[86]

The unexplainable nature of performance and appreciation whereby two critics convey contrary experiences in newspapers and, similarly, audience members can disagree on the value of a performance, is part of the risk element of attendance that makes a fine performance, to an individual, so especially rewarding. It is the 'allusion and elusiveness' that to Scruton 'are important in high culture as they are in the language and rites of a religion'.[87] This is a reason that music can not only have a transformative and transcendental aspect but, in the case of some liturgies (not least evensong, as discussed in chapter 1), can also surpass theological concerns. The power of the musical language attracts many people to the services irrespective of belief. Indeed, the atmosphere of silence before a performer steps onto a stage and between movements of

---

[86]   Ian McEwan, 'Psychopolis', *In between the sheets* (London, 1997), pp. 133–134.

[87]   Scruton, *Modern Culture*, p. 43.

Influences and Perceptions of Music in Society 151

pieces owes much to a sacred liturgical environment where an understanding of timing is essential. The stage of the Wigmore Hall adds to this image with its cupola on which the Soul of Music looks up at the Genius of Harmony. The unknown aspect of mysticism of place is part of the revealing nature of the experience, which is a point that Florence (*On Chesil Beach*) dwells on as she describes the hallowed nature of the hall.[88] As Scruton continues, 'to explain is to alienate: it is to show something as "outside", observed but not internalized. It is to place conception above experience, as in science or historical research. Nothing is significant aesthetically unless embodied in, and revealed through, experience. Hence the need for allusion, which imports a reference without describing it, so leaving the thread of pure experience unbroken.'[89] It is the nature of art ennobling the human spirit that Scruton speaks to, not least in the setting of a public concert that demands, as with religion, a certain decorum and reverence. It is for this reason that when discussions about 'casual' concerts (in which the audience can bring their own food or text on their phone) are propagated, there is a quick response from commentators who explain that if such a concert is offered, they will stay at home. As these people are often from the same socioeconomic constituency that provides funding to arts organizations, their views are usually taken more seriously for fear of losing income in an already delicate environment. The relevance of an audience that comes from a similar socioeconomic background also has a bearing on Fiona's (*The Children Act*) performance for colleagues and the relative power of the music serving as a release from the quotidian frustrations of legal life. Fiona is exposed during the Christmas concert and the measure of closeness to the world of professional musicians is too much. But as she later finds in talking with Jack, no explanation can adequately express the nature of her thought process. It is not simply a difference of appreciation in two individuals understanding the artistic moment but rather the inherent nature of individualism that is the nature of artistic reception.

McEwan's perception of the relationship between the musical and legal worlds is also seen in the writings of Tom McGregor and John Mortimer. Two particular extracts (below) contextualise McEwan's narrative. In a chapter from *Kavanagh Q.C.*, one of the barristers, Julia Piper, is faced with the question of whether to follow her partner to Nairobi. In an exchange with the head of chambers, Peter Foxcott, she asks for counsel on whether to leave her legal life in London behind:[90]

'Get off the treadmill before you end up like all the rest of us,' he had said.

'The rest of you?' Julia had been completely floored.

---

[88] McEwan, *On Chesil Beach*, pp. 49–50.

[89] Scruton, *Modern Culture*, pp. 43–44.

[90] The following extract is from the book on which the series is based.

152 *Music and Religion in the Writings of Ian McEwan*

'Yes.' Peter, smiling at her over his vast desk, had become almost maudlin. 'When

I was up at Caius, I used to write poetry. Doggerel in the main, I don't doubt, but

no less valid for all that. Now I write advices.' Then in his best avuncular manner,

he made up Julia's mind for her. 'Don't sacrifice real life on the altar of career.'

'I thought career *was* real life.'

But he silenced her with an abrupt hand. 'Going through the motions. D'you know why so many of us are obsessed with music, art, literature? We've forgotten how to feel. We have these empty spaces which we try to fill with someone else's experience ... someone else's passion.'[91]

Although it could be argued that only those in the senior professions such as law could afford to attend performances at the Royal Opera House or the Glyndebourne Festival, the vast majority of public performances in the UK are accessible to almost the entire population, even if they are financially supported by those with financial means. In *Lessons*, it is noted how the publisher, Rüdiger, supports the opera.[92]

However, Tom McGregor's narrative in *Kavanagh Q.C.* highlights the environment that Fiona (*The Children Act*) is part of and the desire to retain a part of life that remains fulfilling and meaningful. The 'empty space' is filled with music. Music is not just a sublime panacea (as discussed in chapter 2) but a powerful and motivating distraction from temporal concerns. Nor is it merely a desire for the easy pastorale background music that Alan Bennett criticizes when he refers to what's wrong with Classic FM, the commercial classical music station in the UK. To Bennett, the frequent introductions to pieces being described as 'beautiful'[93] satisfy some listeners that the norm will be preserved. The 'easy-listening'[94] that Serena describes in *Sweet Tooth* can also be seen in this category because to a serious music lover it can appear as somewhat superficial. Describing music in these terms removes the sense of the unknown in appreciating music while also presumably categorizing music into the 'beautiful' and the 'not so beautiful'. Fiona and her tenor colleague offer their annual performances for a larger community of barristers and judges who voluntarily and enthusiastically attend. In a manner similar to McGregor's narrative above, Fiona seeks music because it provides a powerful antidote to her daily life. It does not explain or rationalize her life any more than for McGregor's

---

[91]   Tom McGregor, *Kavanagh Q.C. II* (Bath, 1997), pp. 245–246.

[92]   McEwan, *Lessons*, p. 407.

[93]   Alan Bennett, *Keeping On Keeping On* (London, 2017), p. 202.

[94]   McEwan, *Sweet Tooth*, p. 220.

Influences and Perceptions of Music in Society

character of Foxcott. Rather, it provides a contrast and the filling of a void. In *Titmuss Regained* by John Mortimer, himself a barrister, the comment of an audience member attending the Verdi opera, *Simon Boccanegra*, at the Royal Opera House that 'planning policy shouldn't be discussed in the Crush Bar of the Opera House'[95] stems from a similar appreciation of the otherness that is sought. It detracts from the elevated atmosphere for musical appreciation and this narrative addresses the impression that McEwan creates in *On Chesil Beach* when Florence describes the Wigmore Hall in reverential terms that set it apart from the outside world. Whereas the separation of work and art that Fiona experiences is paralleled in the *Kavanagh Q.C.* narrative that 'Christopher always says he forgets all his business worries after the first two bars of the overture'.[96]

When the Music Stops

Beyond the research aspects of music therapy that the Sacks study (above) discusses in relation to *The Children Act*, McEwan's narratives also raise the question of what happens when music stops being a part of a musician's life, when the power that once captured and embraced emotions and provided much consistent happiness and relief from the outside world has largely vanished. In *Amsterdam*, there is a suicide pact between an ageing composer who has put great hopes in a final large-scale commission to celebrate the millennium and an ageing journalist. In the opera *For You*, an egomaniacal composer is reminded of his earlier brilliance while being trapped by the desires of his Polish housekeeper. In both cases, the musicians are aware of the difficulty of maintaining their reputations while younger musicians seek the work they now have difficulty in securing for themselves. The profession has started to move away from them. In both narratives there is a considerable overlap of topics with Bennett's play *The Habit of Art*, which involves a set of fictional scenes with W. H. Auden and Benjamin Britten meeting later in life. Bennett relied on their respective biographies, which were both written by Humphrey Carpenter.

Britten: Are you out of fashion now?

Auden: At twenty I tried to vex my elders. Past sixty, it's the young I hope to shock. I'm unforgiven by the left because I have long since ceased to rally the troops. Still, I *rankle*, which is not unsatisfying.

Britten: The last thing of mine that was generally liked was the *War Requiem*.

Auden: I missed that.[97]

---

[95] John Mortimer, *Titmuss Regained* (London, 1990), p. 104.

[96] Ibid., p. 100.

[97] Bennett, *The Habit of Art* (London, 2010), p. 49.

154   *Music and Religion in the Writings of Ian McEwan*

Throughout the play, Auden – always the elder in every sense and long the person who had given Britten extremely blunt advice about his career as well as his personal life – challenges Britten to be honest with himself, although at the same time he is enamoured of the idea of a collaboration between the two of them. In the opera *For You*, with a libretto by McEwan and music by Michael Berkeley, the conductor's/composer's personal assistant (Robin) criticizes his employer to the housekeeper (Maria), a woman who is in love with him and cannot see his faults. In *Amsterdam* it is an Italian conductor who reminds the composer that his best days are behind him and the compositional talent he was once famed for as a younger composer is unlikely to be recaptured: 'The inventiveness of youth, so hard to recapture, eh Maestro?'[98] In both settings there is a near desperate need to remain professionally recognized, despite the changing nature of the profession and especially the emergence of younger talents. Maria plays on this insecurity by lavishing praise on the older conductor and composer (Charles), whose fragile ego is easily satisfied. When she describes Charles as a 'genius',[99] it is notable because the term is so rarely applied within the music world except in relation to composers of earlier eras. In this sense, Maria demonstrates her lack of familiarity with the argot of the field but understands the advantage of pandering to Charles's ego. In this respect there is a similarity to Bennett's fictional description of Auden's and Britten's later life when he noted in his diaries:

> Towards the end of *The Habit of Art*, Humphrey Carpenter tells the ageing Auden and Britten that they have reached that stage in their lives when even their most devoted fans would be happy to close the book on them: no more poetry, no more music. Enough.[100]

It is the fine balance in the musical life between the career and the reputation that is especially pronounced for a composer whose legacy is judged not only against those who have gone before them and those that come after, but sometimes cruelly between the different points of their own life. Clive's character in *Amsterdam* struggles with the issue of legacy and what a final work could mean for his reputation, and this becomes an increasingly heavy burden throughout the novel. Edward Said's writings in *On Late Style* speak to the question of whether the accepted notion of wisdom in some last works reflects a maturity born of long experience. Verdi's *Othello* and *Falstaff* brim with a confidence that demonstrates an almost youthful ebullience that to Said 'attests to an apotheosis of artistic creativity and power'.[101] It is this very sense that is so appealing for a composer to recapture late in life, but especially for a composer who is being judged against their earlier work. To that end, the observation of

---

98   McEwan, *Amsterdam*, p. 162.
99   McEwan, *For You*, pp. 45–46.
100   Bennett, *Keeping On Keeping On*, p. 220.
101   Edward Said, *On Late Style* (New York, 2006), pp. 6–7.

Influences and Perceptions of Music in Society **155**

the Italian conductor in *Amsterdam* that the past is 'so hard to recapture'[102] is especially lacerating. In a similar sense, the remark of one of Bennett's characters, the biographer Humphrey Carpenter, in *The Habit of Art*, that success was important to Britten and that through Auden he would achieve a 'passport to posterity'[103] reflects on Said's arguments regarding late style and the feeling of necessity and professional relevance. Charles (*For You*) hungers to be remembered as a great figure while Clive (*Amsterdam*) seeks a final opportunity to prove himself.

But what if lateness does not bring about the great masterpieces of a lifetime but instead wreaks havoc on a reputation? Said questions whether Ibsen's late plays do just this, and that 'far from resolution [they] suggest an angry and disturbed artist for whom the medium of drama provides an occasion to stir up more anxiety, tamper irrevocably with the possibility of closure, and leave the audience more perplexed and unsettled than before'.[104] These are the constant sentiments found throughout both *Amsterdam* and *For You* in narratives that are unencountered in other writings of McEwan because the characters are specifically professional musicians wrestling with music at an older age. Music is still powerful to them, but the relative power of the profession and the public's perception is working against them. In the case of Clive (*Amsterdam*), he is tortured by his inability to achieve what he once did. His state of mind near the end of the book captures the sense of knowing that it is all over and the lofty aspirations, both for the immediate success of his piece and for a work that society would learn from in future generations, is now waning.

> when he sat in front of the manuscript – the handwriting of a younger, more confident and gifted man ... he had been denied his masterpiece, the summit of a lifetime's work. This symphony would have taught his audience how to listen to, how to *hear*, everything else he had ever written.
>
> he was too weary, too emptied out, too old.[105]

In *For You*, McEwan balances the sombre aspect of age for Charles with a comic sexual lack of achievement, conveyed in a style wholly different from the lack of sexual confidence for Turner (*The Imitation Game*) or Edward (*On Chesil Beach*). Rather, it is part of the absurdity of an egotistical composer and conductor with an overblown self-image. Charles is also unable to perform as a composer and committed husband, and McEwan merges all three failings into one personality. The characters of Charles and Clive are very different from each other, but both seek the professional limelight and the related public adulation. As discussed in chapter 4, the character of Charles is no less believable for this portrayal either.

---

[102] McEwan, *Amsterdam*, p. 162.

[103] Bennett, *The Habit of Art*, p. 70.

[104] Said, *On Late Style*, pp. 6–7.

[105] McEwan, *Amsterdam*, p. 142.

156   *Music and Religion in the Writings of Ian McEwan*

The noble quest for understanding sublimity in music whether as a performer, listener or composer, as considered in chapter 2, collides with the egotism of Clive (*Amsterdam*), where his engagement is not for himself as a servant of the music (as it is for Florence in *On Chesil Beach*) but instead for music that will ultimately be his agent for success. The narrative of how this is achieved is no more than a veil for his own vanity, much as Charles's (*For You*) sexual failing is a parallel to his empty musical and personal self.

Mozart

Mozart's music is prominent in *On Chesil Beach* (*String Quintet* and *Haffner Symphony*), *The Imitation Game* (*Fantasia*), and also briefly in *The Comfort of Strangers* and *Amsterdam* where there are references[106] to one of McEwan's earliest coming-of-age musical memories with performances of *The Magic Flute*. Mozart's music serves two ends in McEwan's writings, one of which is the sublime aspect that can remove the listener to another, reliably comfortable place of happiness, or at least personal resolve. The other is a matter of the powerful elevation of emotions that is quite different from his approach to Bach and the *Goldberg Variations*, as discussed in chapter 2.

Mozart's *Fantasia in C minor*, K. 475 for piano is a piece that particularly interested McEwan around the time of writing *The Imitation Game*. He had been listening to a recording of the work and asked his girlfriend at the time (1974) to play the piece for him. When he was collaborating with the director Richard Eyre on a new play, *The Imitation Game*, he felt that the relatively austere opening was 'haunting'[107] and a perfect fit for the play. The play's subject matter centres on the character of Cathy Raine and the balance between her secret work in intelligence at Bletchley Park and her largely private performances of the Mozart *Fantasia*, which she practises over and over again, seeking perfection. The work becomes a focus for her and serves as another code to break, but on a personal level. As Lynn Wells notes, it is an 'auditory correlative of her challenge to improve herself'.[108] The piece has both an emotional and an intellectual aspect for her. As Sacks observed, the neurological aspect of choosing a piece of repertoire for a particular purpose is not accidental, and Cathy relies on the challenge to break a code that she has chosen for herself.[109] Much of her daytime work involves a sustained analysis of structure while trying to break secret codes in a secret environment, but at the end of each working day she returns to practising. Were the piece a traditional sonata in a predictable form then it would be fair to suggest that the 'code' was merely the practice and

---

[106]   McEwan, *The Comfort of Strangers*, p. 2; McEwan, *Amsterdam*, p. 95.

[107]   Quinn, 'Interview with Ian McEwan'.

[108]   Wells, *Ian McEwan*, p. 143.

[109]   McEwan chooses the code for Cathy.

Influences and Perceptions of Music in Society   157

the desire of an amateur pianist to perfect her craft. As McEwan notes, 'music in its written form [is] a kind of code'.[110] However, the *Fantasia* is far from a predictable piece. The harmonic instability of the opening bars is unusual in its degree of chromaticism by comparison to the typical Mozart (or indeed Haydn) piano sonata. Charles Rosen noted that although the writing is as 'symmetrical as one could wish [in a work of the period and style] ... the abrupt, poignant changes of harmony destroy all the stability of the tonic [home key], creating instead a mysteriously expressive atmosphere'.[111] This degree of harmonic intrigue, while at the same time embodying an expressive aesthetic, is a perfect counterpoint to Cathy's daytime working existence because it is both an example of a challenging code and an encounter with a different emotional vocabulary. Through the opening bars of the piece Cathy is able to find the other half of her existence, the expressive one. The troubles of her personal life can be substituted by the power of a complex musical work that she can return to as an intellectual pursuit with the intention of mastering it in the fullness of time. As such, Cathy has a developing relationship with the piece that matures over time while also improving. In this respect there is a similarity with Florence (*On Chesil Beach*) who selects different music for later points of her study,[112] and thus also plans her relationship to the repertoire. Dominic Head observes that *The Imitation Game* is 'underpinned by a preconceived expectation of gender traits [and that these are] clearly a metaphor for the imposition of set gender roles',[113] but through music Cathy, like Florence, has both a degree of independence as well as a confidence towards traditional role reversal. Music becomes a powerful private emotional force that can largely surpass other concerns.

The relative harmonic instability of the *Fantasia* opening continues across the larger work, and the final section offers, according to Rosen, 'not the harmonic tensions of the opening, but the tensions set up by all the different tonalities in the course of the piece. The resolution is less like that of a sonata than of the final section of an operatic finale...[what] we have is a truly abnormal [work] by classical standards'.[114] Considering the difficult balance between Cathy's work, her own life, and her relationship with a colleague, Rosen's inference of the *Fantasia* having some sort of operatic dimension is especially consonant with a work that evokes multiple contrasting emotions (as in opera). The improvisatory nature of the piece, with so many sections (six in Rosen's analysis) and such sustained harmonic ambiguity, suggests to Rosen a dualism – itself a relationship whether musical or otherwise – between the immediate impression of an improvised work and the relative advantages of an organized

[110]   Ian McEwan, *The Imitation Game* (London, 1981), p. 18.

[111]   Charles Rosen, *The Classical Style* (New York, 1998), p. 92.

[112]   McEwan, *On Chesil Beach*, pp. 50–51.

[113]   Dominic Head, *Ian McEwan* (Manchester, 2007), p. 55.

[114]   Rosen, *The Classical Style*, p. 92.

158   *Music and Religion in the Writings of Ian McEwan*

form. In this sense it 'could give such an impression of unity while sounding so rhapsodic'.[115] Thus, the intellectual maze that the piece is based around allows a superior analytical mind like Cathy's not just an intellectual stimulation in a therapeutic sense, according to Sacks's research, but also a powerful challenge to conquer. As Hegel commented, 'what it [music] claims as its own is the depth of a person's inner life',[116] noting that 'object-free inwardness in respect of music's content and mode of expression constitutes its formal aspect'.[117] The deeper Cathy explores the *Fantasia*, the closer she is to the answers in her own personal life. Further, the nature of her repetitive practice is also not merely for a want for perfection, but also because the listening experience of Mozart allows someone with an appreciation of the score to, in Scott Burnham's words, 'anticipate and savour such moments'[118] because their taste is increasingly refined.

The choice of the *Fantasia* by Cathy also shows a degree of creative inspiration and independence on her part when she could have easily moved from a simple Mozart piano sonata to a more difficult sonata. Instead, she chooses a work that is an intellectual puzzle, a small secret in its relative obscurity, as well as something of an improvisation. There is also the stimulating aspect that she studies the music of a Germanic sensibility, although not a heroic figure in a Beethovenian sense. This could be considered as a complement to her daytime work with the thesis that in her duty to the country she must understand both the head, heart, and soul of the enemy in order to be successful. However, that would overlook the supremacy of Mozart as a figure known across many countries by the mid-twentieth century and long before. As the fetus remembers in *Nutshell*, 'There's a special grace in facility [of writing/composition]. All art aspires to the condition of Mozart's.'[119] If that argument is to be explained, then the strength will be in seeing the value of Mozart as a global, universal figure who represents the best of humanity, for his music can be valued across multiple cultures and is therefore not divisive but inclusive. Cathy expands her thinking rather than restricting it.

Haffner Symphony

The responses to music depicted in McEwan's novels are consistently given by his female characters, but Edward's (*On Chesil Beach*) response to the first movement of Mozart's *Haffner Symphony* is a notable exception, as the piece

---

[115]   Ibid., p. 93.

[116]   Georg Wilhelm Friedrich Hegel, *Aesthetics, Lectures on Fine Art*, trans. T. M. Knox (Oxford, 1975), vol. II, pp. 888–910; Carl Dahlhaus and Ruth Katz, *Contemplating Music* (Stuyvesant: Pendragon Press, 1987), p. 340.

[117]   Hegel, *Aesthetics, Lectures on Fine Art*, p. 341.

[118]   Scott Burnham, *Mozart's Grace* (Princeton, 2012), pp. 115–116.

[119]   McEwan, *Nutshell*, p. 151.

Influences and Perceptions of Music in Society   159

is a significant contrast to others discussed in McEwan's writings where purely orchestral works of the Classical period are not included. However, though the piece is played on an LP for him to respond to, it has nonetheless been chosen by Florence. The piece is written in the key of D major, a key associated with jubilation, festivity, and pageantry. The opening of Bach's *Christmas Oratorio*, Handel's 'Hallelujah Chorus' (*Messiah*), and the outer movements of Handel's *Music for the Royal Fireworks* are all pieces in D major with an instrumentation of strings, woodwinds, brass, and timpani. The opening of the *Haffner Symphony* is not only jubilant but has an air of almost demonstrative confidence, and the choice of this work for a character such as Edward to respond to is significant. It is Edward's only great enthusiasm for a piece of classical music throughout the novel, as opposed to his feelings for Florence and whatever she is playing, and this is vastly different from the repertoire he knows her for. This is not a piece belonging to the intimate world of the string quartet. It is also a piece that shows a youthful confidence and was written when Mozart, then thirty-one, was not that much older than Edward.

Anthony Storr noted that 'the way in which music is presented makes possible a greater range of individual reactions ... if everyone taking part is familiar'[120] with the piece. As a consequence, Florence's previous knowledge of the symphony not only allows her a different potential range of responses but by nature of her knowledge of the piece (by comparison to Edward's) she controls a degree of his response. Thus, by selecting a piece she knows and for someone she knows well, she is exerting a measure of control.

The piece itself was created as a result of an earlier commission, now known as the *Haffner Serenade*, K. 250, which was written for the Salzburg wedding of Marie Elizabeth Haffner to Franz Xavier Spath. The bride was the daughter of Sigmund Haffner the Elder, who had once been Mayor of Salzburg and was a supporter of Mozart in his early tours. At the point of Edward hearing this work they were unmarried, and Florence was still a virgin. However, the language McEwan uses in describing Edward's response to the piece is laced with a subtle sexual overtone.

> Florence once more showed him the exposed, glowing orange valves of an amplifier protruding from an elegant grey box, and the waist-high speakers, and she put on for him at merciless volume Mozart's Haffner Symphony. The opening octave leap seized him with its daring clarity – a whole orchestra suddenly spread before him – and he raised a fist and shouted across the room, careless of who heard, that he loved her. It was the first time he had ever said it, to her or to anyone. She mouthed the words back at him, and laughed with delight that he had at last been moved by a piece of classical music.[121]

---

[120] Storr, *Music and the Mind*, p. 67.

[121] McEwan, *On Chesil Beach*, p. 147.

160   *Music and Religion in the Writings of Ian McEwan*

For the composer Michael Tippett, 'symphonic music in the hands of the great masters truly and fully embodies the otherwise unperceived, unsavoured inner flow of life. In listening to such music, we are as though entire again, despite all the insecurity, incoherence, incompleteness and relativity of our everyday life. The miracle is achieved by submitting to the power of its organized flow; a submission which gives us a special pleasure and finally enriches us.'[122] In analysing the language in McEwan's text, it can be noted that at this juncture in the story Florence has never been 'exposed' and is certainly not 'glowing' as if pregnant or indeed radiantly in love either. The 'waist-high' speakers are presumably of the height of her own waist or Edward's. The 'merciless' volume and the fact that he had 'at last been moved by a piece of classical music' suggests that he is bereft of the obvious emotions that should have moved him before and also the exasperation ('at last') that Florence has in comprehending him. The 'protruding' aspect of the amplifiers coupled with the opening ascent of the orchestral passage at the beginning of the symphony suggests Edward's own tumescence. The 'whole orchestra spread before him' can be clearly associated with the later offer that Florence proposed to Edward on the beach: the suggestion that he could sleep with other women so long as he remained honest with her. The opening octave leap can also be seen symbolically as an interval of naked purity, honesty, and strength alongside the reference to the virginal 'first time'. Florence interprets Edward's response with an approach that sees him as weaker and only finally emboldened by a musical score that she chose. The power of the moment is therefore multilayered, for the music is overwhelming to Edward but chosen by Florence. It is akin to one person in a couple providing the other person with photographic images that titillate them. Though the receiver is presumably grateful, it is the giver who has controlled the situation and, intentionally, the response. McEwan interprets this for the reader in language filled with the sensual, complaining, and desperate. But later in the novel it is acknowledged how futile she saw her attempts at introducing classical music to Edward had been:

> She said all this [about her future plans] knowing that classical music meant nothing to him.

> But Florence believed his triumphant shout at the opening of the Haffner Symphony was a breakthrough.[123]

Storr's comments above regarding the nature of familiarity to a given work are extended by Frances Berenson's observation that with 'the character of a relationship which is akin to friendship ... music has essentially human characteristics.'[124] But with her prior knowledge of the piece, Florence by nature has

---

[122] Michael Tippett, 'Art, Judgement and Belief: Towards the Condition of Music', in Peter Abbs (ed.), *The Symbolic Order* (London, 1989), p. 47.

[123] McEwan, *On Chesil Beach*, p. 151.

[124] Frances Berenson, 'Interpreting the Emotional Content of Music', in Michael Krausz

Influences and Perceptions of Music in Society 161

a different relationship with the *Haffner Symphony*. Mozart, though, is also a safe proposition and, in the words of Alan Bennett, 'so safe, so consistent and now so universally esteemed'[125] that even to a novice in classical music such as Edward, Mozart would still be very well known. Edward is introduced to the piece as he would be to a friend of Florence's that he hasn't met before. The image of the non-classical music lover (in either sense) can be seen as an eviscerating criticism of those who do not understand the world of classical music. To be outside the realm of classical music appreciation is portrayed as lacking and, in some respect, embodying an immaturity. 'At last'[126] Edward had understood the value she had long known. In every sense, Edward is portrayed as a boy, not a man. His failure on their wedding night reinforces that. There is a blunt ironic parallel to their wedding night when Edward shouts with frustration while having been unable to make any sort of physical or emotional breakthrough and then shouts again at the opening of the symphony. Thus, not only is Edward portrayed as immature and incompetent but in complete contrast to Florence, for whom the power of music is consistently enveloping, satisfying, and superior.

'All art aspires to the condition of Mozart'[127]

The statement above is made by a fetus in *Nutshell* and borrows from Walter Pater's famous comment that 'all art constantly aspires towards the condition of music'.[128] It is a statement about purity from one whose mind remains one with the limited personal experience of responding to the voices of adults around the womb. The impression the fetus has of adults and indeed of the nature of creation is far from pure or necessarily happy, and so the perception of Mozart as representing a summit of existence is a powerful thought. Here, Mozart represents a higher aspiration in a world of doubt, and there is a surety to knowing Mozart's works because they provide an idea of a better existence now and also to come.

In the Peter Shaffer play *Amadeus* (1981), there is a scene in which the composer Antonio Salieri – portrayed throughout the similarly titled 1984 film as a rival of Mozart who is consumed with jealousy – hears the *Adagio* from Mozart's *Serenade* for thirteen wind instruments, K. 361. Even though there are many exceptional moments in the film, not least the musical performances, the staging of various opera scenes, and the overall script and direction, this scene has stood out for many musicians as a beautiful summation of Mozart's

---

(ed.), *The Interpretation of Music: Philosophical Essays* (Oxford, 1993).

[125] Alan Bennett, *Writing Home*, p. 171.

[126] McEwan, *On Chesil Beach*, p. 147.

[127] McEwan, *Nutshell*, p. 151.

[128] Walter Pater, *The Renaissance Studies in Art and Poetry* (Oxford, 1986), p. 86.

162   *Music and Religion in the Writings of Ian McEwan*

musical gift that sets him apart and indeed above others. The character of Sali-eri comments on how the opening could potentially sound almost comically facile and yet in Mozart's hands a musical language is developed that makes one question whether Mozart's ability was not only God-given but a voice of God on earth.[129]

Maynard Solomon writes that 'what may be most unusual in [some of the superlatively beautiful passages of Mozart] is their wholeness, their encapsulated sense of completion, their inherent resistance to forward motion because they have already approached a state of perfection.'[130] In this vein, how can Edward possibly compete with the power of (a) Mozart? McEwan has given Edward an image of double perfection between Florence and Mozart while drawing a line between Florence and Edward, not only sexually but also in terms of their basic understanding and appreciation of music. Burnham notes 'the music [of Mozart] is somehow pre-made, and it glows with a self-sufficiency that has less to do with unity and more with apartness: untouched, untouchable.'[131] Burnham's description of Mozart could equally be a description of Florence, but it also reflects the differences in the relationship. Mozart gives an impression of completeness whereas the personal relationship is fraught with the incomplete.

The challenge of being able to interpret what a piece (or in the case of the extract from *Amadeus*, a piece and a composer) can mean to a performer or listener is discussed earlier from a neurological perspective in relation to Sacks's study. However, Burnham, whose research has long been focused on music of the eighteenth and nineteenth centuries, attempts (and in the opinion of this writer succeeds) to formulate a coherent understanding of why Mozart's music should seemingly hold a unique or special power over listeners. There is a great difference between the musical styles of the *Fantasia* that Cathy plays in *The Imitation Game*[132] and the *Haffner Symphony* recording Florence plays for Edward in *On Chesil Beach*,[133] but both occupy a particular place in contextualising the narrative. Burnham begins his study by quoting Karl Barth: 'Whoever has discovered Mozart even to a small degree and then tries to speak about him fails quickly into what seems rapturous stammering.'[134] This statement alone from the well-known Swiss Reformed theologian presents the difficulty in explaining, even for a theologian, the nature of Mozart's power over his listener. However, much of what is challenging to analyse is just so because

---

[129]   Peter Shaffer, *Amadeus* (New York, 1981, 2001), pp. 27–28.

[130]   Maynard Solomon, *Mozart: A Life* (New York, 1995), p. 375; Burnham, *Mozart's Grace*, p. 18.

[131]   Burnham, *Mozart's Grace*, p. 4.

[132]   McEwan, *The Imitation Game*, p. 81.

[133]   McEwan, *On Chesil Beach*, p. 203.

[134]   Karl Barth, *Wolfgang Amadeus Mozart*, trans. Clarence K. Pott, foreword by John Updike (Grand Rapids, 1986), p. 27; Burnham, *Mozart's Grace*, p. 1.

Influences and Perceptions of Music in Society 163

music of a superior mind is by nature a stage beyond the normal. A second-rate composer can be more easily understood because the student and scholar can point to strengths and weaknesses and, to a certain extent, so can an audience of music lovers who are tutored in music at a basic level. Mozart though, like other masters such as Palestrina and Bach, appears to create his music almost effortlessly and, perhaps coincidentally, that is also how his music is typically received by listeners. Thus, in the case of Cathy's continual practice, there is a vision of perfection, even if it might be unattainable. However, it is important to observe that the experience of performing Mozart and listening to Mozart are two different subjects.

Many performers will note that Mozart's writing appears deceptively straightforward when in fact it is notoriously difficult, in part because of the appearance of ease. Cathy's constant practice mirrors that of the professional musician in its constancy. The music itself does not have the technical or physical demands of later repertoire and consequently is within her technical grasp. In the realm of piano performance there are performers who can play Mozart piano sonatas sufficiently well but do not even consider the possibility of playing the more technically challenging repertoire of Chopin, Liszt or Rachmaninoff. However, even the performers of the aforementioned later composers' works will still readily admit that Mozart can be something of a conundrum because not a note is wasted or out of place and so the performance has an exposed, unveiled, quality. A minor technical mistake in the work of many composers might be easily forgiven by a listener but a mistake in Mozart is considered far more obvious because the line of purity and compositional elegance is unmistakably broken and with it a certain performing spell of perfection. It is for this reason that, as with Bach, many performers have devoted themselves to the work of certain eras and in this case to the work of an eighteenth-century composer. Although the pianist Alfred Brendel performed an extremely broad repertoire, the latter part of his career focused very largely on works of the Classical or early Romantic era. In his later years, the same could be said of Sviatoslav Richter, and it is often observed that perhaps the reason performers gravitate towards these works in their final years is that from an artistic viewpoint they are able to view the repertoire – that for many is the summit of the literature – with a measure of experience that can only come from age. Although there are exceptions, it should not be assumed that a fourteen-year-old will play a Mozart sonata in the same fashion as an eighty-year-old any more than they would read a poem the same way. The notes might be accurate for both of them, but the actual interpretation of the piece is another matter. The constant practice and reflection of Cathy (*The Imitation Game*) on one piece highlights the nature of a maturing understanding.

It is common for musicians, whether amateur or professional, to return to a piece they once studied decades earlier and play it again with a completely different approach to the score. The notes will always be the same, but the understanding of the musical language will have evolved in its own way. Even if they have theoretically studied little in between, they are a changed person from life's experiences and that is brought into play when they approach the piece almost, as it were, anew. Although maturity cannot be taught, a greater awareness can certainly be encouraged and to that end many teachers recommend that their students also look at the paintings of the same era and country in which the composer lived, or the architecture, in order that the students' perspective is expanded. It is not maturity, even though that is generally what is hoped for, but rather a greater and more enriched education. This is the focus readers can witness in Cathy (*The Imitation Game*), as someone who is already used to applying considerable quiet discipline to her work and then transfers her concentration to learning a Mozart *Fantasia* instead. The time she devotes to studying the music of Mozart who, in the language of her professional work, writes in a perfect code, allows her an ever clearer image of the piece that will mature as she does. At the end of her study her impression of the piece will be different because the internal power of the work will have changed not only her perception of the music but, Sacks would argue, her own emotional response to the piece.

There is also the contrast of a working situation that revolves around a climate of war compared to one of distinct beauty. Roger Scruton argues that through high culture we 'extend the repertoire of emotion'[135] and in referring to Matthew Arnold remarks that 'feeling does not exist in and of itself, in some purely subjective medium, much as we deceive ourselves in thinking the opposite – into believing we are paragons of sensitivity who are accidentally deprived of the means to reveal it. The poet [and also the musician], who causes us for a moment to move in time to his emotion and so to re-make it in ourselves, can open the avenues of expression and unfreeze the veins.'[136] If, in the case of Cathy, the reader considers her life as representing a dualism between work and rest, war and peace, toil and relaxation, then we can also consider Lydia Goehr's description that the 'transfiguring aspect'[137] of music allows Cathy to see beauty not only through Mozart but through the contrast to her daytime work of decoding as well. It is an extension of the Aristotelian view of the right judgement (*orthos logos*) that in Scruton's opinion can also be part of '*feeling* rightly'.[138] As a consequence, a balanced, moral person who has to evaluate and consider a specific dualism in life as Cathy does is supported in her daytime work by a certain 'education of the emotions'[139] that her playing of Mozart provides. To borrow further from Aristotle and Scruton on the allied subject of poetry, it 'does not tolerate the improbable, but it can tolerate the impossible, provided the impossible is also believable'.[140] If this sentiment is

---

[135] Scruton, *Modern Culture*, p. 16.

[136] Ibid.

[137] Lydia Goehr, *The Imaginary Museum of Musical Works* (Oxford, 1992), p. 167.

[138] Scruton, *Modern Culture*, p. 15.

[139] Ibid., p. 16.

[140] Ibid., p. 60.

Influences and Perceptions of Music in Society   165

applied to music, then Mozart can be viewed in the life of McEwan's characters as providing a force that can live at the extreme of beauty if for no other reason than the fact that little, if anything, can surpass it in the same manner. The fictional words of Salieri (above) from *Amadeus* – a play and later a film that was extremely popular and viewed by many more people than the audiences who attend classical music concerts – find a further resonance in Burnham's comments:

> Mozart's music stages suspended moments of revelatory beauty, moments whose second sight is made possible by the presence of a threshold created by modern subjectivity. With this threshold, consciousness becomes an inner space created in contradistinction to the outside world, defining the outside world: to be inside is to know of an outside. Mozart's beautiful moments make this space resonate as an interior realm, activating its divination of a now remote transcendence. This unknowable otherness can only be imitated – with a brush of awe, a prickling of the senses.[141]

Burnham's comments relate perfectly to Cathy's situation because through music she comes to redefine the world she otherwise lives in. In this sense it can also be seen that if she examines the context of Mozart's work historically, then she also comes to rationalize her work when thinking of a German society that can produce war in a contemporary setting. Mozart's music ultimately surpasses temporal concerns because it is superior and this, Scruton would argue, is one of the positive values of higher culture. From an atheist's perspective, like McEwan, it is also possible to contextualise the higher role of art music as something transcendental and therefore near sacred in meaning, whatever that meaning might be to an individual. Scruton writes that the sacred 'focuses emotion beyond the immediate fact' as we also see in higher art, and that it therefore 'enables us both to overcome our fears and at the same time confront what has happened'. In considering Cathy's work this, too, has an immediate resonance because it provides a direct complement and rationale to her otherwise dual experiences. Scruton writes that 'By focusing on profane things' such as lesser art or trivial pursuits 'we ruin what is sacred', not least because our time and emotions are absorbed elsewhere in something less worthy. As a consequence, 'We subject the world to our fears and foibles, and take a step back from the true community towards self-isolation'.[142] By this argument, through an engagement with something consequential, whether religion or the fine arts, the 'threat of nothingness is averted'[143] because we are not only beyond the sensory spheres of superficial diversions of the world but also effectively contributing our minds, and potentially influencing our communities, to a finer model of society. The finer model is a central goal of Cathy's work, both in her

---

[141]   Burnham, *Mozart's Grace*, p. 1.
[142]   Scruton, *Modern Culture*, 61.
[143]   Ibid.

166   *Music and Religion in the Writings of Ian McEwan*

decoding but also in the larger moral argument for her occupation during war-time. This, in turn, is reminiscent of the nineteenth-century concerns regarding the power of music and its relation to music and morals as discussed earlier in this chapter.

Burnham notes that 'what Mozart offers to modernity is the sound of the loss of innocence, the ever-renewable loss of innocence. That such a sound is beautiful may have nothing to do with Mozart and everything to do with us,'[144] and it could be argued that Mozart brings to the fore the best of Cathy's self. At the time of World War II, the setting of *The Imitation Game*, the loss of innocence and time is visceral, palpable, and often immediate. Burnham's comments illuminate the nature of music allowing us – and in this case specifically Mozart's music – to discover the purer side of ourselves. The central *Andantino* section, and the brief F major section with an Alberti bass in the *Fantasia* that Cathy plays, convey this sentiment of innocence, not least with comparatively simple and predictable phrase structures, especially by comparison to the rest of the piece which has both an improvisatory and impassioned aesthetic. Further, the sighing (or weeping) melodic gestures that are so characteristic of Mozart bring to mind the nature of falling tears through the simplest of musical devices. From the perspective of hearing while playing, the musical line is inherently imbued with a complex emotional palette that is nonetheless relatable. Rosen comments on the 'physical delight' to be taken in Mozart's 'sensuous play of sonority, and indulgence in the most luscious harmonic sequences', which aligns with Burnham's comments that 'perhaps no composer used the seductive physical power of music with the intensity and the range of Mozart'.[145] The F major section that Cathy plays and which initially has the oscillating repetitive pattern of an Alberti bass in the left hand and, meanwhile, an especially graceful and limpid right-hand line which floats freely above, as if unhindered, is like the play of a child who can observe any number of external acts but remains acutely focused on their own activity. Burnham's description of Mozart's ability to acquire these complementary states is apposite:

> If Mozart's music has not maintained an explicitly Christ-like presence, it has at the very least been perceived as a locus of goodness. The 'ever renewable loss of innocence'.
>
> Mozart's music can be heard to hover: between innocence and experience, ideality and sensuousness, comedy and tragedy, sympathy and mockery, intimacy and transcendence.[146]

Seen in the context of *The Imitation Game*, McEwan's narrative is therefore one of portraying Cathy as a source of thoughtfulness and wisdom and indeed elevated thinking. Her playing in the Officers' Mess can hardly be considered

[144]   Burnham, *Mozart's Grace*, p. 116.
[145]   Ibid., p. 35.
[146]   Ibid., pp. 166–168.

Influences and Perceptions of Music in Society 167

an indoctrination into the world of high art but it is nonetheless an open door to a broader artistic world than the environment an officer's mess would otherwise provide. Of real consequence is the nature of her own thinking and the balance between multiple intellectual and emotional layers as she pursues the secret life of her work and the even more secret life of her private time in thought, preparation, and practice at the piano. Marshall Brown writes of Mozart's 'revolutionary self-absorption', which has the ability to 'access some preconscious realm, some deeply interior space'.[147] With this in mind, Cathy's presence becomes a source of goodness and betterment in an otherwise functionary environment. The power of music is subtly communicated, and while certainly acting as a stabilizing presence in her own life it is, at the very least, an image of similar poise to those who know her. Given the male domination of the setting, it might also be considered a quiet, maternal presence and a double othering, firstly because it is a woman who brings music to the ears of others and secondly because the style of music is far removed from the typical songs of male officers when off duty and relaxing. Cathy becomes a beacon of a higher calling that in turn is a reminder of why a struggle for freedom in a world war is important. Principles, ethics, morals, and justice allow for the freedoms that Cathy cherishes and which she freely shares with others while nurturing a deeply personal self-discipline towards those goals. The narrative of *Black Dogs*, set in the aftermath of World War II, includes the following extract that offers a complementary perception of the nature of values during an era of war.

> Human nature, the human heart, the spirit, the soul, consciousness itself – call it what you like – in the end, it's all we've got to work with. It has to develop and expand, or the sum of our misery will never diminish. My own small discovery has been that this change is possible, it is within our power. Without a revolution of the inner life, however slow, all our big designs are worthless. The work we had to do is within ourselves if we're ever going to be at peace with each other. I'm not saying it'll happen. There's a good chance it won't. I'm saying it's our only chance. If it does, and it could take generations, the good that flows from it will shape our societies in an unprogrammed, unforeseen way, under the control of no single group of people or set of ideas.[148]

This narrative highlights the nature of the inner self as well as individual responsibility. The 'revolution of the inner life' is what Cathy is embarking on with her continued mastery of the score while the particular choice of work demands sustained introspection. The 'work within ourselves' is seen as the necessary route towards achieving the 'big designs'. Critically, the time it takes Cathy to perfect her professional work during the day and her musical work in her private time is part of a larger effort towards betterment on an individual level

---

[147] Marshall Brown, 'Mozart and After: The Revolution in Musical Consciousness', *Critical Inquiry*, 7 (1980–81), 689–706; Burnham, *Mozart's Grace*, p. 114.

[148] Ian McEwan, *Black Dogs* (London, 1998), p. 173.

that can ultimately be a source for larger societal improvement. It is 'within our power' because it is individual and thus 'no singular group of people or ideas' will govern its success. Rather, Cathy's approach can be seen as setting a standard and a discerning image within her social setting and representative of the 'lasting peace' and advancement that is part of the larger narrative. The transformative nature of musical reception and the choice of repertoire she selects are central to McEwan's portrayal.

4

'DON'T MAKE FUN OF THE FAIR':
THE COMPOSER IN TWENTIETH-CENTURY
BRITAIN

The Legacy of Perception

McEwan's knowledge of the profession of music and musicians is born from a familiarity with the inner workings of the field over several decades. This has arisen through friendships with many professional and amateur musicians, regular attendance at concerts, and his general interest in the field of performance since he was a child. The non-musician who reads his novels is presented with a narrative that relates the world of classical music in an accessible manner while in turn observing and commentating on its familiar scenarios, both positive and negative, to professional musicians who work in the field on a daily basis. Across several texts including novels and libretti his narratives dissect the presence of the classical musician in British society. In so doing he manages to reinforce certain aspects of perception that are generally known to the public while illuminating others. In discussing the libretto for the opera *For You*, that he conceived with the composer Michael Berkeley, and which is centred on a composer who is also a conductor, he commented on the nature of genius, egotism, and self-centredness in a musician as it can appear to others:

> I found it irresistible to write a story about a composer, because I find the act of composing such an interesting metaphor for creativity in its purest sense ... I wanted to explore the world of a creative obsessive and the way people are mesmerized by the power of that sort of genius.[1]

This quote exemplifies the approach of McEwan towards assessing the reason why musicians might be seen differently to others. Chapters 2 and 3 examine the aspects of sublimity and the powerful nature of music on the individual. This chapter evaluates the public perception and expectation of British society towards the professional musical world by examining the portrayals in *Amsterdam* and *For You* most specifically. As McEwan has commented, the composer can be seen as a 'metaphor for creativity' and the 'irresistible' quality of this

---

[1] Ashutosh Khandekar, 'Dual Purpose', *BBC Music Magazine*, 16:9 (May 2008), pp. 38–41.

170 *Music and Religion in the Writings of Ian McEwan*

view is founded upon his knowledge and perception of the subject matter. McEwan's approach in *For You* is to portray a larger-than-life composer whose character has few morals and a considerable ego, and to veil these observations with a measure of humour. In *Amsterdam*, the approach is markedly different as a composer is seen as doubting his own legacy and reputation within the field of classical music, but the stresses that relate to the lives of both composers in modern Britain are similar. The opera and the novel are both a satire and social critique that, as Richard Bradford argues,[2] Thatcherism revitalized. The desire for popularity and recognition is central to the characters' personalities. Dominic Head suggests that although *Amsterdam* is not generally seen as one of McEwan's most critically successful books,[3] it nonetheless portrays the central characters of Vernon Halliday and Clive Linley as 'representative of the professional achievers of the Thatcher-Major era', with the impression that 'professional standards have occluded ethical standards'.[4] As Jack Slay succinctly notes, they are 'men coming of age in the 1960s and 1970s, profiting from the 1980s, and securely ensconced in positions of authority by the 1990s'.[5] The consequence of this situation is that McEwan's criticism of politicians, which occurs throughout his works, meets uncomfortably with the world of the professional musician. This chapter examines how that balance occurs and equally how the public has come to expect a certain image of the composer in contemporary society. In order to establish how this situation has arisen, I shall begin by contextualising the role of the contemporary composer and the arts in Britain that preceded this 'coming of age'.

'Bankrolled by the State'[6] – State Support and Public Expectation

When Noël Coward wrote and performed the song, 'Don't Make Fun of the Fair', around the opening of the Festival of Britain in 1951, his contribution received the sort of mixed reception that would be little different if the Festival were to have happened in 2022. His approach is quintessentially British, with scepticism and sarcasm towards contemporary art and the expectation of a festival that celebrates the contemporary. There is a presumed and expected suspicion. Large-scale events by nature require government funding and with that the world of politics, committees, press coverage, public expectation, and constant scrutiny before during and after the Festival, which supported Coward's cynical text. The inherited legacy of the Festival of Britain was considerable because it was compared in the first instance to the Great Exhibition of 1851. More recently, the Festival was assessed retrospectively by comparing it

---

2   Richard Bradford, *The Novel Now* (Oxford, 2007), p. 30.

3   David Malcolm includes references to the positive and negative press reviews in *Understanding Ian McEwan* (Columbia, 2022) p. 190.

4   Dominic Head, *Ian McEwan* (Manchester, 2007), p. 24.

5   Jack Slay, Jr., *Ian McEwan* (New York, 1996), p. 8.

6   Ian McEwan, *The Child in Time* (London, 1992), p. 25.

The Composer in Twentieth-Century Britain   171

with the celebrations surrounding the Millennium Dome and the 2012 London Olympics. The writings of Robert Hewison (*Cultural Capital*, 2014*)* and Barry Turner (*Beacon for Change*, 2011) provide significant context to its place in twentieth-century British culture and the continued perception of the arts in britain. Coward's approach showed the popular view that is equally sustained in McEwan's narratives, most especially in *Amsterdam*, where a composer is commissioned by the government to write a new work to celebrate the millennium.

The question of whether there is fairness and indeed believability between Coward's and McEwan's texts is important to analyse, not least because of the popular appeal of both writers and their ability to continue to reinforce a public and popular perception. This is especially the case when both Coward and McEwan speak to the question of government funding. Coward's song title 'Don't Make Fun of the Fair' is, of course, the opposite of what the song, across several verses, manages to achieve in great detail through Coward's carefully acuminate critique. The song suggests that the financial resources ('all that's underwritten') are to be unquestioned because the 'dear Festival of Britain' must be allowed to succeed without censure ('don't let anyone sabotage'). The nature of exhibiting talent is frowned upon ('we've never been keen … on showing off our swank') and connected to financial rewards ('money in the bank'). Most critically, it is suggested that the performances could be sufficiently unstimulating that audiences could sleep in the concert hall so long as the outward impression made on foreign tourists remains positive. There is no redeeming element in the presentation of the Festival to the audience, and as the Festival sought to be a beacon of inspiration and entertainment, this is especially damning, even though it can be viewed through a humorous lens.

> Every day in every way
> Help the tourist to defray
> All that's underwritten
> Sell your rations and overcharge,
> And don't let anyone sabotage
> Our dear Festival of Britain.
>
> We've never been
> Exactly keen
> On showing off our swank
> But as they say
> That gay display
> Means money in the bank.
>
> Take a snooze in the concert hall,
> At least it's warmer than home.
> Show the foreign diplomats
> That our proletariat's
> Milder than a kitten.[7]

---

[7]   Barry Day (ed.), *The Lyrics of Noël Coward* (London, 1965), pp. 343–346.

172   *Music and Religion in the Writings of Ian McEwan*

The implicit criticism in Coward's song is little different from the subsequent criticism of the Millennium Dome and the venues of the 2012 Olympics. Head makes the connection that the somewhat doomed Millennium Symphony that is the focus of Clive (*Amsterdam*) inevitably leads to the memory of the problematic Millennium Dome.[8] The ubiquitous questions ask what will Britain be left with for a legacy that will endure and bring forward new ideas and creative possibilities. In the case of the arts, large-scale events draw attention to 1) the government's perception of its responsibility in relation to the arts and artists 2) what the taste of the public is understood to be and 3) to what extent either 1) or 2) should be supported by the state as opposed to privately funded. McEwan's commentaries and narratives take up these points from the Thatcher era to the present day, and his fictional narratives align with the perceptions of professional musicians, not least his collaborator on the oratorio *or Shall we die?* and the opera *For You*, the composer Michael Berkeley. *Amsterdam* includes a composer (Clive) who is hoping for one last great success, whereas *For You* is focused on a composer who is conducting his own music and who, by comparison, has been more successful in his career.

Amsterdam is a novel that examines both the nature of legacy and reputation for a composer (Clive) as well as the role of state support of the arts in Britain. One of the principal reasons that state support for the arts has to be considered essential is that the British tax system does not allow for individuals or corporations to receive the sort of significant tax incentives that are offered in other countries, not least the USA, to support arts organizations. Although the USA offers very little by way of direct support for the arts, especially by comparison to Scandinavian countries, it does allow individuals and corporations to benefit from a tax system that can facilitate a percentage of charitable donations being deductible on annual tax returns. As a consequence, the (in)direct support of the arts in the USA is considerable, but it is susceptible to popular trends and the influence of conservative programming wishes laid bare by wealthy donors. Concert series of popular works of the eighteenth and nineteenth centuries have traditionally been relatively easy to find donors for, whereas a concert series that solely promotes new music is far more difficult to gather support for, despite the fact there will be music of our own time and an artistic voice that represents the current generation. In Britain, the approach has been a muddled one for several decades and not exclusively related to which political party was in government. However, the Festival of Britain provides an important reference point for contextualising McEwan's two narratives with composers, and considering their believability, while appreciating the multiple issues at play for the British composer in the twentieth century.

To understand the values the Festival organizers considered important, it is critical to appreciate the model of the Great Exhibition. The Exhibition had set a standard, adopted by all the successor trade exhibitions in Britain, France, and

---

[8]   Head, *Ian McEwan*, p. 147.

The Composer in Twentieth-Century Britain   173

the United States, of spectacular displays which sought to 'Improve the taste of the middle classes, to inform manufacturers about mechanical improvements and to morally educate the working class'.[9] Postwar, the aspect of moral education or betterment was not a primary concern in Britain as a country that had only recently been fighting in a world war and knew only too well the costs of moral decisions. But the nature of improving taste was unquestionably supplanted by a strong desire to assert a British identity in the arts while broadening a public understanding of the creative world. Coward's description of Britain in his song points out that the adventurous nature of any festival would lead to some successes but also many points of contention. It is impossible to please everyone. However, after a generation of essential government directives related to wartime affairs, the Festival was able to cultivate an environment of individualism. For creative workers, making the 'new' allowed for a measure of personal autonomy.[10] However, as Barry Turner writes in *Beacon for Change*, the question of the role of the arts, despite Britain's long cultural heritage, was a debate in itself:

> What is art? In any other European country, the question would have sounded faintly ridiculous. But in Britain of the 1950s, even a broad definition was elusive. The popular reaction against anything new was shared by many of the cultural elite (one reason why European artists of the inter-war years are so poorly represented in British collections) and extended from the fine arts to music, literature, drama and film, though some even disputed that film deserved consideration as an art at all.[11]

In trying to establish the role of the Festival in relation to the 1851 Great Exhibition, Robert Lutyens, architect, identified the essential difference as attempting a balance between 'the enthusiasm of blond, bearded art students in duffle coats and the scepticism of so-called reactionaries'.[12] This comment highlights the fact that, to Lutyens, no critical constituency was likely to be satisfied. In this respect, the nature of Coward's scepticism was not only felt more broadly in the artistic community but mirrored a public perception that hampered the efforts of the director, Gerald Barry, from the outset. The debates about the role of art music in British society and the question of whether a reasoned political and critical debate can produce an excellent end result are relative to both *Amsterdam* and *For You*. When funding is consistently limited and politicians with specific motives are involved, many compromises become unavoidable, as will be examined with particular reference to *Amsterdam*. In *For You*, the cynical edge of Coward is translated towards the contemporary artist. It is for these reasons that Turner quite rightly described the Festival as

---

[9]   Barry Turner, *Beacon for Change* (London, 2011), p. 11.

[10]   Robert Hewison, *Cultural Capital* (London, 2014), p. 5.

[11]   Turner, *Beacon for Change*, p. 185.

[12]   Ibid., p. 127.

174   *Music and Religion in the Writings of Ian McEwan*

a beacon but observed that in the long-term, Barry's vision, as its director, was only partially fulfilled. It was an almost impossible remit given the degree of public scepticism.

> For the first time since the war, ordinary citizens were given a vision of the future which took them beyond the everyday concerns of keeping body and soul together. They might not have liked everything they saw but they were made aware that design was for living, that the arts need not to be elitist and that technology was stronger in promise than in threat. The Festival was a beacon for change. The light may have flickered over the years, but for those five glorious months in 1951 it was bright and strong.[13]

Part of the challenge of the Festival was providing a series of events that could draw high critical praise and offer something new while drawing an audience that was suspicious of what it perceived as overt originality. Above all, the audience sought a measure of comfort and entertainment in a postwar environment. The Festival provided both in ample measure but in terms of the legacy in relation to high art, the potential boost that could have been provided was limited by the relative inaction of successive governments. Although, as a result of the Festival, the Arts Council and the Council for Industrial Design came into their own as cultural lobbies, with access to government funds, and in the following decade grants to museums, galleries, and the performing arts increased fourfold,[14] the legacy of sustained cuts to the arts from the Thatcher era onwards, coupled with the problematic competitive nature of the 'Cool Britannia' approach of Blair's government, left the arts in Britain begging for support, despite a worldwide reputation for excellence and innovation. For the conservative establishment who felt that the 'arts were a costly extravagance with no hope of a political return,'[15] it is unsurprising that 'elegant fun' was a phrase that cropped up frequently in Barry's speeches and articles out of necessity, with the hope of seeming popular. In this he echoed Samuel Johnson, who had spoken admiringly of the Vauxhall Gardens as 'that excellent place of public entertainment ... peculiarly adapted to the taste of the English nation, there being a mixture of curious show and gay exhibition, music, vocal and instrumental, not too refined for the general ear ... and good eating and drinking for those who choose to purchase that regale.'[16] Johnson, Barry, Coward, and, as will be shown, McEwan all speak to a country where the arts are consistently viewed as an entertainment rather than a cultural need or indeed part of a valued national identity that should merit consistent support. The criticism towards innovation amidst cynicism and wariness about anything new can be

[13]   Ibid., p. 258.

[14]   Ibid., p. 236.

[15]   Ibid., 245.

[16]   Ibid., p. 89.

seen as aligned with the history that Johnson referred to, with the historical expectation of entertainment first.

When considering the state of the Church of England as discussed in chapter 1, it is interesting that Turner considered Coventry Cathedral to be the apotheosis of the overall festival,[17] and that despite the challenges that Coventry has faced since the war, the cathedral remains a continuing embodiment of the arts in contemporary society. It was the site for the premiere of Britten's *War Requiem* while also being home to John Piper's baptistry window, Graham Sutherland's tapestry, and Basil Spence's provoking design for a new cathedral, positioned alongside the old cathedral that had been so severely damaged by bombing in 1940.

Politics, the Arts, and State Funding

The idea that fine arts could be a necessary force for good has been especially challenged since the Thatcher government limited the amount of artistic activities taught in state schools and especially removed the ability for children to study an instrument at no cost. In this respect, Robert Hewison's comments that beauty makes our public servants nervous[18] and that governments are not committed to 'enhancing the quality of life'[19] has especial resonance within McEwan's writings. In *The Child in Time* it is commented that:

> The idea that the more educated the population the more readily could its problems be solved had quietly faded away. It belonged with the demise of a more general principle that on the whole life would get better for more and more people and that it was the responsibility of governments to stage-manage this drama of realised potential, widening possibilities. The cast of improvers had once been immense and there had always been jobs for types like Stephen and his friends. Teachers, museum keepers, mummers, actors, itinerant story-tellers – a huge company and all bankrolled by the State. Now governmental responsibilities had been redefined in simpler, purer terms: to keep order, and to defend the State against its enemies.[20]

The 'cast of improvers' that had been cultivated and supported during the Festival was dealt a hard blow by the Thatcher government, with the removal of support for the arts and the promotion of an ideology that art worth sustaining could sustain itself. Johnson's comments (above) still apply because the arts that are easiest to sustain are dependent on a broad appeal. Supporting what is popular is natural to politicians but it does not necessarily encourage advance-

---

[17] Ibid., p. 240.

[18] Hewison, *Cultural Capital*, p. 6.

[19] Ibid., p. 17.

[20] McEwan, *The Child in Time*, p. 25.

176 *Music and Religion in the Writings of Ian McEwan*

ment at all. McEwan's narrative suggests that society was better off when it considered 'widening possibilities' that the government took ownership in. Encouraging the imagination supports broader thinking more generally, both by individuals and society at large, as opposed to the 'simpler' thinking that had replaced it.

When Lord Melbourne commented in 1835, 'God help the minister that meddles with art', the country was still very largely, and almost entirely for the remainder of the century, dependent on the goodwill of philanthropists to support local arts bodies and was soon (1840) to have a Prince Consort who was deeply committed to the arts. But as philanthropy during the twentieth century became a smaller competitive field, a vacuum for the support of the arts has emerged. This has occurred despite the considerable benefits to social welfare and cohesiveness. The history of philanthropy from civic leaders in the nineteenth and early twentieth centuries was seldom followed in the second half of the twentieth century to the same degree. Yet as Kingsley Amis's[21] Professor Welch observed in *Lucky Jim* (1954), published just three years after the Festival, the relationship of music to an understanding of a society should be unavoidable:

> It may perhaps be thought that the character of an age, a nation, a class, would be but poorly revealed in anything so apparently divorced from ordinary habits of thought as its music, as its musical culture.

Nothing could be further from the truth.[22]

As Robert Hewison has commented: 'politics and the arts are both ways of making meaning. Above all, politics and the arts have a common interest in shaping a society's wider culture – culture, that is, not just as a way of life, but as a way of organizing life',[23] while also noting that in Enlightenment thinking, the arts occupy a separate place to politics and the market, and have universal and eternal values.[24] The narrative in *The Child in Time* (above) describes a society where these values have been removed. Published during the years of Blair's 'Cool Britannia', when the government's approach to the arts was inconsistent, the legacy of the Thatcher era remained largely unbroken. McEwan's narrative draws on the memory of better times when, as in his own experience,[25] folksongs were learned in schools and subsidy for the arts provided opportunities for people through much of the country. It is not simply a matter of funding performances and exhibitions but the vision of a better society that McEwan

---

[21] Kingsley Amis is described in *Sweet Tooth* (New York, 2012, p. 84) as 'a comic novelist, brilliantly observant with something quite merciless about his humour'.

[22] Kingsley Amis, *Lucky Jim* (New York, 1954), p. 171.

[23] Hewison, *Cultural Capital*, p. 3.

[24] Ibid., p. 20.

[25] Iain Quinn, 'Interview with Ian McEwan' (2018).

The Composer in Twentieth-Century Britain   177

describes, and which is enriched through an exposure to broader experiences. It is this view that the director Richard Eyre, who worked with McEwan on *The Imitation Game*, communicated when highlighting the disparity between the aspirations of society and the realities of government funding decisions:

> We can justify the subsidized arts on the grounds of cost effectiveness, or as tourist attractions, or as investments, or as commodities that can be marketed, exploited and profited from, but the arts should make their own argument. They are part of our life, our language, our way of seeing; they are a measure of our civilization. The arts tell us truths about ourselves and our feelings and our society that reach parts of us that politics and journalism don't. They entertain, they give pleasure, they give hope, they ravish the senses, and above all they help us fit the disparate pieces of the world together; to try and make form out of chaos.[26]

The impact that this troubled environment has had on composers has been significant because with a lack of sufficient support there has also been a rise in criticism towards bodies that have received funding. The response to Harrison Birtwistle's opera, *Gawain*, in its revival at the Royal Opera House in 1994, was a signal moment and helps to contextualise the relationship between a composer and the state as seen in *Amsterdam*, and *For You*, an opera that lays bare aspects of the creative process. Birtwistle was one of Britain's most decorated composers, having received both a knighthood and the Companion of Honour (CH). Two protestors, Frederick Stocken and Keith Burstein, both composers, styled as 'The Hecklers', arranged a demonstration against the atonal musical style of the opera. Stocken commented: 'We want to see a return of classical music with popular appeal, not this arch-modernist stuff which gives you a migraine.'[27] The challenge to the arts was presented quite starkly in this statement whereby the popular was set against the modernist with no discussion of composers who might provide a *via media*. The comment highlights the great divide post-Thatcher that has emerged between the popular composer of classical music who is met with suspicion because of financial success and the modernist who is distrusted because of their relative lack of interest in populism. When Clive (*Amsterdam*) speaks of his desire to create a tune that will be remembered long into the future and help people understand the nature of music,[28] he addresses a hope that he can find the narrow path between the general public's appreciation and the response of colleagues and critics.

Performances at the Royal Opera House receive state funding and so this episode briefly raised questions about the nature of state funding of the arts,

---

[26] Richard Eyre, 'Report on the Future of the Lyric Theatre in London' (1988); Hewison, *Cultural Capital*, p. x.

[27] Esther Oxford, 'A noisy night at the opera: Esther Oxford reports on a clash that is looming between traditionalist music lovers and avant-garde rivals at Covent Garden', *Independent* (10 April 1994).

[28] Ian McEwan, *Amsterdam* (London, 2005), p. 21.

178   *Music and Religion in the Writings of Ian McEwan*

in a similar vein to the almost annual questioning of exhibits at Tate Modern. However, Turner's comments above about the nature of art in Britain ('What is art?') are part of this debate because as Dr Johnson succinctly illuminated, the very nature of public expectation of the arts in Britain is towards 'fun' and entertainment rather than a deeper meaning that, in the case of *Gawain*, could be achieved by supporting a work of our own time even if its value might (only) be defined as momentary or transitional. It nonetheless reflects an artistic voice of the period, and history has shown us that contemporary audiences have often struggled with art of their own time. Tastes, though, cannot be forced on people, and while Michael Berkeley has noted[29] that the style of Birtwistle's music has not appealed to McEwan, the music of Thomas Adès and George Benjamin certainly has. Berkeley considers that McEwan, along with many in the general public, has a limited enthusiasm for contemporary music that does not embody a degree of lyricism and recognizable melodic content. However, even though their collaboration on the opera *For You* involved a score that had a fragmented approach to tonality, McEwan came to hear and appreciate the differing musical language, which Berkeley was unsurprised by given McEwan's other intellectual pursuits.[30]

While McEwan does not write extensively about the composers of contemporary music, but rather music of the Baroque and Classical periods, his approach towards narratives that feature composers shows an understanding of the different aspects of perception and reception of modern composers. The following comment to the composer, Clive (*Amsterdam*), is an example of the specific nature of perception that McEwan demonstrates:

> 'You're the composer? ... My eleven-year-old granddaughter studied your sonatina for her grade exam in violin and really loved it.'

> The thought of children playing his music made him feel faintly depressed.[31]

Most contemporary composers of art music do not aspire to have their music played solely by children for the purpose of passing an examination, after which their piece is customarily discarded as another takes its place for a subsequent examination. This explains Clive's depressed response.[32] The fact that this piece might end up being the most well-performed piece of his output, known to future generations of professional musicians, and have a measure of commercial success, is not a parallel to the acceptance of a major work by the profession at large for a piece that is regarded as being of substance and therefore contributing to the greater canon. The comment has a certain belittling effect on Clive because it lessens, though not necessarily cheapens, the art that he is contrib-

---

[29]   Iain Quinn, 'Interview with Michael Berkeley' (2018).

[30]   Ibid.

[31]   McEwan, *Amsterdam*, pp. 9–10.

[32]   Ibid., 10.

The Composer in Twentieth-Century Britain   179

uting to, especially as it comes from a minister whose government is supporting an important new commission for him. In a similar vein of artistic-societal disconnectedness, a reference in *Black Dogs* also demonstrates the separation between the artist and the entertainer. The description (below) mirrors a regular occurrence at the BBC Proms when a piano concerto is performed. The applause suggests that part of the nature of the arts is the public appeal of spectacle. The 'well-meaning' aspect that describes the action has a cynical tone to it that relates to an impression that a performance cannot be taken too seriously – or simply will not be taken seriously – by the sort of audience that claps at trivial occurrences. McEwan bolsters that idea by criticizing it as 'foolish'. Thus, he refers to an event that he assumes a reader will be familiar with, but with some judgement. As the clapping when a piano lid is raised occurs at popular concerts (like the Proms), this reinforces the societal challenge of perception for the professional musician, and especially the fragile world of the composer, in a sceptical society.

> From the crowd ... there came a round clapping. It was of the foolish, well-meaning kind you might hear from a concert audience when the grand piano is lifted on to the stage.[33]

Audiences at the Wigmore Hall, where McEwan frequently attends concerts, and which is a focus of *On Chesil Beach*, do not cheer or applaud when a piano lid is raised but Proms audiences have for many years. It is in good fun (to borrow from Dr Johnson), and that part of the nature of the Proms, just as the speech from the conductor on the Last Night of the Proms, has become a tradition along with flag waving. But McEwan draws a line between the sophisticated environment of the Wigmore Hall that he discusses in detail in *On Chesil Beach* and the popular environment of many classical music concerts. The popular and entertaining aspects are brushed aside whereas the elevated world of chamber concerts or the choices individuals make for the music they perform or listen to (as discussed in chapters 2 and 3) are considered in detail.

The nuances of the public reception of music and musicians are central to an understanding of the life of the professional musician, not least because of how they relate to fragile artistic personalities such as Charles (*For You*) and Clive (*Amsterdam*). It also illustrates the critical focus of a telescopic vision towards the self that is typical in the nature of artistic devotion as seen most especially with Florence in *On Chesil Beach* but also with Charles and Clive. In this regard, McEwan reinforces a perception that aligns with sentiments within the profession. The composer, Elizabeth Lutyens, remarked that 'composing is so absorbing that there is simply no room for anything else,'[34] and this state-

---

[33]   Ian McEwan, *Black Dogs* (London, 1998), p. 82.

[34]   Murray Schafer, 'Elizabeth Lutyens', *British Composers in Interview* (London, 1963), p. 106.

180   *Music and Religion in the Writings of Ian McEwan*

ment summarizes the nature of the preferred personal freedom and individuality that both Charles and Clive seek.

A contrasting approach towards state funding of the arts is portrayed in *Sweet Tooth*. McEwan's narrative raises the subject of CIA involvement in the cultural cold war. When Serena is approached by her superiors to consider the possibility of recruiting British authors to unknowingly write for government-supported publications, the CIA-backed *Encounter* magazine, edited by Melvin Lasky, is given as an example of past and established practice. The conundrum that authors faced in relation to their professional independence and integrity is described as follows in *Sweet Tooth*:

> *Encounter* was funded by the CIA. There was a stink, a lot of arm-waving and shouting, various writers took flight with their consciences.[35]

Encounter was part of an (initially) secret programme of cultural propaganda in Western Europe, funded with more resources 'than anyone would ever realise'.[36] A CIA centrepiece in the cultural Cold War was the Congress for Cultural Freedom which was run by a CIA agent, Michael Josselson, from 1950 until 1967. With offices in thirty-five countries and over twenty published magazines, it arranged art exhibitions, owned a news and features service, organized international conferences and bestowed prizes on musicians and artists, while also arranging numerous public performances.[37] The impact on American composers was considerable, especially in cultural showcases in Berlin. Samuel Barber, Leonard Bernstein, Elliott Carter, Aaron Copland, George Gershwin, Gian Carlo Menotti, and Virgil Thomson all had their works premiered in Europe under the auspices of the US government.[38] As McEwan portrays in *Sweet Tooth*, this involved employees of the government learning the 'delicate art of stroking the egos of intellectual prima donnas [while organizing] tours by an American ballet company, and orchestras, [presenting] modern art shows and more than a dozen conferences' that could be described as occupying the 'hazardous terrain where politics and literature meet'.[39] However, one of the most significant events promoted was a 1949 conference held at the Waldorf Hotel in New York City, billed as the Cultural and Scientific Conference for World Peace, with well-known figures from the USSR and the USA. Although the luminaries included Arthur Miller and Leonard Bernstein, other figures were 'critical or distrustful of an American government that was asking its citizens to treat a former invaluable ally as a dangerous enemy'.[40] Indeed, in the 1946–1947 concert season of the New York Philharmonic children's concerts

---

[35]   Ian McEwan, *Sweet Tooth* (New York, 2012), p. 85.

[36]   Ibid., p. 287.

[37]   Frances Stonor Saunders, *The Cultural Cold War* (New York, 2013), p. 1.

[38]   Ibid., p. 18.

[39]   McEwan, *Sweet Tooth*, p. 229.

[40]   Ibid., p. 228.

The Composer in Twentieth-Century Britain   181

there were two performances featuring Russian music titled 'Music of Russia – Our Great Ally'. For musicians, the conference was ultimately seen as a critical moment for understanding the pressure on Soviet musicians. The distinguished Russian composer Dmitri Shostakovich was questioned directly on the earlier unattributed published statements in the state publication, *Pravda*. It had described the composers Paul Hindemith, Arnold Schoenberg, and Igor Stravinsky as 'obscurantists', 'decadent bourgeois formalists', and 'lackeys of imperialist capitalism' whose music should 'therefore be prohibited in the U.S.S.R'. In his ashen-faced response Shostakovich murmured in Russian: 'I fully agree with the statements made in *Pravda*.'[41] As McEwan describes the situation, he was 'shown to be miserably trapped between his conscience and his fear of displeasing his KGB handlers and what Stalin would do to him when he got home'.[42] However, in his memoirs published thirty years later, Shostakovich commented that 'I still recall with horror my first trip to the USA. I would not have gone at all if it hadn't been for intense pressure from administrative figures of all ranks and colours, from Stalin down. People sometimes say it must have been an interesting trip, look at the way I am smiling in the photographs. That was the smile of a condemned man. I felt like a dead man.'[43] McEwan's narrative continues; 'the CIA had been backing its own highbrow notion of culture since the end of the forties. The idea had been to try to lure left-of-centre European intellectuals away from the Marxist perspective and make it intellectually respectable to speak up for the Free World. Our friends [the Americans] have sloshed a lot of cash around by way of various fronts.' However, when the funding source and the nature of *Encounter* had become public knowledge the idea lost its appeal, although the works that had been created were now part of the canon. A considerable amount of money had been invested in the CIA project, and McEwan's portrayal[44] rests heavily on providing the narrative of the circumstance without an obvious judgement.

The approach of British intelligence in *Sweet Tooth* is one with a 'modest budget, no international festivals, no first-class flights, no twenty-pantechnicon orchestra tours, no bean feasts'[45] and as such far smaller in ambition than the US model. The CIA official turned broadcaster, Tom Braden, remarked that the United States was 'the only country on the planet that didn't understand that some things work better when they're small'.[46] This contrasting approach suited the British on multiple levels. Braden noted that CIA projects had become overblown and overfunded, although that option may have been music to the ears of the British intelligence officers who were scraping by on modest

[41]   Saunders, *The Cultural Cold War*, p. 42.

[42]   McEwan, *Sweet Tooth*, p. 229.

[43]   Saunders, *The Cultural Cold War*, p. 43.

[44]   McEwan, *Sweet Tooth*, p. 86.

[45]   Ibid.

[46]   Ibid., p. 230.

182   *Music and Religion in the Writings of Ian McEwan*

financial resources. Far from being welcomed, the Americans had become resented because of their heavy-handed approach.[47] In *Sweet Tooth*, the British would focus on young writers at the start of their careers who needed financial backing and some time off to focus on their writing.[48] When Serena (*Sweet Tooth*) asked why such a programme could not simply be arranged through the Arts Council, it was explained to her that the literature section was overseen by Angus Wilson, a man who fitted the bill as a relative Establishment figure having been a former naval attaché, a member of the Athenaeum, and also associated with Bletchley Park. As such, he bridged the literary and secret government worlds. However, when Wilson had been approached about the secret plan to fund writers he 'all but threw [the intelligence officer] out of a third-floor window'[49] over the suggestion. The intelligence officer commented to Serena on the irony that when Britain acted in this way it was criticized, and yet the Soviets financed concerts of the Red Army Chorus at the Royal Albert Hall which were sold out.[50] Although McEwan's narrative does not question the nature of support for the arts, it does question the illogical nature of the opposition argument given that 'here in Britain no one was ever troubled by the Foreign Office paying for the BBC World Service, which was highly regarded'[51]and promoted British interests and community around the world.

Tonality

The subject of tonality, or more specifically, atonality, is brought front and centre in an especially detailed description in *Amsterdam*, during which McEwan not only demonstrates his significant knowledge of the arguments at play in the fields of contemporary music but also how this would be understood from a composer's perspective. Clive considered himself a successor to Ralph Vaughan Williams and largely ignored the criticism that suggested that as a modern composer he needed to be more avant-garde.[52]

To consider himself an heir of Vaughan Williams demonstrates not just self-confidence, but a certain arrogance given the reverence that the late composer was and is held in. Vaughan Williams had an extremely successful career in multiple areas of the profession, including being a collector of folk songs, musical editor of the *English Hymnal*, an internationally respected symphonist, as well as a composer of vocal, chamber, and instrumental music, and a pub-

---

[47]   Ibid.

[48]   Ibid., p. 87

[49]   Ibid., p. 89.

[50]   Ibid.

[51]   Ibid., p. 230.

[52]   McEwan, *Amsterdam*, p. 21.

The Composer in Twentieth-Century Britain   183

lished author. Although Clive might consider himself to follow in these footsteps, there is no complementary commentary within *Amsterdam* that suggests anyone else holds that opinion or that he has worked across quite so many fields. However, Clive's observation regarding the support of modernism in the music colleges is true insofar that they allowed composers to develop their compositions, and indeed research, irrespective of the need for performance or relative commercial success. One of the leading advocates for new music that did not necessarily have to be performed by performers but rather through computers, and not necessarily heard by a 'live' audience but in recordings, was the Princeton-based composer Milton Babbitt. His seminal article, 'Who cares if you listen?'[53] succinctly summed up a perceived need, strongly supported by the academic community, to break away from the restrictions of writing with a large audience in mind. In Britain, those composers who did not adhere to the new prescript, which separated the historic relationship of the composer from the performer and the audience, were considered outside the core of modernists. However, several achieved considerable success nonetheless and included William Alwyn, Richard Arnell, Malcolm Arnold, Wilfred Josephs, and Leonard Salzedo. They were composers who were also well known in the fields of film and television music. In the case of Salzedo, the opening of his *Divertimento for three trumpets and three trombones* served as the music for the Open University broadcasts from the 1970s to the 1990s. These composers' relative commercial success and consequent public presence outstripped the few composers who were experimenting with technology, but academia provided a consistent and effectively subsidized home for many composers.

The words (below) of Herbert Howells – a composer who was largely known for his many tonal compositions written for cathedral and collegiate choirs – in preparation for a BBC radio programme that looked at the extremities of modernism in new music, bear resonance as the same arguments are still being waged in the twenty-first century. Howells did not rule out avant-garde music, but he cautioned against extreme examples:

Atonality: This is the real threat to continued sympathy and contact as between listener and composer. The ordinary listener's extreme difficulties in the presence of a language whose structures, symbols and syntax are foreign to him.

The search for repose and beauty in contemporary music can yield further 'reconciliation' if made with an open mind. It is paradoxically true that, though the strongly contrapuntal bias of modern music has often put a limit upon our receptive powers, it is in the new counterpoint that an unexpected beauty can be found ... the quieter voice of modernity is best heard and most appealing.[54]

---

[53]   Milton Babbitt, 'Who cares if you listen?', *High Fidelity*, 8:2 (1958), 38–40.

[54]   Lewis Foreman (ed.), *From Parry to Britten – British Music in Letters, 1900–1945* (Portland, 1987), pp. 195, 197.

184   *Music and Religion in the Writings of Ian McEwan*

Howells continues by giving examples of works by Walton ('a master of this type of appeal'), and selected movements of Stravinsky, Hindemith, Berg, Vaughan Williams, and Constant Lambert as models of modern music that can relate to a contemporary audience. The value placed on quiet solemnity is seen to be no less relevant in Howells' interwar (1936) commentary than McEwan's observations at the end of the century, as discussed in chapter 2, or the successes of John Tavener or Henryk Górecki. Of Clive (*Amsterdam*), McEwan continues, 'Surely its [new music's] advocates, rather than he himself, were the reactionaries. In 1975, [Clive] published a hundred-page book which, like all good manifestos, was both attack and apologia. The old guard of modernism had imprisoned music in the academy where it was "jealously professionalized", "isolated" and rendered "sterile", [and] its vital covenant with a general public arrogantly broken.'[55]

These comments have a critical invective that relates to McEwan's own tastes as observed by Michael Berkeley,[56] and it is a blunt censure. It is not just that modernism was 'professionalized' by the academy but the inference that by its removal from the critical reception of the public it would have a certain irrelevance. It would be 'isolated' and, most critically, 'rendered sterile'. The summative argument that the essential contract between the composer, the performer, and the audience was 'broken' has remained an ongoing debate within the music profession for decades. However, McEwan's portrayal of this circumstance is presented with a weight of evidence that is recognizable to musicians.

A 'covenant with the general public'

The fracturing of a 'covenant with the general public' is a crucial statement in McEwan's writings and commentaries concerning music, because while showing the positive elements of music in the lives of characters and in society generally, as discussed in the previous two chapters, here he presents a blunt narrative on what is unacceptable. Whether McEwan's own preferences are towards Mozart or the avant-garde is irrelevant in this statement. Rather, it is the central matter of communication, of translation of a musical language from the composer's mind to that of the performer or listener and the place of that relationship. McEwan illustrates the challenge in *Amsterdam* with the description of a concert that had received a subsidy, and which included a piece that involved the brutal treatment of both a piano and a violin for an extended period.[57] Not only is the relationship with the audience, whether performer or listener, fragmented, but even the instrument is subject to brutalization. That this

---

[55]   McEwan, *Amsterdam*, p. 22.

[56]   Quinn, 'Interview with Michael Berkeley'.

[57]   McEwan, *Amsterdam*, p. 22.

artistic approach is described as relating to the Holocaust, with the argument that this was the only form of music making that could now be considered, reinforces the scepticism. McEwan presents the composer of an avant-garde piece in the weakest of all lights. Aside from the issue of hitting one instrument with another, the composer is reliant on the emotional response of the performer and the listener to first think of the Holocaust and then align their emotions with the piece being played and heard. McEwan shows little interest in programmatic music either in his novels or his own personal tastes. As such, this avant-garde piece is viewed with a brazen cynicism, and McEwan draws a clear line between art that is appreciated and art that is incomprehensible to him. Such is his familiarity with the topic that when read through the eyes of a professional musician, there is an unremitting edge of sarcasm to the narrative.

As with many of the scientific topics that McEwan discusses, the commentaries he expresses regarding modern music – a difficult term because some composers can be considered modern in approach and others (simply) contemporary figures – touch quite knowingly on a debate that has been at the forefront of artistic concerns in Britain since government funding for the arts began after World War II. The presence of atonal music was already a well-established part of the larger musical world, if not consistently the concert world. Roger Scruton offered a commentary that spoke to the perceived challenges: 'the first effect of modernism was to make high-culture difficult: to surround beauty with a wall of erudition. The hidden purpose was twofold: to protect art against popular entertainment, and to create a new barrier, a new obstacle to membership, and a new rite of passage to the adult and illuminated sphere.'[58] There are exceptions to this rule, and Benjamin Britten is the most notable British example because he managed to achieve considerable success even though he wrote tonal music and did not pander towards sentimental styles. The significance of Britten in McEwan's writings can be observed pointedly in *Lessons* when Miriam Cornell discusses a visit to Aldeburgh.

> She described driving to Aldeburgh to hear Benjamin Britten give a talk about string quartets. Roland said that the name meant nothing to him. She drew him closer to her and kissed his nose and said, "We've got a lot of work to do on you".[59]

However, in terms of repertoire written post-1970, Scruton argues that modernists felt betrayed, not by modernism itself but by popular culture that needed to be resisted at all costs. To that end, if the public showed little enthusiasm for modernism, it reflected a larger need for modernism to rescue it from a downwardly spiralling society. Scruton's critical comments on constructionist paintings could equally be applied to music that achieves only small audiences because the public rightly or wrongly consider it inaccessible. 'The "presence"

---

[58] Roger Scruton, *Modern Culture* (London, 2005), p. 85.

[59] Ian McEwan, *Lessons* (New York, 2022), p. 135.

186   *Music and Religion in the Writings of Ian McEwan*

of the works is an *official* presence, and their very dullness serves to emphasize their message, which is that art is no longer a reflection on human life but a mechanism for excluding it.'[60] The potential challenge to Clive (*Amsterdam*) as well as to Charles (*For You*) is to surpass the inaccessible label of artistic remoteness. Charles is less concerned by this, although mostly because of his ego, but for Clive, seeing his commission for the millennium as a last chance at professional renewal, and perhaps as a result, great fame, it is considerable. However, the burden of state support is one that further complicates matters for the politicians, the public, and the composers. Writing in 1990, Jeremy Paxman noted:

> The plain fact is that the arts on their present scale are just unviable: the national appetite is greater than the national capacity. The development of state sponsorship for the arts after the Second World War has been one of the many success stories of the Welfare State. But it not only created a caste of arts bureaucrat, it insulated the artist from the most basic fact of life, that to survive he or she must have customers.

> The Arts Council was the most benign of patrons, studiously refusing to interfere with the creative process. It distorts the natural relationship between the state of the economy and the conditions of the arts, [and] allowed them to flourish while the circumstances of the nation continued to deteriorate.[61]

This comment is supported by a statement of Malcolm Arnold, a composer well known in the concert world and for his many film scores. The 'natural relationship' that had previously existed had largely been 'broken'.[62] (McEwan).

> perhaps this is the reason so few people want to listen to modern music. The composer has insulated himself to such an extent that he has become incomprehensible to the ordinary musical public. I think this is so, and, as such, I put it as a criticism of modern music, which regards truth as more important than beauty.[63]

To those composers who achieved any measure of popular success, such as Górecki (see below), an unconscionable Rubicon had been crossed for proponents of new music. It is no coincidence that one of the reasons that Andrew Lloyd Webber was so readily criticized in the 1980s by the classical music establishment was not just because of his financial success but because Margaret Thatcher – the Prime Minister responsible for the greatest cuts to the arts in schools – considered him her favourite composer because he was self-sufficient and popular. This was in no small measure because he didn't require any state funding. Further, as a politician who had styled herself as being against the

---

[60] Scruton, *Modern Culture*, p. 90.

[61] Paxman, *Friends in High Places* (London, 1990), p. 309.

[62] McEwan, *Amsterdam*, p. 23.

[63] Schafer, 'Malcolm Arnold', *British Composers in Interview* , p. 154.

The Composer in Twentieth-Century Britain   187

old class system, her attacks on the ultra-traditional world of classical music, especially as it was often viewed in relation to wealthy patrons at the Royal Opera House, supported her larger agenda of at least wanting to be perceived as being a representative of the people working on behalf of the marginalized. But, as noted in *Amsterdam*, 'In the small minds of the zealots, Clive insisted, any form of success, however limited, any public appreciation whatsoever, was a sure sign of aesthetic compromise and failure'[64] because success was met with suspicion. This was a curious irony of the Thatcher era because the nature of success in the world of professional classical music is not measured by financial achievement.

An outcome of the estrangement from the public can be seen in the conservative and cautious approach towards programming that can then prevail. John Drummond, then director of the prestigious Edinburgh Festival observed: 'We put on the sort of concerts that won't frighten the directors' wives'[65] and as a consequence keep the margin of failure, but also ambition, very limited. As Paxman commented, a consequence of the state's approach towards the Arts Council enabled audiences to gradually shrink, thus fulfilling the government's argument (and that of its allied bodies) that the arts were no longer relatable. Roy Strong noted that the government's 'attitude to public funding of the arts was rather like Lenin's attitude to religion, that if you created the right conditions, it would just wither away'.[66] The result was that many artists felt, in the words of the director Peter Hall, 'demoralized, cowed, [and] sullen',[67] as their own artistic goals had been hindered by inconsistent support. For McEwan, 'England under Mrs Thatcher leaves me with a nasty taste'.[68] The legacy of that era and the suspicion of the creative arts world has continued to linger in British society and McEwan's portrayal of a contemporary composer, such as Clive, summarizes the difficult balance between populism, success, and professional recognition. But the arguments and the ironies are also part of the landscape of national identity that McEwan is portraying. As Alan Bennett commented:

> We're conceived in irony. We float in it from the womb. It's the amniotic fluid. It's the silver sea. It's the waters at their priest-like-task, washing away the guilt and purpose and responsibility. Joking but not joking. Caring but not caring. Serious but not serious.[69]

Clive's career shows the failure of a system whereby new music can only be heard in camera or with specific external support and where the audience, and potentially the performer (in the case of music 'performed' using computers),

[64]   McEwan, *Amsterdam*, p. 22.

[65]   Quoted in Roy Shaw, *The Arts and the People* (London, 1987), p. 62.

[66]   Paxman, *Friends in High Places*, p. 305; Interview with Roy Strong.

[67]   Ibid., p. 304.

[68]   John Haffenden, *Novelists in Interview* (London, 1985), p. 187.

[69]   Alan Bennett, *The Old Country* (London, 1978), p. 58.

188   *Music and Religion in the Writings of Ian McEwan*

are completely excluded. The analysis of the legacy of the British composer in *Amsterdam* continues: 'In art music, only the first half of the century would figure significantly and then only certain composers, among whom Clive did not number the later Schoenberg and "his like".[70] This comment relates to the nature of syllabi and textbooks which identify specific trends in music history, typically on a broad scale. Clive knows that his approach will not be seen as sufficiently progressive to merit inclusion, which in part explains why he has written a book of his own in order to justify his position.[71] Clive's own history in the profession has already been the source of criticism and before he has even written a note of his commission for the millennium, the musical establishment has been sceptical of the ability of the commissioning committee to fulfil their remit.[72] On multiple levels the possibility of complete success has been written off and this in turn might well be regarded as a pivotal factor in his ultimate decision to enter a suicide pact, because the future holds little possible artistic reward for him.

> Even his supporters, at least in the '70s, granted the terms 'arch-conserva-tive', while his critics preferred 'throwback', but all agreed that along with Schubert and McCartney, Linley could write a melody.

> The committee dismissed by the music establishment as middle-brow, above all longed for a symphony from which could be distilled at least one tune, a hymn, an elegy for the maligned and departed century that could be incorporated into the official proceedings, much as 'Nessun dorma' had been into a football tournament.[73]

In a similar vein to the criticism of contemporary composers within the academy, these contrary comments draw on the professional perception of music that has popular appeal. Much as Clive was ambivalent about his music being played by children,[74] the discussion of the committee towards a commission that could be likened to the first concert of the Three Tenors at the 1990 World Cup is a professional nightmare for him, not least because it sets an impossibly high bar for him to compete with.

Changing Perceptions of the Composer

For many composers the perceived public success or relevance of their work might only be captured through one piece in their career which both they, the public, and critics universally feel is a triumph. The fickle nature of critical

[70]   McEwan, *Amsterdam*, pp. 21–22.

[71]   Ibid.

[72]   Ibid., p. 14.

[73]   Ibid., p. 21.

[74]   McEwan, *Amsterdam*, pp. 9–10.

The Composer in Twentieth-Century Britain   189

and public responses means that the timing of a success might be curious and unexpected. Many people in Britain had not heard of John Tavener when his music was performed at the funeral of Diana, Princess of Wales in 1997. Yet the piece that brought his music into many households, the 'Song for Athene', was written in 1993. Despite the success of the piece, the composer had a mixed view of it in later life, commenting that 'I'm fed up with hearing *Song for Athene* every time I turn on *Essential Classics* in the morning ... it's a piece I wrote for a friend [and] it *belongs* to a funeral,'[75] rather than a morning broadcast or a concert.

Tavener's earlier association with The Beatles on their album *The Whale* (1970) was relatively unknown by the 1990s, although followers of classical music were familiar with his work for cello and orchestra, *The Protecting Veil* (1988), written for the Proms. Following the funeral of Diana, not only was the 'Song for Athene' a staple piece in the repertoire of choirs around the world, but other choral works of Tavener became increasingly popular, not least his short anthem, *The Lamb*. In each case, both pieces used musical repetition in an especially tonal manner and audiences and choirs found this approach to harmony a tonal panacea in an otherwise noisy and consuming age. Tavener was considered by many to be both 'serious' and 'accessible', a description and distinction that Clive (*Amsterdam*) longs for with his desire to be perceived as an heir to Vaughan Williams.[76] The inner debate of Clive's regarding the intelligible nature of tonal harmony is consonant with McEwan's own commentaries about the nature of harmony and lyricism[77] and Michael Berkeley's opinion of McEwan's taste.[78]

Clive falls into the category of a composer who has made his mark and reputation many years before but is eager for a final achievement before he comes to the end of his career. However, the offer of a commission from the government to celebrate the millennium is for him a two-edged sword. It is a commission with unusual expectations because it must satisfy the perception that politicians and the general public have of him rather than being in any sense avant-garde. The response to Birtwistle's *Gawain*, discussed above, is an example of how public funding of ambitious musical performances can potentially backfire. Composers who were associated with the academy and the avant-garde postwar could also be perceived as un-English or not relating to the English, which is a particular threat to a composer like Clive who is writing in response to a government commission. Almost by default he will lose the respect of colleagues. To write ambitiously will be perceived as aligning with trends that the public are unenthused about. Even at the Festival of Britain, the enthusiasm

---

[75] Andrew Palmer, 'John Tavener', *Encounters with British Composers* (Woodbridge, 2015), pp. 438–439.

[76] McEwan, *Amsterdam*, p. 21.

[77] Quinn, 'Interview with Ian McEwan'.

[78] Quinn, 'Interview with Michael Berkeley'.

190   *Music and Religion in the Writings of Ian McEwan*

for the Lion and Unicorn exhibit of unusual artefacts owed more to an amusement garnered by eccentricity than a prevailing engagement in the creative aspect. Commenting in 1963, Elizabeth Lutyens wrote about composers who composed in a more advanced tonal language:

> One was hardly ever performed; one was jeered at by the players, if silently; one was considered 'dotty' and, the chief thing, one was considered un-English. Those were the days when people talked a lot about the renaissance of British music, whereas we were writing in what was considered a 'mittel-European' style. Of course, a style derived from Bach or Brahms wasn't considered un-English. But to adopt the procedures of, say, Schoenberg was almost the antichrist, except for refugee composers.[79]

A 2014 interview with Simon Bainbridge includes his observation that when he was a student, there was a rising interest in contemporary music from the continent but ultimately a tipping point forty years later. This transition is captured by McEwan in the character of Clive (*Amsterdam*), as someone who is torn between the creative aspect of his personality and the pressure of critical reception for a contemporary piece. Bainbridge's observation about the earlier era being one of 'real discovery' is the opposite to the environment that Clive now finds himself in when trying to fulfil a commission that will mark his contribution to the field. It is a complex balance.

> I went to study at the Royal College of Music in 1969 ... the giants of the post-Second World War period – Berio, Stockhausen, Ligeti, Pousseur, Kagel and Boulez ... dominated the way we thought about music ... but Peter Maxwell Davies, Harry Birtwistle and Sandy [Alexander] Goehr were equally important to me.

> Forty-odd years later, there seems to be a lack of connection with contemporary composition. When I was a young composer I went to everything, and the Queen Elizabeth Hall was sold out whenever Berio was in town. In other words, there was a sense of real discovery. That's all gone, and I can't explain why that's happened.[80]

Clive's work is to be a celebration of the past, past ideals and relatively unmovable British tastes, rather than anything ambitious, as the clock turns to a new year. If he succeeds then he will have given a musical voice to the nation at an important moment in history, but if he fails in any respect, then there will be no second chance. Whereas a piece receiving a normal premiere that lacks a positive critical reception could well be performed another time, a piece that receives a highly publicized premiere that is poorly received is almost guaranteed to be ignored long into the future. Michael Tippett wrote of the relative inability of the public (and arguably the music profession, too) to sustain inter-

---

[79]   Schafer, 'Elizabeth Lutyens', *British Composers in Interview*, p. 105.

[80]   Andrew Palmer, 'Simon Bainbridge', *Encounters with British Composers*, p. 24.

The Composer in Twentieth-Century Britain   191

est in a large number of works by a single composer. His comments address the question that haunts Clive in relation to the reception of his new work and the nature of whether it will 'connect' with the public.

> what happens to all of us writing music at the present time is that only a certain number of our works can break through into that part of the concert world which we call repertory. We connect, therefore, more popular works with certain people.[81]

Amsterdam, For You, and The Habit of Art

Amsterdam (2005) and the libretto of *For You* bear similarity in studying the nature of ego and the professional and personal lives of composers and there are many points where their texts also relate to the perception of composers in Alan Bennett's play, *The Habit of Art*. Each focuses on composers in the later stages of their careers. Bennett's play includes commentaries from W. H. Auden, with whom Benjamin Britten is having imaginary conversations, that when compared to Auden's letters to Britten, further expand upon the presentation of the modern composer in McEwan's writings. As a student, McEwan had interviewed Britten, and Britten was a godfather to Michael Berkeley, McEwan's collaborator on *or Shall we die?* and *For You*. In a letter to Britten in 1942 that is read during *The Habit of Art*, Auden summed up the challenge of remaining humble despite the affections of others:

> Wherever you go you are and probably always will be surrounded by people who adore you, and praise everything you do. Up to a certain point this is fine for you, but beware. You see, Bengy dear, you are always tempted to make things too easy for yourself in this way, i.e. to build yourself a warm nest of love (of course when you get it, you find it a little stifling) by playing the lovable talented little boy.[82]

Each composer of the three portrayed in these works has concerns about the public's perception of them, especially when they are expected to generate equal enthusiasm for any new work they compose when it is weighed against their earlier works, but it is a fickle field. A work that might ultimately achieve a tremendous reputation as a contribution to the canon might initially receive a terrible reception at the premiere, the most obvious example of this being the riot in 1913 at the Théâtre des Champs-Elysées, Paris, for the premiere of Igor Stravinsky's *Le Sacre du printemps* (*The Rite of Spring*) with choreography by Vaslav Nijinsky. Today, the supremacy of this work is readily acknowledged and there are frequent peformances around the world. However, for a living com-

---

[81] Schafer, 'Michael Tippett', *British Composers in Interview*, p. 98.

[82] Donald Mitchell and Philip Reed (eds), *Letters from a Life – Selected Letters of Benjamin Britten Vol. 2* (London, 1991), pp. 1015–1016.

poser there is not only the question of earning a living and whether there will be a subsequent commission and continuing opportunities for their next work to be heard, but also maintaining their reputation and professional standing among critics and colleagues, as discussed above, in relation to Clive (*Amsterdam*). With this can also come self-doubt about their earlier work, as is seen with Charles (*For You*) when he sings of his compositions in earlier years and observes the emotional distance that is now part of his own self-assessment :

> It does not touch me,
> this music of my younger self,
> when my name was unknown
> I hear it clearly, each intricate part,
> I understand it, even admire it,
> but I cannot feel its passion,
> the longing, the sharp hunger,
> the lust for newness of that young man.[83]

The narrative here is the complete opposite to Florence in *On Chesil Beach*, when she is a young professional musician. Whereas Florence lives for music and has little concern in sexual endeavours or even a monogamous life for her husband, Charles has lived on the edge, and McEwan portrays this existence with a degree of vacuity that, while not removed from the life of a young musician, is not of the same substance as Florence's world of disciplined practice and high aspirations. Florence makes no mention of 'longing', 'passion', 'hunger', or 'lust' but rather sees her role in an almost sacred capacity and indeed the Wigmore Hall as a temple to art, an image many would recognize today.

In a letter from Auden to Britten, the poet writes about the balance between the two worlds and the necessary sacrifices that must be made in order to succeed in both the professional and personal worlds, with the implicit criticism that Britten needed to consider both aspects of his personality if he was to achieve greatness.

> As you know I think you [are] the white hope of music; for this very reason I am more critical of you than of anybody else, and I think I know something about the dangers that beset you as a man and as an artist because they are my own.

> Goodness and Beauty are the results of a perfect balance between Order and Chaos, Bohemianism and Bourgeois Convention.

> Bohemian chaos alone ends in a made jumble of beautiful scraps; Bourgeois convention alone ends in large unfeeling corpses.[84]

Received by Britten when he was a young man, this letter contextualises the perception of a senior figure guiding a younger artist and cautioning against

---

[83]   Ian McEwan, *For You* (London, 2008), p. 5.

[84]   Mitchell and Reed, *Letters from a Life – Selected Letters of Benjamin Britten*, p. 1015.

The Composer in Twentieth-Century Britain   193

behaviour that can betray artistry, much as career decisions have plagued both Clive (*Amsterdam*) and Charles (*For You*). Clive had immersed himself in the shallow world of celebrity culture and Charles's life was one of chaos and indulgence. Auden's commentary is apposite because it shows the shifting perceptions towards musicians from early success to potential later obscurity.

The Favoured Foreigner

The British have long hailed celebrated musicians from abroad. The unattributed but well known epithet of Britain in the nineteenth century as the 'land without music' was certainly not true in terms of the number of British composers at work but could well have suggested that it was a country where a cosmopolitan spirit was present in the arts, especially in larger cities. But the role of the foreign-born musician has often been praised. The decision of Royal Mail to include the German-born Handel in a commemorative collection of British composers in 1985 alongside Elgar, Delius, and Holst is an example of how the larger public impression has been influenced. But the lingering perception regarding foreign musicians is certainly present in literature, and contextualising this view is essential for assessing how British composers have seen themselves. In Patrick Hamilton's *Craven House*, a scene of domestic music making has the following exchange, which highlights a notion that great musicians were consistently born abroad.

> 'Give us that Chopin you gave us the other night. I expect you know Chopin well, don't you, Major?'
>
> 'He was a Pole, wasn't he?'
>
> 'Yes, I believe he was.'
>
> 'Yes, all these great musicians are Poles or something aren't they?'[85]

The composer, Howard Blake, sums up the dilemma for the modern British composer with observations that reflect Elizabeth Lutyens's comments above[86], regarding the potential for an un-English sentiment towards composers that fostered any sort of modernist interest. By comparison to Lutyens, Blake is very well known, not least because of his score for the Raymond Briggs animation, *The Snowman*.

> I think people in this country find the whole idea of being a composer rather weird. They don't understand how composers write music – they think there must be some trick to it. In other European countries, particularly Italy and Germany, people are far more at home with composers. When I did a con-

---

[85]   Patrick Hamilton, *Craven House* (London, 2017), p. 30.

[86]   Schafer, 'Elizabeth Lutyens', *British Composers in Interview*, p. 106.

194　*Music and Religion in the Writings of Ian McEwan*

cert in Germany recently, members of the audience came up and talked to me intelligently about the music ...That doesn't happen to me in England. People think 'That must be a mistake' or 'I wonder what we're supposed to think about *that*.'[87]

McEwan builds on this perception in a commentary within *Amsterdam*:

Shakespeare was a genius, of course, and Darwin and Newton, he had heard it said. Purcell, almost. Britten, less so, though within range. But there had been no Beethovens here.[88]

This narrative reinforces the notion of Britain as a literary or scientific nation rather than a musical one. The seventeenth-century composer Henry Purcell is consistently regarded as the first great English composer and there are many musicians who feel that it was not until Benjamin Britten's work in the twentieth century that another great composer could be witnessed. However, in this text McEwan shows the impossibility that Clive faced. Someone who was erudite enough to know Darwin and Newton had judged two of the most revered names in the British musical canon as comparatively lesser figures.

'The thinking man's Gorecki'[89]

The question of whether Clive's talent is being compared to Górecki is an especially pointed critique by McEwan. The Polish composer Henryk Mikołaj Górecki (1933–2010) was largely unknown outside of Poland and specialist musical circles until 1991, when the soprano Dawn Upshaw's recording of his *Third Symphony – Symphony of Sorrowful Songs*, with David Zinman conducting the London Sinfonietta, was released. Although Górecki's music had been increasingly popular in Europe and the USA during the 1980s, this particular recording, issued fifteen years after the piece was written, sold 700,000 copies within two years.[90] This was an extraordinarily high number of sales for a classical release at the time. Of this success the composer commented that 'perhaps people find something they need in this piece of music ... somehow I hit the right note, something they were missing. Something somewhere had been lost to them. I feel that I instinctively knew what they needed.'[91] However, at the point of first publication of *Amsterdam* (1998) there was already a steady flow of criticism within the musical establishment about a composer who had

---

[87]　Palmer, 'Howard Blake', *Encounters with British Composers*, p. 98.

[88]　McEwan, *Amsterdam*, p. 133.

[89]　Ibid., p. 13.

[90]　Ronald Blum, 'The impact of Górecki's Symphony No. 3', *Chicago Sun-Times* (26 June 1994).

[91]　Eamonn McCusker. 'Symphony No.3: Sorrowful Songs', *CD Times*, (6 July 2007).

The Composer in Twentieth-Century Britain 195

achieved commercial success, not least through one piece but more critically a piece that was so obviously tonal. The British radio station *Classic FM* launched the following year (1992) and found there was sufficient audience enthusiasm in hearing the work that they aired the piece weekly, although very few of Górecki's other works were played on air at all at that point. Meanwhile, his choral work, *Totus Tuus* (1987), began to enter the repertoire of British cathedral and collegiate choirs. As Robert Maycock noted in his *Independent* review of a concert that the composer attended, there was a standing ovation following a performance of Górecki's work which met with a measure of embarrassment to both the composer and, Maycock suggests, many in the music establishment for their previous response to Górecki's success:

> When Henryk Górecki stood up to acknowledge the performers of his Third Symphony, the entire packed Barbican audience rose spontaneously with him. The cheering raged on when he reached the platform, looking touched and only a little as though he might get used to the experience.
>
> What have they, or we, been searching for, that so much emotion can break out on finding it? Criticism, to its embarrassment, has been more concerned about putting down the piece (or its success) than trying to understand.[92]

Maycock touched on an important point, noting the considerable response of the audience, and yet the sustained criticism that Górecki had endured in England. The history of the British reception of new music is notoriously thorny in any generation and as the composer William Walton commented: 'Music critics are quite beyond me ... Heaven help the composer who is in the wrong camp!'.[93]

Commercial success for a composer in Britain is consistently understood to mean a lowering of standards, especially post-Thatcher with the conundrum of Andrew Lloyd Webber's success, as discussed earlier. Howard Blake commented that he had 'always thought [he] had two lives: one making money and another writing music.'[94] Yet many leading composers have been recognized by the government. Senior honours were received by Michael Tippett, Peter Maxwell Davies, Harrison Birtwistle, and Judith Weir. Benjamin Britten received a Companion of Honour. All are composers whose work was perceived by the mainstream of the profession to have created a distinct identity and contribution to the field rather than any prerequisite of being well-known to the general

---

[92] Robert Maycock, 'Scarpia: A night to discomfort the critics: A triumphant reception for Henryk Gorecki's Third Symphony and a startling recital for massed Dansettes and projector', *The Independent* (10 June 1993), online at <https://www.independent.co.uk/arts-entertainment/scarpia-a-night-to-discomfort-the-critics-a-triumphant-reception-for-henryk-goreckis-third-symphony-1490720.html> [accessed 17 December 2020].

[93] Schafer, 'William Walton', *British Composers in Interview*, p. 80.

[94] Palmer, 'Howard Blake', *Encounters with British Composers*, p. 99.

196   *Music and Religion in the Writings of Ian McEwan*

public. It is the curious irony of the British approach to the arts that a composer might be starved of commissions for several years, frequently because of the lack of funding available in the arts, and yet can also be recognized by the government at the highest level, or indeed with honorary degrees from leading universities. Britten offered a blunt commentary that captured the challenges a professional composer faced. As noted above, McEwan refers to Britten in *Amsterdam*[95] with limited enthusiasm. He had also interviewed him as a student.[96]

> Perhaps people in this country don't warm to things quite the way they do on the Continent but that is not so depressing as the basic philistinism which exists in this country. It is not a matter of appreciating Schoenberg; it is a deep prejudice to any kind of music. It is possible to encounter people in this country who don't know anything about music and are proud of it. I remember at a tennis party at Lowestoft once, about the time I was leaving school, I was asked what career I intended to choose. I told them I intended to be a composer. They were amazed! 'Yes, but what else?' Attitudes of that kind die hard, but oh, how one wishes the basic philistinism of this country would wither away. Perhaps it will![97]

'The ex-Beatle'

In the case of Clive, the respect afforded him by Julian, the Foreign Secretary, is severely tinged by the comparison that is then made between Clive and an ex-Beatle, who was the favourite for the commission with other members of the cabinet.[98]

Clive had not emerged in the profession to a wave of popularity, or after having been viewed as a figure of the avant-garde, and as such cut his professional teeth surrounded by, and in spite of, the stringent expectations of the academy. Consequently, he is in neither of the two larger artistic camps. Rather, he is a figure that is perceived as being at ease with the world of celebrity pop culture. Indeed, he has already had encounters with celebrities from the world of popular music who have visited his house.[99] These associations do not help the impression of Clive as a serious musician but rather increase his reputation as a charlatan and 'throwback'[100] in a noble profession. The potential crossover from the world of popular music or even musical theatre has seldom been

[95]   McEwan, *Amsterdam*, p. 133.

[96]   Quinn, 'Interview with Ian McEwan'.

[97]   Schafer, 'Benjamin Britten', *British Composers in Interview*, p. 124.

[98]   McEwan, *Amsterdam*, pp. 45–46.

[99]   Ibid., p. 45.

[100]   Ibid., p. 21.

successful, as was observed in the lack of sustained success for Andrew Lloyd Webber's *Requiem* [1985] or Paul McCartney's *Liverpool Oratorio* [1991].

Neither of the texts in the Webber or McCartney (an ex-Beatle) works were provocative by comparison to McEwan's/Berkeley's oratorio, *or Shall we die?*, but the reception of their pieces in the world of classical music was relatively inconsequential, despite an initial and predictable avalanche of publicity surrounding the premieres because of the public reputation of the composers. Michael Berkeley believes this was because of the challenge of composing outside a style with which a composer is familiar and notes how in his study with Richard Rodney Bennett, it was explained that writing shorter works with a limited harmonic language and little development of material was very different from composing a large-scale work, especially one for orchestra, chorus, and soloists.[101] This argument can also be seen vice versa, as few composers of symphonies write popular songs, although that is in large part because of the professional stigma associated with the genre, despite the considerable financial benefits that could ensue. Both Paul McCartney and Andrew Lloyd Webber had achieved considerable success in their home fields but the suspicions around their compositional abilities in the realm of larger forms in classical music were quickly confirmed.

Clive's desire for his fifteen minutes of fame blinkers the artistic goal that his colleagues can see eludes him: '*This is my music.* He was walking towards a representation of himself ... the "Nessun Dorma" of the century's end.'[102] But even Puccini (the composer of 'Nessun Dorma') is no equal to Clive, who instead wants a piece akin to the masterwork of Beethoven's ninth symphony, albeit with a hint of mystery in order that the listener already feels they are familiar with it.[103] However, this would not have been the 'perfectly unborrowed' nature of the creative process that Coleridge speaks of. As McEwan writes in *Science*, 'originality is inseparable from a powerful sense of the individual, and the boundaries of this individuality are strongly protected'[104] both by the creator and by their followers. In the finished piece, Clive's melody would sound to the innocent ear as though it had been anticipated or developed elsewhere in the score as he ponders Beethoven's *Ode to Joy*. However, whether it is truly 'original' or 'individual' will become a source of criticism. If McEwan's observations in *Science* are examined in this context, then the lack of originality of Clive's work will make it inseparable from the criticism he fears. Clive is driven not by an individual artistic vision but by 'ambition'.

---

[101] Quinn, 'Interview with Michael Berkeley'.

[102] McEwan, *Amsterdam*, pp. 156–157.

[103] Ibid., p. 20.

[104] Ian McEwan, *Science* (London, 2019), p. 38.

198 *Music and Religion in the Writings of Ian McEwan*

a few steps up, a few steps down. It could be a nursery tune. It was completely without pretension, and yet carried such spiritual weight. Such was the nature of his mission, and of his ambition. Beethoven.[105]

The 'pretension' Clive refers to is in reality his own. The comparison to Beethoven is almost laughable – and arguably intentionally so – because Beethoven's output is filled with masterworks, not simply one successful piece. Clive is still hoping to write one seminal piece that he can be revered and respected for, generation after generation, so that he, in turn, can finally be within the pantheon of greatness, like Vaughan Williams.[106]

The Amateur Interest

McEwan also presents another aspect of society when he portrays a devoted amateur's interest in music. The knowledge of a police officer being aware of Clive's work exposes the nature of a society [in the case of Britain] where despite uneven approaches to the arts by successive governments, a senior police officer nonetheless is aware of figures who are recognized as influential in the world of culture.[107] This example further highlights the impression of Britten – one of the very few British composers whose name was known to the general public – as a figure recognized throughout the country. There is also the characterization of a police officer who reads Blake and is someone who is sufficiently culturally aware that he knows of Britain's most celebrated twentieth-century composer, Benjamin Britten. Clive discussed his own setting of Blake's *A Poison Tree* and its performance by Britten's longtime partner, Peter Pears, with the officer.[108] While this exchange is believable, it is also consistent with McEwan's larger approach to the arts as accessible. Meetings with policemen do not typically involve conversations about Blake or Britten but McEwan presents this circumstance as completely natural.

Whether Clive's piece will move audiences, let alone empower anyone or enrich their lives, is of little consequence to the minister who sees the piece as no more consequential than the many trivial aspects of his diurnal administrative planning. That noted, if it proves to be a success then Garmony will vicariously share in the adulation afforded to Clive. It is an initially shortsighted view of the minister because the success of a new symphony that had been commissioned by the government – a rarity in itself – could promote the image of the government as a body seen for its wise and relatively ambitious support of one of the country's composers. It could also increase Clive's own professional

---

[105] McEwan, *Amsterdam*, p. 76.

[106] McEwan, *Amsterdam*, p. 21.

[107] Ibid., p. 178.

[108] Ibid., pp. 151–152.

standing and this in turn could produce related benefits, such as further commissions. The fact that Clive has been considered in the first instance speaks to the public knowledge of his work within political circles, which makes him influential even if he is not universally admired. As a consequence, there is already a measure of power to Clive's position. Richard Eyre, a self-proclaimed socialist, noted that some degree of necessary power was ultimately found when he became artistic director of the National Theatre and that there was a certain advantage to not being on the margins of the profession:

> It feels like an essential rite of passage, that you do eventually join the Establishment. You just long not to be treated as trivial and marginal and silly. My abiding motto is that Biff cartoon where an ageing hippie is looking out and saying 'we are the people we warned ourselves against.'[109]

McEwan's narrative in *The Child in Time* about the role of state support of the arts[110] and the reference in *Amsterdam*[111] to funding cuts in the arts being reported in a newspaper also speaks to the issue that Eyre commented on and is highlighted in McEwan's narrative about policy decisions: 'The art of bad government was to sever the line between public policy and intimate feeling, the instinct for what was right.'[112] In this respect, the commentary of the former Foreign Secretary, Douglas Hurd, on announcing McEwan's Booker Prize for *Amsterdam* (which includes the character of a Foreign Secretary) by describing it as 'a sardonic and wise examination of the morals and culture of our time'[113] is especially biting.

The Private Life

In the case of Charles (*For You*), the personal side of his life is part of the opera itself in terms of his lack of friendships with any degree of equality and the presumption of subservience from everyone around him. His assistant, Robin, his housekeeper, Maria, and his sick wife, Antonia, are also all dependent on him. His treatment of each of them is consistently appalling, with each having to navigate his temperament at one level or another. In his relationships with other musicians (discussed below) he is swiftly dismissive. As Robin sings early in the opera, there is a typical formula: 'Humiliation, then forgiveness, then seduction.'[114] Over time, Charles has had many affairs which his wife Anto-

---

[109] Interview with Richard Eyre.

[110] McEwan, *Amsterdam*, p. 14.

[111] Ibid., p. 112.

[112] McEwan, *The Child in Time*, p. 3.

[113] Sarah Lyall, '"Amsterdam" by Ian McEwan Wins Booker Prize', *The New York Times* (28 October 1998).

[114] McEwan, *For You*, p. 7.

200   *Music and Religion in the Writings of Ian McEwan*

nia has come to accept in some measure as a predictable pattern. She sings: 'Working late again … Working is our household euphemism'[115] for an affair. When Antonia finally catches him in bed with another woman, she sings with a sarcasm that lists his multiple faults over time and the feeble excuses he has provided to her: 'We agreed you'd never bring your work home. Is this the flute whose husband owns a bank, or the harp with the autistic son, or the cello with the house in Wales?'[116] None of the musicians are mentioned by name, possibly because she doesn't know their names but equally because, like her on some level, they are simply passing through this life. Meanwhile, his housekeeper Maria sees him as a genius.[117] It is a scenario of an abusive relationship that can also be seen in Kingsley Amis's *Lucky Jim* when, in relation to painters, it is commented that 'great artists always have a lot of women, so if he can have a lot of women that makes him a great artist, never mind what his pictures are like.'[118] Amis takes the predicament one stage further by suggesting that the quality of work is also irrelevant if the person is already accepted as 'great' and Charles unquestionably believes he is on some level.

In the nature of dispensing with people who no longer serve the ends of the composer, there is a notable similarity in McEwan's portrayal of the artist as artistically absorbed and Bennett's portrayal of Britten. Like McEwan's character of Charles, the character of Britten in Bennett's play *The Habit of Art* is seen as someone who would simply cut people from his social circle with little warning, although Auden's narrative defends the separation of art from relationships and the nature of excuses being presumed as acceptable.

> Carpenter: When he [Britten] falls out with someone the ex-friend becomes a corpse. Never spoken of again. Still, he's an artist.
>
> Auden: Rubbish. Art is never an excuse for cruelty.[119]

Although there are many similarities between McEwan's composers in *For You* (Charles) and *Amsterdam* (Clive) and no shortage of narcissism and relative self-doubt for each, Clive is not the socially ruthless individual that Charles is. Indeed, one might argue it is the typical caricature and popular perception of a power-driven conductor and a self-doubting composer that is then bolstered within a popular novel. Clive is described in a manner that includes many truisms about the world of classical music and the fickle behaviour of artistic egotism which, after all, only exists because it is allowed. McEwan's portrayal of Clive aligns with Bennett's comments for Auden when it is remarked that in relation to concerts, 'It would have been possible to back

---

[115] Ibid., p. 12.

[116] Ibid., p. 34.

[117] Ibid., p. 45.

[118] Amis, *Lucky Jim*, p. 125.

[119] Alan Bennett, *The Habit of Art* (London, 2009), p. 24.

The Composer in Twentieth-Century Britain 201

out of his engagements by assuming the license of the free artistic spirit, but he loathed such arrogance.'[120] McEwan is aware that concerts are cancelled by well-known performers for seemingly trivial reasons, but the portrayal of Clive shows a modesty towards colleagues that Charles's outbursts and criticisms of musicians in rehearsals do not.

The Sexual Element

The implied innuendo in *For You* is treated in an intentionally humorous fashion. Charles's abuse of position is seen within the context of a man whose sexual abilities have begun to fail him. When his wife, Antonia, facetiously describes Joan, the horn player Charles has slept with, as the 'horn of plenty' – and notes 'not since Britten's [*Serenade for Tenor, Horn and Strings*] and Mozart's [concertos] did the horn have such a friend',[121] McEwan shows a knowledge of the repertoire that is suavely used in a literary context. It is an intricate use of critical commentary that also has an insider's knowledge of the profession, which 'is expanded upon when Antonia sings: 'No, my dear, it is you who are cheap. Has he offered you yet your solo of thirty-two bars? And promised a concerto?','[122] as the ultimate prize for a soloist trying to make their individual mark in a crowded profession. McEwan demonstrates a knowledge of the world of the contemporary performer and the potential manipulation of circumstances by someone in a position of power. Joan is swiftly portrayed as a musical Judas by dishonestly advancing her own career while betraying the integrity of her art. However, Joan has already condemned Charles for his own sexual inadequacies[123] and here, albeit in a more comic light, there is a familiar trope with the sexual difficulties faced by Edward in *On Chesil Beach* and Turner in *The Imitation Game*, although in this instance with the added question that it might be due to the man's senior years. The comic aspect within *For You* was deliberate, and in a joint interview McEwan asked Berkeley if this might be the first operatic 'no-show'.[124] Such was the concern that the moment when Charles failed to perform might be lost on the audience that there were surtitles although, as McEwan later noted, 'It was a condition. It's not so distracting. A saccade is all that's required.'[125]

> Joan: They say an erection never lies. But this is also eloquent, when you shrink before my touch.

---

[120] McEwan, *Amsterdam*, pp. 61–62.

[121] McEwan, *For You*, p. 34.

[122] Ibid., p. 35.

[123] McEwan, *For You*, p. 31.

[124] Ashutosh Khandekar, *BBC Music Magazine*, 16:9 (May 2008), pp. 38–41.

[125] Daniel Zalewski, 'The Background Hum', *The New Yorker* (15 February 2009).

202   *Music and Religion in the Writings of Ian McEwan*

Charles: This has never happened to me before.

Joan: That's what men always say.[126]

In the intermission of the first performance of the opera, McEwan and Berkeley had dinner. Berkeley commented that in the sex scene the percussionists used 'an instrument called a lion's roar', but it had been inaudible. 'You pull a string through a drum head, and it makes this odd sound. It needs to be loud, like someone grunting during wild sex.' McEwan responded 'A lion's roar! I wished I'd known that when I wrote the libretto.'[127] Berkeley added: 'it strikes me that so many contemporary composers don't explore the tension between comedy and tragedy enough. You can only have real blackness if it comes after a flash of light, and music can deliver this sort of abrupt contrast supremely well in conjunction with words.' He further noted that the libretto was not like McEwan's novels because opera is delivered with a 'degree of hyperbole … the emotions are heightened [and] many dramatic things happen in a short space of time.'[128] The opera also captures both Charles's and Antonia's own approach to little acts of revenge, and as McEwan observed, the notion that 'if you're not a monster you're not good.'[129] Although the succinctness of a typical opera libretto only allows for a relatively limited exploration of deep character, McEwan nonetheless relies on the perception of abuse of power that, as Berkeley noted,[130] was symptomatic within larger society. McEwan's comment above indicates the possible exaggeration of Charles's character but it is not an inaccurate depiction.

Both McEwan and Bennett draw on an image of the music profession in a sexualized manner and there is an interesting parallel to McEwan's writing in the sexual dialogue in Bennett's play *The Habit of Art*. The critique, though no less blistering, is not from a lover but from the older Auden in his comments to the younger Britten, which are laced with innuendo. In terms of a criticism of behaviour that mirrors Antonia's, Bennett's narrative also treats abuses of position with an overall presumption that assumes the enabling of others who 'looked the other way'. The following extract focuses on Britten's *Death in Venice* and the particular use of a boy:

Auden: This is an old man lusting after a boy, and Apollo has got fuck all to do with it.

Author: There were boys all through his [Britten's] life to whom he gave his heart. Sometimes he was loved in return. And licensed.

---

[126]   McEwan, *For You*, 31.

[127]   Zalewski, 'The Background Hum'.

[128]   Khandekar, *BBC Music Magazine*, 38–41.

[129]   Zalewski, 'The Background Hum'.

[130]   Quinn, 'Interview with Michael Berkeley'.

The Composer in Twentieth-Century Britain   203

Henry: And that's when Aldeburgh looked the other way.[131]

The nature of casual relationships with members of the orchestra is also seen with the conductor Guilio Bo (*Amsterdam*), as he comments: 'I think the second oboe, the young girl, is very beautiful but the playing is not perfect ... Tonight she will have dinner with me.'[132] Berkeley observed how the work is undeniably satirical and pinpoints the weaknesses of the individual conductor. In his conversations with McEwan about the music profession over many years, the nature of the behaviour of some conductors had amused McEwan, but in the case of the opera, the libretto manages to lance the very nature of the abuse of power that had also been commonplace in many areas of society.[133]

The Maestro

In both McEwan's and Bennett's narratives the composer is seen as wholly fallible and, in that vein, the veil of artistic mystery is removed and honesty unavoidably prevails for the composers. Both writers treat the image of the composer as someone who is overblown but also personally weak. In *Science*, McEwan describes how the 'fiercely individualistic world of novelists, poets, artists and composers who know in their hearts that they are utterly reliant on those who went before them [presents an image of] a human face.'[134] The artist is seen as someone who, without the structure and self-discipline of their own craft, easily collapses into one personal dilemma after another. Vanity and over-confidence take over. Clive (*Amsterdam*) is easily flattered by being referred to as 'maestro'[135] when he is on the continent and enjoys the deference of orchestral members by comparison to those in Britain. The nature of these exchanges is also addressed by Bennett, when Auden asks if Britten is ever called 'maestro', to the rejoinder, 'On occasion. [but] Not in Aldeburgh.'[136] In Britain, there is the strong expectation that respect would have to be earned, and that any failures on the part of a conductor could lead to potential discontent and distrust within the orchestra, especially if the conductor was particularly arrogant. It is for this reason that Charles never allows his orchestral players to comment but rather asserts his authority and retains a relatively dictatorial control of the rehearsal. The comments (below) made to Joan earlier in the opera about her playing might appear abrupt and rude to many reading them for the first time, but they would not shock a seasoned orchestral player who has observed many conduc-

---

[131] Ibid., pp. 67–68.

[132] McEwan, *Amsterdam*, p. 161.

[133] Quinn, 'Interview with Michael Berkeley'.

[134] McEwan, *Science*, p. 48.

[135] McEwan, *Amsterdam*, p. 158.

[136] Bennett, *The Habit of Art*, pp. 46–47.

204   *Music and Religion in the Writings of Ian McEwan*

tors of different generations and from different countries over several years. Norman Lebrecht discusses the fallible nature of conductors at length throughout *The Maestro Myth*,[137] and further instances can be seen in the DVD *The Art of Conducting*[138], which shows footage of conductors in rehearsals throughout the twentieth century. The responses of Robin, Charles's assistant clarify that this rehearsal dynamic is nothing new. Following a mistake by Joan in a passage which Charles had written with near-impossible technical demands, there is an exchange:

> Joan: I did my best with what you wrote.
>
> Robin. Not this. Please God, not this again –
>
> Joan: I'll try again. Please let me try again.[139]

The idea of a strongly worded exchange within the rehearsal is something that McEwan had relayed to John Updike in a personal letter while he was writing the text:

> In the libretto I've been writing, the composer, who is conducting his own work at a rehearsal hears a false note and sings, 'And stop and stop and stop! God fucking damn, I called a halt. /Am I standing here for nothing, waving my arms?' For the US production I was asked to devise a polite alternative, and meekly suggested 'for goodness sake'.[140]

The Image of the Virtuoso

In *Saturday*, the neurosurgeon, Henry Perowne, refers to the pianist Glenn Gould as one of his pianists of choice when listening to Bach's *Goldberg Variations*.[141] Gould had a particular following among classical music lovers that was enhanced by the mystique that for most of his career he only recorded instead of performing live. However, the comments of a childhood friend that young Gould 'always sought to create an impression of fierce independence' and was someone for whom 'human interaction and intimacy were totally inessential' are modified towards a later impression of someone who 'craved contact' but 'on his own terms' and 'often succeeded in drawing someone into his orbit',[142] a trait of social control and manipulation that is often seen with Charles (*For*

---

[137]   Norman Lebrecht, *The Maestro Myth* (London, 1991).

[138]   *The Art of Conducting – Great Conductors of the Past* [DVD], Teldec (2002).

[139]   McEwan, *For You*, p. 7.

[140]   Letter from Ian McEwan to John Updike (7 January 2007).

[141]   McEwan, *Saturday* (London, 2006), p. 22.

[142]   Peter F. Ostwald, *Glenn Gould – The Ecstasy and Tragedy of Genius* (New York, 1997), pp. 58–59.

You). Part of Gould's ability stemmed from an inherent charm coupled with a playfulness and intellect that attracted people, providing that he could remain in complete control and, once the parameters were established, his will could be largely unchallenged. His biographer, Peter F. Ostwald, noted that 'in this way he could also make inordinate demands on his friends and when the time came, as it inevitably did' where criticism and viewpoints were expressed that Glenn could not tolerate, he would quickly break off the friendship.[143] In this respect there is a considerable similarity with both Britten in Bennett's portrayal and diary writings and Charles (*For You*), as friends were consistently kept around only for a period in which they served a supportive, emboldening or reassuring purpose. In relation to the idea of self-proclaimed genius, in whatever personal interpretation, Gould's notion of what he described as 'aesthetic narcissism' not only applies to the characters of Britten, Charles, and Clive but is familiar to many in the field of classical musical overall. In a statement of considerable grandeur that could easily have been uttered by Charles, Gould once noted that 'through the ministrations of radio and the phonograph, [and as such the removal of the live audience as part of the composer-performer-listener equation] we are rapidly and quite properly learning to appreciate the elements of aesthetic narcissism – and I use that word in the best sense – and are awakening to the challenge that each man contemplatively creates his own divinity'.[144] Beyond the self-perception or relative delusion of the musician making a contribution that is equal to the gods, there is also the dependable reassurance of those close to them, whether in blatant adulation or in creating an environment, to build ever greater reaches to this self-centredness. In *For You*, Antonia remarks how as Charles's ambition began to know no bounds, those around him became negligible to him,[145] and Clive's failure to report an assault because he was trying to think of a melody is equally removed and narcissistic.

As much as Gould was considered a product of another age, Charles and Clive are also removed from societal norms in their own self-perceptions. The eulogy given by John Roberts at Gould's funeral in Toronto speaks to the nature of an all-embracing commitment to art, although when referring to him as a 'man apart', there is a tacit confirmation of the nature of the isolationism, self-discipline and, ultimately, individualism that can be seen in Charles and Clive. Further, this is recognized with the statement that this approach to life of self-perceived sacrifice is pure and even moral. The image of the artist is not only enabled by the individual but supported by those around them.

> having carried the burden of genius all this life. He realized he was a man apart. Everything about him was different ... a truly modern man and a re-

---

[143] Ostwald, *Glenn Gould*, p. 59.

[144] Glenn Gould, 'Let's Ban Applause!' *Musical America* (February 1962), reprinted in Tim Page, *The Glenn Gould Reader* (New York, 1984), p. 246; Ostwald, *Glenn Gould*, p. 139.

[145] McEwan, *For You*, p. 40.

206   *Music and Religion in the Writings of Ian McEwan*

markable innovator ... very concerned with the human condition, and, in his own way, the purest and most moral person I have ever encountered.[146]

Gould had a fantasy of attending his own funeral and this was partially fulfilled by a playing of the Aria from his recent recording of the *Goldberg Variations* at his funeral. Not only did this mean that those attending would hear the sound of his playing but, given his tendency to hum while he played, also his voice.[147] For his biographer, Ostwald, while the early recording of the *Goldberg Variations* catapulted Gould's reputation into the sphere of select pianists who garnered international attention, the later recording propelled him 'into the world of immortal pianists'.[148] The nature of legacy and reputation that so many artists strive for, including Charles and Clive, is seen here in a contemporary setting that demonstrates McEwan's narrative to be wholly plausible and, to a musician reading this narrative, believable.

The Figure of Farce

An essential part of McEwan's narrative about Charles, and also Bennett's description of Britten, rests with the eccentricity that a life largely removed from the humdrum of society can easily engender. Both writers indulge in scenes that bring the composers to a level of comedy by highlighting their circumstances, not through a veil of necessary mystery or indeed 'aesthetic narcissism', to draw on Gould's self-description, but rather by pointing out curious aspects that cannot help but make the reader amused at the sometimes-removed nature of the artistic world. In McEwan's writing, it once again highlights the related narcissism of those around the composer as Maria (the maid) is driven to secure Charles for herself. She believes she is able to make him uninterested in other women so that his music, his contribution to the world, would be solely for her.[149] To that end, rather than appeal to his artistic, emotional or intellectual self, she will instead focus on his sexual appetite. All of this for Maria will be worth it because her adoration will be rewarded by a closeness to what she perceives as 'genius'.[150] It is her fifteen minutes of vicarious fame.

The moment of great self-indulgence, or perhaps tremendous self-belief, comes when Charles is to conduct the rehearsal for the world premiere of his *Demonic Aubade.* While the orchestra applauds him following his brief comments of thanks, he raises his baton and the piece begins. This action would

---

[146] John Roberts, memorial service tribute to Glenn Gould, 15 October 1982, in the Glenn Gould Archives, File 1979-20, 44, 40, National Library of Canada; Ostwald, *Glenn Gould*, p. 331.

[147] Ostwald, *Glenn Gould*, p. 331.

[148] Ibid., p. 119.

[149] McEwan, *For You*, pp. 51–52.

[150] Ibid., 45.

The Composer in Twentieth-Century Britain   207

be highly favourable to an orchestra because, in general, orchestral musicians do not like to be talked to at great length but rather while they are playing. In the film *The Art of Conducting*,[151] numerous conductors are shown rehearsing symphonic works or commenting on their conducting style. It is consistently noted that if a conductor needs to speak with an orchestra, it is far more effective to do so while they are playing, if at all possible, not least because it is a preferred use of limited rehearsal time. As such, Charles begins his relationship with the orchestra on the best footing. However, this is soon turned into a moment of bizarre self-adulation as he starts to narrate his own piece, suggesting, in no small measure, that it resembles creation and life itself. In an especially amusing development, Charles provides his own statement of artistic faith and excuses for the faults in his personal life. Considering that part of his approach to the profession has been sleeping with orchestra members, the personal aspects of his oration are especially perturbing and self-indicting.

> He must be ruthless!
> No religion, no purpose except this:
> make something perfect before you die.
> Life is short, art is for all time –
> History will forgive my ways because
> My music outstared the sun.[152]

The absurdity of such a moment in a rehearsal would be met with inner laughter from an orchestra, not least with the justification that in pursuing art above all else, his other actions can be forgiven. This overly poetic and self-enraptured approach is also seen in *Amsterdam*, with Clive's work for the millennium celebrations. With a seeming lack of recent commissions and little interaction with musicians who are not in some way subservient, as opposed to being equal to him, and therefore willing to challenge him, Clive's thoughts are equally self-centred. They are in the manner of a pre-concert talk that describes a piece to be heard.

> It was only a bridging passage to the finale; what fascinated him was the promise, the aspiration – he managed it as a set of ancient worn steps turning gently out of sight – the yearning to climb on and up, and finally arrive, by way of an expansive shift, at a remote key and, with wisps of sound falling away like so much dissolving mist, at a concluding melody, a valediction, a recognizable melody of piercing beauty that would transcend its unfashionability and seem both to mourn the passing century and all its senseless cruelty, and to celebrate its brilliant inventiveness.[153]

The 'valediction' that would 'transcend unfashionability' speaks of a conviction that would justify the relative inadequacies that critics might see in the piece.

---

[151] *The Art of Conducting.*
[152] McEwan, *For You*, p. 62.
[153] McEwan, *Amsterdam*, p. 20.

208   *Music and Religion in the Writings of Ian McEwan*

The 'senseless cruelty' of criticism can also be removed by the 'brilliant inventiveness' of the age, even if inventiveness is not something that Clive has been known to pursue in his compositions. The whole statement borders on a comic narcissism.

In a sincere reflection, the comments of the composer Alexander Goehr on the compositional process speak to the greater art of composition as it is more typically considered and received. The sense of an overwhelming presence in the compositional process is present but sincerely conveyed. 'For me [the] experience [of composition] exceeds all other satisfactions that I know or can imagine ... for, at this moment, I find myself overcome by an oceanic sensation of oneness with all around me.'[154] The nature of genuine absorption is pronounced in Goehr's comments and similarly addressed by Robert Saxton, who relates the vanity seen in McEwan's portrayals of Charles and Clive to be something necessarily avoided in the professional pursuit.

> In a sense, composers write for themselves. They're on a voyage of discovery, their appetites have been whetted and they just have to carry on. Of course, it's heartening to have one's work – rather than one's personality, as sometimes seems too frequent these days – recognized, but seeking acclaim mustn't be on the agenda.[155]

With these portrayals McEwan demonstrates his knowledge of the motivations that can cloud a composer's judgement. In presenting them in a sometimes-comic fashion there is also a certain cynicism and a respective dualism. As noted above in relation to the concert of new music with the mistreatment of a piano and violin,[156] and the portrayal of music and musicians as discussed in chapters 2 and 3, McEwan draws lines under experiences that are portrayed as valuable and observes others that should be questioned.

McEwan's portrayals of the life of the contemporary composer strike the professional nerve that Berkeley[157] refers to and are, to a professional musician, easy to recognize. But so too is McEwan's narrative of government support of the arts, the expectations of politicians and the balance of the ideal and necessary in a composer's life. Most critically, McEwan reveals a broad understanding of the relationship between the public at large and the composer as it is frequently seen in twentieth- and twenty-first-century Britain. In the libretto *For You* and the novel *Amsterdam*, he weighs in on the very nature and challenges of the music profession, and the public's perception. As a result, the reader or listener (in the case of the opera) who is uninitiated in the world of classical music encounters a world that has its own argot and understanding as well as ceaseless intrigue.

---

[154] Alexander Goehr, *Independent* (1 June 1991); Storr, *Music and the Mind* (Toronto, 1992), p. 97.

[155] Palmer, 'Robert Saxton', *Encounters with British Composers*, p. 423.

[156] McEwan, *Amsterdam*, p. 22.

[157] Quinn, 'Interview with Michael Berkeley'.

APPENDIX

INTERVIEW WITH IAN McEWAN
27 JULY 2018

Iain Quinn: What are your earliest memories of music?

Ian McEwan: I don't come from a cultured background. Both of my parents left school at fourteen. My father was a military man who joined the ranks of the army in the early 1930s. Like a lot of British soldiers, he had a mouth organ and played old favourites in the vamping style. He was a sociable man and liked to get together with mates in the sergeants' mess. Whenever he was encouraging me to take up an instrument he would tell me that I would always have friends if I could play the piano. What he had in mind was being surrounded by twenty mates singing 'It's a long way to Tipperary'. So at the age of thirteen I began teaching myself the mouth organ – I had one of those chromatic Larry Adler instruments. It was extremely frustrating. I was starting to listen to the blues and couldn't understand how harp players made the wonderful sounds they did. Later, I realized you could buy blues harmonicas in different keys with scales of flattened thirds and sevenths.

My mother liked what she called 'nice music' and although she didn't know the names of composers in general she did have a record of Grieg's piano concerto that I remember playing from when I was ten.

I also recall listening to *Family Favourites* on the radio in North Africa. People would write in and say something like 'Please play whatever for Henry and Doris stationed in Singapore'. I think my sister, who is ten years older than me and was living in England, asked me to choose a song. I thought hard about it. I had a secret pre-sexual crush on Doris Day. It seemed natural to ask for her 'Secret Love'. It was a thrill to hear it, and to hear my name on the radio.

The 1944 Education Act spawned a number of important song books for children and even in a primary school in far away Tripoli we had an hour or two a week singing English, Scottish, Irish, and Welsh folk songs. They bore little relevance to our surroundings of cacti and date palms, but we hardly noticed. I remember 'Cockles and Mussels' and 'Three gypsies stood at the castle gate'. How we loved belting out 'The Vicar of Bray', even though we didn't understand a word of it! What was lovely about those song books was that they were part of a unifying cultural heritage.

212   *Music and Religion in the Writings of Ian McEwan*

I lost religion at about the age of eleven. I disliked hymns because they seemed patently not true. There were certain tunes I loved. But three hundred boys grinding their way through hymns at 8 a.m. was a sound experience I came to loathe. At university I sang in Dvořák's *Mass in D*, Bach's *Mass in B minor*, and Mozart's *Versperae Solennes*. Singing Beethoven's *Ninth Symphony* with the Brighton Festival Chorus and Daniel Barenboim was a highlight. At Woolverstone Hall there was a very talented teacher, Michael Channon. When I arrived at the age of eleven (bewildered, with my parents two thousand miles away) he was directing *The Magic Flute*. Because the school was small, everyone was involved. We had two music lessons a week and Michael Channon would get all the small boys to sing through the arias – as if they were hit numbers from a musical. I assumed these were school songs. We sang in English: 'Man and wife and wife and man, Together make a godly span.' ['*Bei Männern welche Liebe fühlen*']. I had never heard an opera before but I came to adore *The Magic Flute*. Eight years later, when I was at university, I heard the opera at the Royal Opera House. As soon as those fat, juicy opening chords of the overture sounded, I was in tears. The buried memory of homesickness overwhelmed me. Even now, those chords can make me wet-eyed. I was far from home and very lost.

I started piano lessons at school at the age of twelve. My piano lesson was at 5.30 which was also the time of tea – the last meal of the day. I was reliant on other boys to put together a plate of food – a completely hopeless project. I complained to my father, but as a soldier who had once known in barracks all about not getting enough to eat he knew his priorities. My piano lessons were instantly cancelled. Michael Channon stepped in and offered to give me two hours a week himself for free, and at a convenient time. But he made this extraordinary suggestion in front of other boys and I was too shy to accept. I regard that as one of those dividing moments in my life. If only I'd had the courage to say yes.

When I was seventeen I taught myself to play the flute. Later I had a few lessons. I learned some of the easier Bach and Handel sonatas but slowly lost interest. Perhaps if I had been playing in an octet it would have been different, but playing on your own throws you back on the quality of your tone – and mine was poor.

IQ: A number of nineteenth-century musicians regarded Bach not simply as a man but as a god. Do you find it easy to relate to that sentiment?

IM: I can understand that point of view. I came by it gradually. I'm still reeling from hearing Angela Hewitt play the *Goldberg Variations* last night at her sixtieth birthday concert [Wigmore Hall, 26 July 2018]. We've become friends over the years. I mentioned her 'wise and silky' playing of Bach in my novel, *Saturday*. She's been to stay with us and has rehearsed on our upright – a real privilege to sit and listen.

Interview with Ian McEwan   213

I was sixteen the first time I heard Bach. At school I'd been a quiet, under-performing boy, barely noticed by the teachers. Suddenly I went through one of those mental explosions that can come in adolescence. It was like a switch had been thrown. Suddenly I was passionate about music, hungry for it, desperate to hear more. I went to see Michael Channon and asked him where I should start. His answer was Bach. My first passion was Book One of The Well-Tempered Clavier. Next, the three violin concertos, the Double, the E major, the A minor. Next, the violin partitas, then the cello suites, then the Brandenburg Concertos. So began an involvement and delight which, fifty-five years later, is still there. I also started listening to Jacques Loussier and so began my fondness for mainstream jazz.

My state boarding grammar school was centred around a lovely Palladian house in beautiful Suffolk countryside. It was run from London by the London County Council and took mostly bright working-class kids from so-called broken homes, as well as a small number from the lower and middle ranks of the Forces and a scattering of boys from more bohemian backgrounds. It was a now-discredited notion that you could take such kids, give us a public school type of education (actually it was better than that) and send us all to university or medical college. 'Embourgeoisement' was the name of the process. But it was an extraordinary success. The school's ethos was cool and witty, quite streetwise. Many of the boys were confident Cockneys who knew a lot about music. I heard Chuck Berry, and Barrett Strong, and The Marvelettes well before I heard cover versions by The Beatles and the Stones in their early albums. Twelve and 8 bar blues throbbed through the place. Keith Richard's musically astute autobiography describes the sorts of sounds of the late fifties that shaped his playing. It was just the sort of music that was played at my school. So while I was listening to Bach it was against the background of a lot of blues, Motown, and jazz – Muddy Waters, Skip James, The Miracles, Coltrane, Miles Davis. I felt there was a strong connection between bebop and the Bach partitas. Of course, Bach was a great improviser.

Also popular at the school was a traditional jazz band, The Feetwarmers. Through them I developed a taste for Jelly Roll Morton and set about teaching myself the banjo. I even auditioned for The Feetwarmers. The number we played was Sweet Georgia Brown – it has a nice major to minor shift in the first two lines. I was nervous and also tried to be cool by not glancing at the fret. I was one position out – the band was in F, I was in F sharp. I wasn't asked to join.

IQ: Where did the interest in the Mozart *Fantasia*, K. 475 come from? (*The Imitation Game*)

IM: I had a recording by Ivan Moravec. My girlfriend at the time, in 1974, was Elaine Streeter, a very accomplished pianist who was studying music therapy. I often asked her to play the *Fantasia*, and that only increased my love of the piece. I remember she had a baby grand – this was a highly unusual possession

214 *Music and Religion in the Writings of Ian McEwan*

at the time. And a marvellous one. In the late seventies, Richard Eyre came to the BBC to make one-off TV films for *Play for Today*. At the time we were both living in the same part of London, Stockwell. He asked if I'd write something for him. This project became *The Imitation Game*. The *Fantasia* was still very much with me. I liked the dramatic opening and the haunting melody that floats in above the Alberti bass. Harriet Walter played the central role of Cathy Raine, a young woman who wants to play a significant role in the war but finds it impossible. Women were mostly shunted off into peripheral low-skilled jobs. As a senior army officer recommended at the time, 'Let no man do what can be done by a woman.' We've had all this fuss just recently about a woman who delivered Spitfires from factory to aerodrome. But why not? Perhaps attitudes have not changed as much as we think.

Writers of my generation, who grew up in the shadow of the war and wanted to examine its effect on the national narrative, often turned to Angus Calder's book *The People's War, Britain: 1939–1945*. It was among the first of the histories to suggest that the war was not entirely about us all 'pulling together'. Powerful class and gender matters were played out. My heroine ended up at Bletchley, doing a humdrum job, as thousands of women there did. The intelligence breaking and analysis in the famous huts was, with one or two exceptions, done by men. But the code Cathy Raine breaks is the Mozart *Fantasia*. Within it, she can do something difficult and interesting.

IQ: Do you think her relationship with music is similar to the surgeon in *Saturday*, where there are particular performances he wants for particular moments?

IM: The other day, as I was going into the auditorium to hear Angela play the *Goldberg Variations*, a stranger said, 'You're here because of *Saturday!*' I was indeed interested in the surgeon as a kind of artist. My character operates to Angela's performance of the Aria. Over many months of research for the novel, I watched a neurosurgeon, Neil Kitchen, at work. I sent him some pages of an early draft to check. He told me I'd made one important mistake. There's a substance called Betadine, a bright yellow antiseptic liquid. I had described the surgeon, about to make an incision in the patient's scalp, making a yellow line with a paint brush. Neil was insistent. He always used a sponge on a clamp. Clearly a matter of believing is seeing. The *Goldberg* Aria suggested all the delicacy and intelligence of a surgeon about to begin his work.

IQ: Britain has an especially large audience for popular classical concerts and also a tradition of sneering at new works, especially by modern British composers, sometimes before they've even heard the pieces. Do you have any thoughts on why this might be the case?

IM: Well, obviously, sneering should have no place in any serious culture. I've listened to a lot of contemporary music. Thomas Adès and George Benjamin

Interview with Ian McEwan 215

have given me much pleasure. And I greatly admired the work of Michael Berkeley, with whom I've collaborated. Back in the 1960s and 1970s there developed a rigorous modernism of an uncompromising sort. Beyond atonality. In the late 1970s I was at a concert in which a man beat the leg of a piano with a baseball bat. Composers working with even a trace of tonality were aggressively dismissed. Too many composers lost touch with their audiences. But things have moved on a long way since. I heard a Thomas Adès piece, *These Premises are Alarmed* [1996] – a brilliant title – and we the audience went wild and loved it. The pulse and orchestral colour were brilliant.

But no tone row or aleatoric piece has ever moved me the way Schubert or Bach or Stravinsky have. What I like about Strauss, Debussy, and Bartók is that wild sense of music pushing against the outer limits. But to have limits you've got to have form. Much purely atonal music seems to have its emotional range confined to a mere expression of anxiety. I have the same problem with jazz. Where the harmonic progressions hold sway in bebop, I'm happy. When they dissolve, and the musicians set about freely expressing themselves, my interest fades. This is the same difficulty I have with *Finnegan's Wake* – a tragic waste of genius.

People who never 'got' classical music quite reasonably find it rather hidebound. The dinner jackets and conspicuous-consumption picnic hampers at Glyndebourne or Garsington at Wormsley may seem like a bad advertisement to some. But when the context is right, everyone can be swept away by what we call high culture. Remember the World Cup when [Puccini's] 'Nessun Dorma' was number one in the charts. There was Auden's 'Stop all the Clocks' in *Four Weddings and a Funeral*. Look what happened to Samuel Barber's *Adagio*. I'm sure that the *Goldberg* Aria or any of the variations could be a popular hit delivered in the right way.

IQ: Do you think the British have a particular value for their own culture and if so what parts of it?

IM: Well, we're a very layered society. You could live your life within a particular subculture of art or classical music without needing to confront the fact that ninety per cent of the population doesn't know a thing about it. I could walk down Clapham High Street and stop a lot of people before I found someone who'd heard of Angela Hewitt. I'd need to go even further before I found someone who'd heard of me or my stuff. Yet, within each intact world, we find lively, skilled and innovative cultures. In movie post-production, for example, you get twenty-five musicians coming to the dubbing theatre to record sometimes very difficult music. They've never played together before. Their level of sight-reading is simply astonishing. In the separate world of the theatre, writers and directors know they can call on extraordinary levels of talent. I pay little attention to pop singers these days. Some are immensely talented and famous, they stride the earth like gods. And I've never heard of them.

IQ: A colleague of mine in English literature was recently asked about [the musical] *Hamilton* [2015] and responded, 'What is it?'

IM: Exactly. There are millions who have yet to hear even Vivaldi's *Four Seasons*. But they have other sources of joy. That's what makes culture so hard to define. I was at a small club recently to hear Van Morrison. (There are plenty of classical musicians who have never heard of him!) I looked around at the audience, at people deeply knowledgeable about blues, jazz, and gospel. This was an expert audience. Many of them had no need of the *Goldberg Variations*, of sitting very still in a concert hall, barely breathing, trying not to cough for ninety minutes on end. Both audiences profoundly satisfied, all needs met.

But the classical tradition is bejewelled with masterworks of Western civilization. They stand among our supreme achievements. Whether ninety per cent of the population has never heard them makes no difference. It's always been like that. My friend Martin Amis and I often disagree on this. He believes we're in terminal decline, that the 'moronic inferno' is raging, that people are more stupid than they've ever been. I think so-called high culture was always a minority pursuit. In music, if we are to speak of decline in this country, it's in the disappearance of free music lessons in schools. Kids from culturally under-nourished backgrounds once could name their instrument and the lessons would become available for them. It was a truly civilized arrangement and now it's gone.

IQ: As has the singing. I had singing at my junior school in Cardiff and it was identical to what you've described in Libya except we were also singing pieces like 'Waltzing Matilda'.

IM: Yes, we sang that too and also Tallis's 'Canon'. That was fun as a round.

IQ: Well it's a team environment that's non-competitive and that's now hard to find.

IM: It drew on and animated a common heritage. The problem is that it's now ideologically under attack because it excludes songs from the Indian sub-continent and Nigeria or North Africa. But that should be simple – include them all!

IQ: To what extent do you want your readers to consider a moral or ethical question in reading your novels that extends beyond the overarching narrative? I think especially of those who focus on one or two sentences in *Black Dogs* and miss the greater landscape.

IM: Sure. I cling to the idea of the novel as a form of ethical investigation. Inhabiting other minds is a moral act. But you're right, certain questions are posed, then become embedded in the perpetual present of the internet, and then circulate. I've been asked a thousand times, 'Why do your novels open

Interview with Ian McEwan 217

with such incredibly intense scenes?' I reply that nearly all of them don't, but it makes no difference. It's an occupational hazard that all writers face. You get used to it.

IQ: You've mentioned Nabokov a few times. There's nothing in Nabokov that deliberately intends to shock but rather there's a presentation of ideas from which the reader can make their own decisions. *Lolita* is an obvious example of this. It struck me that you adopt a very similar approach and that your narrative is no more gory or detailed than it needs to be but instead it's up to the reader to decide where does this actually land morally or ethically. As such the 'normal' and 'expected' are presented because they do happen. In tandem with that, it's of course highly plausible that a surgeon would listen to Bach as in *Saturday*.

IM: If I were a patient I'd rather have my operating neurosurgeon listen to the *Goldberg Variations* than Freddie and the Dreamers. Would I want someone's hands in my brain if they were listening to Barry Manilow?

IQ: Do you see the presence of muzak as being a concern in terms of the diminishing listening abilities of the general public?

IM: I'm constantly asking waiters in restaurants to turn the music off. Not down, but off. Other customers are always glad. I was somewhere recently where I made my request and there was scattered applause.

IQ: Is the film ending for *On Chesil Beach* the one that you prefer in returning to the novel after many years or are you happy with either?

IM: Some people didn't like it, some did. In the novel, the young bride, Florence, vanishes from the page and the novel follows on in a summary of Edward's unfulfilled life. It's less satisfying to do that in a movie. They need to see each other one last time and mourn their losses of almost half a century before. He goes to Wigmore Hall, to her last concert. Her now famous string quartet plays the piece – the Mozart D major quintet – that she once promised she would play for him. They don't talk or meet, they simply exchange a long gaze and shed a tear. In the movie's very last minute, I was also keen to have that beautiful melody from Rachmaninov's *Symphonic Dances*. I prefer the two piano version – here played by Graeme Mitchison and his friend James Sherlock. Graeme died earlier this year. He was a gifted scientist and a brilliant amateur musician. By unhappy chance, another element of sadness in the movie's final moments.

IQ: Would you say it was a matter of creating a similar emotional response to the one in the novel and it's a different medium with different demands?

IM: Yes, you reach for the same effects, but by other routes. Both novel and movie illustrate how life can be changed by doing nothing. Edward watches Florence walk away. He can't stop her because he's too angry. His life changes for the worst.

IQ: Why do you include references to music in your novels? Is it to help to define a character?

IM: Sometimes it helps to define a character – especially in *On Chesil Beach*. But mostly it's a helpless matter, beyond conscious scheming. Music is diffused through all aspects of my life. It plays the same part as poetry or landscape or for that matter love. It's an intensification of what or who we are. Perhaps religion plays the same role for others. Music seeps into my novels because it's a fixed element of my interior life – and the novel, pre-eminently, is an interior form.

IQ: The musical references in the novels nearly always relate to instrumental works rather than any works with text. Do you think this allows the reader to develop a greater imagination because they're not being coaxed along by a text?

IM: I spend more time listening to instrumental rather than choral music, although I do go to a fair amount of opera. However, my greatest pleasures have come from the piano, piano and violin, piano trios, string quartets and quintets. These days, I prefer a Mozart piano sonata to a Mozart symphony. I feel as though I've heard them all too many times. I'd rather be at Wigmore Hall than the Barbican. Perhaps this is a distillation of what I like in writing – a fusion of the lyrical and the precise, the intimate and the profound – difficult combinations.

IQ: The nineteenth-century writer, Eduard Hanslick, argues in *Vom Musikalisch-Schönen* [*On the musically beautiful*] that the music sets the sentiment of a piece, say a Schubert song which begins with a piano introduction, even before the text has entered and so the emotions of the listener are already in place from the outset and that arguably it could even be a different text. I wondered about this with your collaboration with Michael [Berkeley], whereby the sentiment of the text is already set before it's heard.

IM: When we were writing the opera, I suggested to Michael a structure of ten scenes of ten or twelve minutes. Over a period of a year, I was emailing them to him as he was composing. Michael occasionally sent me sound files of synthesized sections he'd just completed – and they had their reciprocal effect on me. Music and words shaped each other.

But music remains the greater force. Last Christmas, Annalena and I decided we would shock everyone by me singing and she playing the last of the *Winterreise* songs, *Der Leiermann* [*The Hurdy-Gurdy Man*]. It's by far the

Interview with Ian McEwan 219

simplest in the cycle. We tried it a few times but kept bursting out laughing at my ineptitude. The piano part is far lovelier than the singing part, especially when *I* was singing. We came across a recording by an Irish singer, once very famous – Harry Plunket Greene. He recorded an English version of *Der Leiermann*. He had an untrained voice, rather like Burl Ives. His was a slight but touching account of the piece, which you can hear on YouTube. Listening to him made me grasp the truth of what you're saying: when it's music and text, the music is almost everything. Schubert's simple introduction, like a sad and hanging question, says it all and not even Plunket Greene, not even I, could ruin it completely.

On interviewing Benjamin Britten ...

IM: I interviewed Benjamin Britten once and it was a complete disaster. I was in my first year at the University of Sussex. The student radio station, which mostly played rock music, asked me to interview Britten because he was coming on a visit. I'd never interviewed anyone in my life. I was overawed. Back then I knew more about Britten through the poet George Crabbe than through the music, but I loved *Curlew River* [1964] which I'd heard at the Aldeburgh festival that same year, 1970. I liked the opera *Peter Grimes*. My school had performed *Let's make an opera* [1949], which I hated because it seemed rather prissy. So armed with that meagre involvement, as well as a love of the Suffolk coast, I was shown in to the Presence. Britten was sitting next to Pears. I had a quarter of an hour. What amazed me was that he seemed nervous or very guarded or perhaps profoundly bored. It was a faltering interview. The more I fumbled, the shorter Britten's responses. There came a point when I'd used up all my questions. We were both tongue-tied and a terrible silence came down. The only time we loosened up a little was when we talked about Crabbe. The student radio station was not wild about poetry. My dog's dinner of an interview never made it onto the airwaves.

INTERVIEW WITH MICHAEL BERKELEY
17 JULY 2018

Iain Quinn: What is your perception of Ian's knowledge of classical music?

Michael Berkeley: Well, I think Ian's knowledge is fuelled very much by his passion for music and in particular for Bach, who he sees as supreme. This is informed in part by the fact that he has played the flute and did when I first knew him and still does, I think. The passion is very evident in that he goes to a lot of concerts, particularly chamber music and particularly in the Wigmore Hall which he loves. In fact, we wrote the *Three Cabaret Songs* [2013] together, one of which is about the Wigmore Hall. I think music is pretty central to his life and that he feels, in the famous adage, 'art should aspire'. I've always found that after he's been to a concert he talks about it with real knowledge and authority. I don't think he's interested in great huge symphonies or the avant-garde. It's not really his sensibility. On the other hand, some friends of mine saw him at a Wynton Marsalis jazz concert recently. Jazz he certainly likes and we even thought about doing an opera on Chet Baker at one point and so his interests are pretty wide and they are informed by a kind of fascination with the workings of music. One of the things he always said to me when we were working together was that he just loved working with musicians. I think he's really fascinated about how they come together, how they interact, how they speak in dialogue which I supposed he's very interested in as a novelist. I think he was largely self-taught and it was something he felt passionate about. It's more to do now with the living experience. He'll go frequently to hear Angela Hewitt and András Schiff play Bach. He's completely obsessed with it. Some of these people have become friends of his and so that has doubled or tripled the effect of the music. People will go and play at his house. So, music is central to him.

IQ: Does he see music as a source of private solace or the higher art or is it appealing to be part of another creative world that isn't literature?

MB: I think it's partly the abstract nature of music that brings the listener to bring what they want to it whereas in literature the emotions are spelled out for the reader. I think the thing about chamber music is that it's such an intimate

222   *Music and Religion in the Writings of Ian McEwan*

soul-searching medium. There's no hiding place. I don't think Ian likes irrelevant extraneous gestures, although they do occasionally come into his novels. I think he likes the economic, the programmatic. He loves lyricism and I think one of the reasons we worked together was because he felt I could write a tune, quite simply.

IQ: What would you say is IM's perception of the profession? The *For You* libretto is strikingly accurate and believable.

MB: It's very interesting because, for instance, Andrew Clements, in the *Guardian*, who had a partner, Amanda Holden, who is a good librettist, didn't like the libretto. Other people thought it was extremely funny and very clever. It is a caricature and it is satirical but it does, as you say, touch a raw nerve. But it's also about the usurping and the abuse of power that does happen in every walk of life. But I think Ian did know about various conductors and their behaviour which of course amused him. Of course a lot of opera ends bleakly, if you think of the well-known ones like *Tosca*. But there's a cathartic element in music we enjoy.

IQ: Were you surprised when you first read it?

MB: I found it immediately suggested ideas to me. The way we worked was that we did all of the collaborative side in long walks and discussions before he wrote anything. I remember in the Chiltern woods we discussed what we might do with *For You*. For a long time what he really wanted to do was write a successful musical. That's how we came to discuss Chet Baker and one or two other things but we could never find anything that was just quite right. I think, in a way, Ian has – and you get this in the novels – a wish to be writing something that's successful and very popular and that's very important to him and – this may go back to your previous question – he found the contemporary opera and even the opera world rather sort of recherché and narrow. I noticed he hadn't been to a lot of opera. He didn't know it. If David Malouf, my other librettist, had one advantage over Ian it was largely that he knew everything. He had been on the board of the Sydney Opera House. Ian loves music but I found that he didn't know a great deal about opera and so it was a learning job in a way. So, once we had had these long discussions there would be silence and then he'd come up with a finished project, jolly nearly, and of course if I had reservations he was always happy to have a look at them. But, because he has such a precise mind – and this goes back to your question about why he likes chamber music – because his mind is so ordered, because he has an almost academic, medical, research aspect to his mind – I don't think it's a coincidence that his son Will is a research scientist in Cambridge – he has got that sort of inquisitive nature which is about how things are put together and why they work. So, when we were doing *or Shall we die?* he read up on Newtonian science and the atom. I would find it quite extraordinary with him because I

Interview with Michael Berkeley   223

would go for a walk with him and he'd come out with all this information that he had assimilated and thought about. Similarly, when he was writing *Solar*, I remember going for a walk with him and he talked about these massive solar banks in the desert, long before they became evident to the general public. He's very much on top of that.

IQ: Do you think he sees the role of the author as an educator?

MB: Well, I don't think that can be what you set out to do. But in *Saturday* he went and worked with a brain surgeon, although that's what he'd enjoy doing anyway. One of his best friends, Ray, is a neuroscientist and they go for long walks and discuss life. One of the things that I think made our relationship work, given that I was not able to offer an absolute cornucopia of scientific information, was that he feels rather in awe of musicians. He is fascinated by them.

IQ: Do you think he's sorry he didn't go farther with his own musical study?

MB: I think he found his natural thing in writing. You see my late wife, Deborah, was his agent and she saw his development from UEA [University of East Anglia]. I always saw that I was in a position of some privilege in his mind simply by view of being a musician.

IQ: Which novels of IM did you know before writing the two pieces?

MB: Yes, I think I had read most of them then and certainly now. I particularly like *On Chesil Beach* because it was the period when I was young too and he was also young. But also the idea of the contrary musical interests as I played in a rock group while being classically trained. That dichotomy was interesting for me.

IQ: Have you introduced IM to new works of the repertoire/performances?

MB: Yes, there were pieces over the years.

IQ: Is there any repertoire you know he dislikes?

MB: I don't think he likes huge expansive even floppy canvases, although having said that Ian can go to a concert and be completely transported by something I wouldn't have thought he would have liked. I don't think he's into opera or contemporary music. I think I have mentioned Birtwistle to him, but I've never had the thought that it really interested him. Most people see lyricism – and I think he does – as a continuation of tonality and that's a problem for a huge part of the musical audience. Once tonality seems to go out of the window they get lost, like landing on Mars. I think in *For You*, which has a fragmented

224   *Music and Religion in the Writings of Ian McEwan*

tonality, he got to know it by coming to rehearsals and began to see why it was as it is and he's too intelligent not to begin to acquire the ability to hear a new language, but I don't think he relates to it naturally. Another thing that he has said in my presence was that he is used to being the Major General and when you work with a composer you're the sort of Lance Corporal. For someone who likes to control things, like Ian, to be on top of things, with a life that's quite ordered, it means a different sort of approach.

IQ: In the case of the oratorio, did you both feel that there needed to be an artistic response to the times?

MB: Absolutely. The commission came from the LSO chorus and Richard Hickox and I turned to Ian because he'd become a really good friend at that point through Deborah. I wanted to stretch myself and work with a good young writer who was interesting and whose work I liked. I particularly liked those early short stories, *Between the Sheets* and *First Love, Last Rites*. I nearly did the music for a film of *The Cement Garden*, which didn't happen although I went to the set though. He seemed a natural to work with but he said, 'I don't think we can avoid what seems to be the overwhelming conundrum of nuclear weapons'. I was very happy to be taken down that path. As I said, he completely explored everything to do with the bomb and the scientists' work. I actually still like the piece very much. There are some things I would do differently but Jac van Steen did a performance in Cardiff, a couple of years ago, which was terrific and he got the tempi just right. Richard [Hickox] was a great choral conductor but he wasn't very rhythmically incisive, I don't think. The bit where we have the parody of a Victorian hymn and the rock group sort of bursts in sounded really rather clumsy in the first performances and when Jac did it it was completely natural.

IQ: Was the first performance under Hickox very different to his recording, from your perspective?

MB: Yes, but this was very different again to the recording. I think the piece in one sense was very successful, the audience liked it and it was done several times. However, I think one or two critics were irritated that this had become a major event before I had won my spurs in their minds and partially because Ian was the flavour of the month. So, it got a rather mixed critical response. I still like it and the point where the mother finds the burnt child and the Blake is set like Bach chorales was very telling too. He drove that from the subject view of the matter.

IQ: How much of the oratorio is supposed to have a cynical element to it? What is the rock section supposed to symbolize?

Interview with Michael Berkeley 225

MB: The Victorian hymn was Ian's way of pointing up the overbearing righteousness of people advocating nuclear war. The rock idea was more from me, following on from that, and what I wanted to do was make it sound grotesque and so add another layer of cynicism in a way. The complacency of what he was saying was underlined first in the sense of the Victorian hymn but also with a horribly jaunty rock bursting in.

IQ: Given the very strong association of the States to the nuclear situation, was it in any sense supposed to represent an American influence?

MB: Yes, I think it was their attitude that he most worried about, definitely. Afterwards, he was actually very excited by it [the oratorio] and I think he felt it did what he wanted it to do. In preparation, I would play through things on the piano for him but what he wasn't prepared for – and people who aren't real musicians never are – is what happens when something is then heard with an orchestra. That always takes them aback because they might be able to read a single line of music but are completely dumbfounded when they hear music suddenly come alive with an orchestra. Ian was always very excited by that.

IQ: ... more so than seeing a novel on the screen?

MB: Yes, I think so, much more so because it's the other way around almost. If you are reading a novel you are using your imagination to add the pictures and that is invariably, if it's a good novel, more powerful than anything that comes up on the screen. Whereas with music you're being given an aural picture that you probably couldn't imagine.

IQ: Would you say that the governing process in working on the opera and the oratorio was to make people think at the end rather than simply telling a story? A lot of his novels leave it to the reader to decide what's morally right or wrong. Was that also the case here?

MB: Yes, I think that's absolutely it. You want to lay these things out and people have to decide and what you hope is that through the power of music they become moved and that's especially the case with *or Shall we die?*

IQ: Do you think the oratorio text was intentionally provoking?

MB: Yes, I did and I thought it would. There was quite a lot of comment at the time about should anyone be making these sort of political statements in music. In retrospect I would probably think differently about doing that now but I was young and it was an exciting idea. The trouble is that it tends to garner the kind of attention that you don't necessarily want. For instance, we had a lot of people writing who felt that they or their loved ones had been saved by the bombing of Hiroshima. There was quite a right-wing backlash and a lot of

226   *Music and Religion in the Writings of Ian McEwan*

people said it was a CND oratorio but it wasn't and we weren't members of CND. It was not as simple as that. This was a piece very much in the tradition of [Tippett's] *A Child of Our Time* [1939/41/44] or the [Britten's] *War Requiem* [1961/62]. In other words, it was not actually taking a 'you must think this way' approach but using history – for instance, the mother finding the child – to sound a warning note about nuclear proliferation and that it could annihilate us. Of course it brought about a political argument of the reverse saying that nuclear arms kept us safe. So yes, it did get us into a bit of a left versus right argument.

IQ: Do you think it's dangerous in Britain for a composer to attach themselves to a contemporary issue as opposed to, for instance, just setting a Shakespeare play?

MB: I think that sometimes it's important to follow your conscience if you feel that's something you can't avoid and that's what we felt then.

IQ: Do you think that's still the case with Ian now?

MB: Yes, I do actually. Because Ian writes well he gets asked to comment on a huge amount of things perhaps more than others. He will always write you an interesting, though-provoking piece and that comes out in the writing. He feels he's a product of his times and he cannot ignore them.

IQ: Do you see the 1980s and 1990s as a turning point in the role of classical music in Britain in terms of music appreciation? Have we become more and more a promenade or pleasure garden culture by comparison to many other countries in Europe?

MB: Yes, I think this fits in with a move towards instant gratification and we know this from the way that the BBC and ITV feel they have to change a shot every twelve seconds because people will be bored and so you very rarely get something like *Private Passions* on television, something like *Face to Face*. It gets more and more difficult actually. Ian rises above that because he's a best-selling author but for the rest of us the challenges of putting on music that is provocative, music that asks questions, are more and more difficult. I think everything has become more commercialized but there's also something else. In a way, minimalism has done us a terrible disservice, however wonderful it may be in some ways. It's easy-listening contemporary music. People will think they're putting on contemporary music because they're putting on a piece of John Adams – an incredibly skilful composer and I like him – but I don't like all minimalism and I can't abide Philip Glass or Michael Nyman either but I can understand it. The trouble is that it's a sort of popular art form now which I think has supplanted music that is more demanding, more challenging.

Interview with Michael Berkeley 227

IQ: You could argue that *Short Ride in a Fast Machine* is exactly what the public wants as it's quick, doesn't last too long and then you can get back to Brahms.

MB: Yes, that's it. You begin to see this in the people that are being commissioned now, especially in a culture of quotas, instead of good composers rising to the top whoever they are. The overriding principle has to be quality not numbers. Very few people now will sit down and read a Shakespeare sonnet or listen to a Beethoven sonata because it doesn't offer an immediate response to them.

IQ: Where do you think the long-standing cynicism towards new art comes from in Britain?

MB: I have thought about this a lot doing *Private Passions*. Whereas very few people pick anything beyond Britten – you can almost count them on the fingers and toes of two hands and two feet, I think it starts with the fact that we didn't really have a court system that felt it was important to employ or patronize musicians. Hunting and shooting was what they did.

IQ: Do you think it's problematic that in the case of Handel and later Haydn and Mendelssohn it was patronage of a foreigner?

MB: Yes, maybe, absolutely. I think we're more conservative about art in this country. If you think about the way the French were with Boulez and IRCAM it's very different. That said, I find the Germans' almost total need for contemporary things goes the other way. I've heard a lot of rather bad music in Germany that came from a sort of studious application of atonality and contemporary ideas. But here, I don't understand it because there is a huge audience that goes to the Tate Modern. We are much more advanced now as a society in our appreciation of the visual arts because we are bombarded with complex images every day on television and on the internet and in the cinema. Music is more problematic but it's interesting that when contemporary ideas are allied to a narrative or a visual image we don't question them. I always think of the shower scene in *Psycho* with the strings playing on the back of the bow or the wrong side of the bridge and we can take the musical language there but if you heard it in a concert hall people would think it was ugly.

IQ: There's an interesting reverse parallel there within the world of church music where people will criticize a particular setting of the evening canticles by Stanford over another and yet have no issue hearing the same musical language in a concert hall or on the radio.

IQ: Do you think some of this relates more broadly to the ever-present remnants of the class system and the present state of Britain whereby criticism in a dissatisfied society is seen as an essential right?

228   *Music and Religion in the Writings of Ian McEwan*

MB: I think that's true and also that music requires time and effort, especially music that you're not familiar with.

IQ: Do you think that the inclusion of Ian's novels on school syllabi has given a prominence to musical works that many younger readers and indeed their friends and family may not have previously encountered? Is it a subtle education as it relates to the identity of a character?

MB: Yes, that's an interesting observation. I think he is also someone that can write the most astonishingly gripping openings to books. If you think of the child being lost in the supermarket or the man in the balloon, those are such staggering opening sections. Real life is about bleakness too. A lot of Ian's best writing seems to pivot on a mistaken sentence, a misunderstanding and that's what makes it so painful.

IQ: How do you account for the relative lack of success of works like the Andrew Lloyd Webber *Requiem* [1985] or the Paul McCartney *Liverpool Oratorio* [1991], given that they're not provocative texts and yet associated with well-known figures?

MB: If they had been good it would have been different but the fact that you can write a hit pop tune does not mean you can write a symphonic work.

IQ: Do you mean that they're not significant enough to enter the classical canon and that meanwhile the popular canon has no interest in a requiem or an oratorio and so they have no natural place?

MB: Yes. When I was studying with Richard Rodney Bennett he said you have got to understand that writing a sixteen bar verse and chorus is a completely different thing than writing a piece with extended form and development in it. It's a completely different gift and very few people can do both. In a sense Mozart did sort of do that in some ways. To be very brutal about it, I don't think those pieces sound like one or the other. It's like opera singers trying to sing light music. It's often as painful as hearing a rock singer singing opera.

BIBLIOGRAPHY

Primary Sources

McEwan, Ian. *Amsterdam*. London: Vintage, 2005.

McEwan, Ian. *Atonement*. London: Vintage, 2016.

McEwan, Ian. *Black Dogs*. London: Vintage, 1998.

McEwan, Ian. *The Child in Time*. London: Vintage, 1992.

McEwan, Ian. *The Children Act*. London: Jonathan Cape, 2014.

McEwan, Ian. *The Cockroach*. London: Jonathan Cape, 2019.

McEwan, Ian. *The Comfort of Strangers*. London: Vintage, 2006.

McEwan, Ian. *Enduring Love*. London: Vintage, 2004.

McEwan, Ian. *First Love, Last Rites*. London: Vintage, 1997.

McEwan, Ian. *For You: The Libretto*. London: Vintage, 2008.

McEwan, Ian. *The Imitation Game: Three Plays for Television*. London: Pan Books, 1981.

McEwan, Ian. *The Innocent*. London: Jonathan Cape, 1990.

McEwan, Ian. *Lessons*. New York: Alfred A. Knopf, 2022.

McEwan, Ian. *Machines Like Me*. London: Jonathan Cape, 2019.

McEwan, Ian. *A Move Abroad: or Shall we die?* and *The Ploughman's Lunch*. London: Picador, 1989.

McEwan, Ian. *Nutshell*. London: Jonathan Cape, 2016.

McEwan, Ian. *On Chesil Beach*. New York: Nan A. Talese, 2007.

McEwan, Ian. 'Psychopolis', in *In Between the Sheets*. London: Vintage, 1997.

McEwan, Ian. *Rose Blanche*. London: Red Fox, 2004.

McEwan, Ian. *Saturday*. London: Vintage, 2006.

McEwan, Ian. *Science*. London: Vintage, 2019.

McEwan, Ian. *Solar*. New York: Nan A. Talese, 2010.

McEwan, Ian. *Sweet Tooth*. New York: Nan A. Talese, 2012.

Interviews

Quinn, Iain. 'Interview with Ian McEwan', 2018.

Quinn, Iain. 'Interview with Michael Berkeley', 2018.

Secondary Sources

Amis, Kingsley. *Lucky Jim*. Garden City, NY: Doubleday, 1954.

Amory, Mark (ed.). *The Letters of Evelyn Waugh*. New Haven and New York: Ticknor & Fields, 1980.

230   *Bibliography*

Babbitt, Milton. 'Who cares if you listen', *High Fidelity*, 8:2 (1958), 38–40.

Bennett, Alan. *The Old Country*. London: Faber and Faber, 1978.

Bennett, Alan. *The Laying on of Hands*. London: Profile Books, 2001.

Bennett, Alan. *The Habit of Art.* London: Faber and Faber, 2009.

Bennett, Alan. *Keep On Keeping On*. London: Faber and Faber, 2016.

Bennett, Alan. *Alleluia!.* London: Faber & Faber, 2018.

Berenson, Frances. 'Interpreting the Emotional Content of Music', in Michael Krausz (ed.), *The Interpretation of Music: Philosophical Essays.* Oxford: Oxford University Press, 1993.

Berkeley, Michael. *Private Passions.* London: Faber and Faber, 2005.

Betjeman, John. *John Betjeman's Collected Poems.* London: John Murray, 1970.

Blum, Ronald. 'The Impact of Górecki's Symphony No. 3', *Chicago Sun-Times*, 26 June 1994.

Bradford, Richard. *The Novel Now*. Oxford: Blackwell Publishing, 2007.

Bradley, Arthur, and Andrew Tate. *The New Atheist Novel Fiction Philosophy and Polemic after 9/11*. ed. Andrew Tate. London: Continuum, 2010.

Bruce, Steve. 'Serious Religion in Secular Culture', in *Scottish Gods: Religion in Modern Scotland, 1900–2012*. Edinburgh: Edinburgh University Press, 2014.

Burnham, Scott. *Mozart's Grace*. Princeton: Princeton University Press, 2012.

Cage, John. *Silence*. Middletown: Wesleyan University Press, 1961.

Childs, Peter. *The Fiction of Ian McEwan: A Reader's Guide to Essential Criticism*. London: Palgrave Macmillan, 2006.

Childs, Peter. *Ian McEwan's Enduring Love*. London: Routledge, 2007.

Clarke, Peter. *Hope and Glory: Britain, 1900–2000*. London: Penguin, 2004.

Coe, Jonathan. *Middle England*. London: Viking, 2018.

Coleridge, Samuel Taylor and Elisabeth Schneider (1964), 'On the Constitution of the Church and State', in *Selected Poetry and Prose*, New York: Holt, Rinehart & Winston.

Day, Barry (ed.). *The Lyrics of Noël Coward*. London: Heinemann, 1965.

Debussy, Claude. 'Monsieur Croche the Dilettante Hater', trans. B. N. Langdon Davies, *Three Classics in the Aesthetic of Music*. New York: Dover, 1962.

Dreyfus, Laurence. *Bach and the Patters of Invention*. Cambridge: Harvard University Press, 2004.

Ferrey, Benjamin. *Recollections of A. N. Welby Pugin, and His Father, Augustus Pugin*. London: Edward Stanford, 1861.

Foreman, Lewis (ed.). *From Parry to Britten: British Music in Letters, 1900–1945*. Portland: Amadeus Press, 1987.

Freud, Sigmund. 'Civilization and its Discontents', trans. and ed. James Strachey et al., *The Standard Edition of the Complete Psychological Works of Sigmund Freud*, 21. London: Hogarth Press, 1961.

Freud, Sigmund. 'Formulations on the Two Principles of Mental Function', trans. and ed. James Strachey et al., *The Standard Edition of the Complete Psychological Works of Sigmund Freud*, 12. London: Hogarth Press, 1961.

Friedman, Dustin. 'E.M. Forster, the Clapham Sect, and the Secular Public Sphere', *Journal of Modern Literature*, 39:1 (2015), 19–37.

Froude, Richard Hurrell. *Remains of The Late Reverend Richard Hurrell Froude, M. A.* London: J. G. and F. Rivington, 1839.

Goehr, Lydia. *The Imaginary Museum of Musical Works.* Oxford: Clarendon Press, 1992.

Gould, Glenn. 'Liner notes', *Bach: The Goldberg Variations.* Vinyl recording, Columbia ML 5060, 1955.

Gould, Glenn. 'Let's Ban Applause', *Musical America*, February 1962.

Gould, Glenn. 'The Goldberg Variations', *The Glenn Gould Collection.* Compact Disc, 13, Sony Classical SLV 48.

Greene, Graham. 'The Paradox of Hope', *Collected Essays.* London: Penguin, 1970.

Greene, Graham. *Stamboul Train.* London: Penguin, 1978.

Greer, Germaine. *The Female Eunuch.* New York: McGraw Hill, 1970.

Groes, Sebastian. *Ian McEwan.* Contemporary Critical Perspectives, 2nd edn. London: Bloomsbury, 2013.

Haffenden, John. *Novelists in Interview.* London: Routledge, 1985.

Hamilton, Patrick. *Craven House.* London: Abacus, 2017.

Harris, Robin (ed.). *The Collected Speeches of Margaret Thatcher.* London: Harper Collins, 1997.

Hayes, Bill. 'Oliver Sacks – A Composer and his Last Work', *The New York Times*, 24 October 2017.

Head, Dominic. *Ian McEwan.* Manchester: Manchester University Press, 2007.

Head, Dominic. *The State of the Novel – Britain and Beyond.* Oxford: Wiley-Blackwell, 2008.

Head, Dominic (ed.). *The Cambridge Companion to Ian McEwan.* Cambridge: Cambridge University Press, 2019.

Hegel, Georg W. F. *Aesthetics: Lecture on Fine Art*, trans. Thomas Malcolm Knox. London: Clarendon Press, 1975.

Hewison, Robert. *Cultural Capital: The Rise and Fall of Creative Britain.* London: Verso, 2014.

Hill, Susan. 'At the Still Point of the Turning World', in Christopher Lewis and Stephen Platten (eds), *Flagships of the Spirit: Cathedrals in Society.* London: Darton, Longman Todd, 1998.

Howard, David. 'Ian McEwan', *Book and Magazine Collector* (London), 84:30–36 (1991).

James, Henry. *Cathedrals and Castles.* London: Penguin, 2009.

Jenkins, David. *God, Politics and the Future.* London: Wilton, Morehouse-Barlow, 1988.

Khandekar, Ashutosh. *BBC Music Magazine*, 16:9 (May 2008).

Larkin, Philip. *Collected Poems.* London: Faber and Faber, 1988.

Leader, Zachary (ed.). *On Modern British Fiction.* Oxford: Oxford University Press, 2003.

Lebrecht, Norman. *The Maestro Myth: Great Conductors in Pursuit of Power.* London: Citadel Press, 1991.

Levitin, Daniel J. *This is Your Brain on Music.* New York: Dutton, 2016.

Bibliography

Lindbeck, George. *The Nature of Doctrine: Religion and Theology in a Postliberal Age*. Philadelphia, PA: Westminster Press, 1984.

Lyall, Sarah. '"Amsterdam" by Ian McEwan Wins Booker Prize', *The New York Times*, 28 October 1998.

Malcolm, David. *Understanding Ian McEwan*. Columbia: University of South Carolina Press, 2022.

Maycock, Robert. 'Scarpia: A Night to Discomfort the Critics: A Triumphant Reception for Henryk Gorecki's Third Symphony and a Startling Recital for Massed Dansettes and Projector', *The Independent*, 10 June 1993, online at <https://www.independent.co.uk/arts-entertainment/scarpia-a night-to-discomfort-the-critics-a-triumphant-reception-for-henryk-goreck-is-third-symphony1490720.html> [accessed 17 December 2020].

McCue, Jim. 'Sex, Psyche and Salvation', *The Times* (London), 8 May 1990.

McCusker, Eamonn. 'Symphony No. 3: Sorrowful Songs', *CD Times*, 6 July 2007.

McEwan, Ian. 'Ian McEwan on Religion in the Twenty-First Century', *The Guardian*, 2014, online at <https://www.youtube.com/watch?v=L-qNht-38CeE> [accessed 17 December 2020].

McGregor, Tom. *Kavanagh Q.C. II*. Bath: Chivers Press, 1997.

Meade, M. Nathaniel. 'Noise Pollution: The Sound Behind Heart Effects', *Environmental Health Perspectives*, 115 (2007).

Mendelssohn-Bartholdy, Felix (1965), 'Letter to Marc-André Souchey, October 15, 1842', in *The Musician's World*, ed. Hans Gal. London: Thames & Hudson, 1965.

Mortimer, John. *Titmuss Regained*. London: Viking, 1990.

Nin, Anaïs. *A Spy in the House of Love*. London: Penguin, 2001.

Orwell, George. *A Clergyman's Daughter*. London: Penguin, 1990.

Ostwald, Peter F.. *Glenn Gould: The Ecstasy and Tragedy of Genius*. New York: W. W. Norton, 1997.

Page, Tim (ed.). 'Of Mozart and Related Matters: Glenn Gould in Conversation with Bruno Monsaingeon', in *The Glenn Gould Reader*, New York: A. P. Knopf, 1984.

Palmer, Andrew. *Encounters with British Composers*. Woodbridge: Boydell Press, 2015.

Paxman, Jeremy. *Friends in High Places*. London: Penguin Books, 1991.

Paxman, Jeremy. *The English: A Portrait of a People*. London: Penguin Books, 1999.

Paxman, Jeremy. *The Political Animal: An Anatomy*. London: Penguin Books, 2007.

Phillips, Adam. *Unforbidden Pleasures*. London: Penguin, 2016.

Plant, Raymond. 'The Anglican Church and the Secular State', in George Moyser (ed.), *Church and Politics Today: Essays on the Role of the Church of England in Contemporary Politics*. Edinburgh: Clark, 1985.

Reed, Philip and Mitchell, Donald (eds). *Letters from a Life: Selected Letters and Diaries of Benjamin Britten, Volume 2*. London: Faber and Faber, 1991.

Bibliography 233

Remnick, David. 'Naming what is there: Ian McEwan in Conversation with David Remnick', in Roberts, Ryan (ed.), *Conversations with Ian McEwan*. Jackson: University Press of Mississippi, 2010.

Rennert, Jonathan and Weir, Gillian. 'Interview on Music, Muzak, Noise, Silence and Thought', *Organ Club Journal*, 4 (1993).

Reynolds, Joshua. *Discourses on Art*. New York: Collier Books, 1961.

Reynolds, Margaret and Noakes, Jonathan. *Ian McEwan: The Essential Guide*. London: Vintage, 2005.

Rosen, Charles. *Sonata Forms*. New York: W. W. Norton, 1980.

Rosen, Charles. *The Classical Style: Haydn, Mozart, Beethoven*. New York: W. W. Norton, 1998.

Rowland, Christopher. 'Friends of Albion', in Christopher Lewis and Stephen Platten (eds), *Flagships of the Spirit: Cathedrals in Society*. London: Darton, Longman Todd, 1998.

Rushdie, Salman. *The Satanic Verses*. New York: Macmillan, 2007.

Rushdie, Salman. *Joseph Anton*. New York: Random House, 2012.

Ruskin, John. *The Stones of Venice*. Sunnyside, Orpington: George Allen, 1886.

Russell, Bertrand. *Why I Am Not a Christian*. London: George Allen & Unwin, 1957.

Růžičková, Zuzana and Holden, Wendy. *One Hundred Miracles: A Memorial of Music and Survival*. London: Bloomsbury, 2019.

Ryan, Kiernan. *Ian McEwan*. Plymouth: Northcote House, 1994.

Sacks, Oliver. *Musicophilia: Tales of Music and the Brain*. New York: Alfred P. Knopf, 2007.

Said, Edward. *On Late Style: Music and Literature Against the Grain*. New York: Pantheon Books, 2006.

Saunders, Frances Stonor. *The Cultural Cold War: the CIA and the World of Arts and Letters*. New York: The New Press, 2013.

Schemberg, Claudia. Achieving 'At-one-ment': Storytelling and the Concept of the Self in Ian McEwan's *The Child in Time, Black Dogs, Enduring Love* and *Atonement* (thesis). Frankfurt: Peter Lang, 2004.

Scott, Derek B. 'The Power of Music', in *Musical Style and Social Meaning*. Farnham: Ashgate, *c*.2010.

Scruton, Roger. 'Review of Enduring Love', *The Sunday Telegraph*, 16 September 2001.

Scruton, Roger. *Modern Culture*. London: Bloomsbury, 2005.

Scruton, Roger. *England: An Elegy*. London: Continuum, 2006.

Scruton, Roger. *Our Church: A Personal History of the Church of England*. London: Atlantic Books, 2013.

Slay Jr., Jack. *Ian McEwan*. New York: Twayne, 1996.

Shrimpton, Nicholas (ed.), *William Blake Selected Poems*. Oxford: Oxford University Press, 2019.

Smith, Graeme. 'Margaret Thatcher's Christian Faith – A Case Study in Political Ideology', *Journal of Religious Ethics*, 35:2 (June 2007).

Sontag, Susan. *Regarding the Pain of Others*. London: Penguin Books, 2005.

234 *Bibliography*

Spark, Muriel. *The Bachelors*. Edinburgh: Canongate, 2015.

Storr, Anthony. *Music and the Mind*. Toronto: The Free Press, 1992.

Tew, Philip. *The Contemporary British Novel*. London: Continuum, 2004, 2007 (2nd ed.).

Tippett, Michael. 'Art, Judgement and Belief: Towards the Condition of Music', in Peter Abbs (ed.), *The Symbolic Order: A Contemporary Reader on the Arts Debate*. London: Falmer Press, 1989.

Turner, Barry. *Beacon for Change: How the 1951 Festival of Britain Helped to Shape a New Age*. London: Aurum Press, 2011.

Vincent, John. 'The Thatcher Governments, 1979–1987', in Peter Hennessy and Anthony Seldon (eds), *Ruling Performance: British Governments from Attlee to Thatcher*. Oxford: Basil Blackwell, 1987.

Waterhouse, Keith. *There Is a Happy Land*. London: Sceptre/Hodder & Stoughton General Division, 1957.

Wells, Lynn. *Ian McEwan*. Basingstoke: Palgrave Macmillan, 2009.

Wells, Lynn. *New British Fiction*. London: Palgrave Macmillan, 2010.

Wilde, Oscar. *The Soul of Man Under Socialism*. Boston: J. W. Luce, 1918.

Wilkinson, Revd Steve. 'A Perfect Knight – Roger Scruton', *The Spectator*, 18 January 2020.

Williams, Peter. *Bach: The Goldberg Variations*. Cambridge: Cambridge University Press, 2001.

Zalewski, Daniel. 'The Background Hum', *The New Yorker*, 15 February 2009.

Web-Based Sources

Barone, Michael and Preston, Simon. 'Simon Says', *Pipedreams*, 19 April 1999, online at <https://www.pipedreams.org/episode/1999/9916> [accessed 17 December 2020].

Bates, Stephen. 'Primate Who Discarded Anglican Image as Tory Party at Prayer', *The Guardian*, 12 July, online at <https://www.theguardian.com/uk/2000/jul/13/religion.world> [accessed 17 December 2020].

Bell, Matthew. 'Margaret Thatcher's Funeral: Maverick Bishop's Sermon Will Not Be', *The Independent*, 14 April, online at <https://www.independent.co.uk/news/uk/politics/margaretthatchers-funeral-maverick-bishops-sermon-will-not-be-vetted-by-no-10–8572220.html> [accessed 17 December 2020].

Dawkins, Richard and McEwan, Ian. 'Interview with Ian McEwan', Richard Dawkins Foundation for Reason and Science, online at <https://www.youtube.com/watch?v=o7LjriWFAEs> (2 February 2009) [accessed 17 December 2020].

Hill, Amelia and Connolly, Kate. 'Rattle Fires Parting Shot at Brit Art Bratpack', *The Observer*, 25 August, online at <https://www.theguardian.com/uk/2002/aug/25/arts.artsnews> [accessed 17 December 2020].

Bibliography

James, Aaron. '"Unbelieving Bishop" Title "Unfair" Says Former Dean'. *Premier Christian News*, 5 September 2016, online at <https://premierchristian.news/en/news/article/unbelieving-bishop-title-unfair-says-former-dean> [accessed 17 December 2020].

MacCulloch, Diarmaid. 'How God Made the English', 2012, BBC, online at <https://www.bbc.co.uk/programmes/b01hbkvt> [accessed 17 December 2020].

Robinson, Martin. 'Killjoy Pope Crushes Christmas Nativity Traditions: New Jesus Book Reveals There Were No Donkeys beside Crib, No Lowing Oxen and Definitely No Carols', *Daily Mail Online*, Associated Newspapers, 21 November 2012, online at <https://www.dailymail.co.uk/news/article-2236195/New-Jesus-book-reveals-donkeys-crib-lowingoxen-definitely-carols-Christmas.html> [accessed 17 December 2020].

Taylor, Richard. 'Churches – How to Read Them', 2010, [TV programme], online at <https://www.bbc.co.uk/programmes/b00tnp8f> [accessed 17 December 2020].

The Art of Conducting: Great Conductors of the Past (2002), [DVD], Teldec, online at <https://www.youtube.com/watch?v=LynqU4AjvtA> [accessed 17 December 2020].

The Queen's Christmas Broadcast 2018. The Royal Family, 3 January 2019, online at <https://www.royal.uk/queens-christmas-broadcast-2018> [accessed 17 December 2020].

Welby, Justin. 'Archbishop of Canterbury: I Am Not Too Political', *The Guardian*, 2 December 2018, online at <https://www.theguardian.com/uk-news/2018/dec/02/archbishop-of-canterbury-i-am-not-too-political-justin-welby> [accessed 18 December 2020].

INDEX

Adès, Thomas   178, 214–215
Alwyn, William   183
Amis, Kingsley
   Lucky Jim   91, 136, 176, 176*n*, 200
Amis, Martin   25, 216
Argerich, Martha   82
Armstrong, Karen   15, 37, 38,
   72–73, 91
Arnell, Richard   183,
Arnold, Malcolm   183, 186
Arnold, Matthew   112, 129, 164
Auden, Wystan Hugh   20, 73, 131,
   133, 153–155, 191–193, 200–203,
   215

Bach, J. S.
   Goldberg Variations, BWV 988   6,
      81–87, 115–116, 135, 156, 204,
      206, 212, 214–217
Babbitt, Milton
   Who cares if you listen?   183
Baker, Chet   221, 222
Bainbridge, Simon   17, 190
Bartók, Béla   106, 112, 215
Beethoven, Ludwig van   81, 88, 109,
   114, 143, 158, 194, 197–198, 212,
   227
Benjamin, George   178, 214–215
Bennett, Alan
   Alleluia!   56, 130
   Habit of Art, The   18, 20, 130–131,
      153–155, 191, 200, 202
   Keeping On Keeping On   152, 154
   Laying on of Hands, The   33
   Old Country, The   69
Berenson, Frances   160
Berkeley, Michael   82, 89, 109, 135,
   143, 178, 184, 189, 191, 197, 208,
   215, 218

For You   7, 8, 20, 50, 60, 79, 111,
   117, 126, 136, 145, 148–149,
   153, 154, 155, 156, 169, 170,
   172, 173, 177, 178, 179, 186,
   191, 192, 193, 199, 200, 201–
   202, 203–204, 205, 206–208,
   222, 233
or Shall we die?   11–12, 24, 31,
   32, 33, 41, 50, 51, 55, 57, 58, 59,
   60–65, 68, 69, 70, 71, 90, 102,
   106–108, 111, 131, 172, 191,
   197, 222, 225
Private Passions   83, 122, 226, 227
Berlioz, Hector   120
Betjeman, John   1, 12, 15, 23, 30, 35,
   36, 43, 45, 47, 54, 74, 75
   Exeter   47, 48, 49
Blake, Howard   17, 193–194, 195
Blake, William   42, 45, 61–62, 91,
   133, 198, 224
Blum, Ronald   194
Burgess, Anthony   88
Bradford, Richard   7–8, 23, 170
Bracke, Astrid   6
Bradley, Arthur, and Tate, Andrews
   11, 24, 25
Bridge, Frank   63, 106, 112
Britten, Benjamin   20, 50, 63, 106,
   112, 131, 153–154, 155, 175, 185,
   191, 192, 194, 195, 196, 198, 200,
   201, 202, 203, 205, 206, 219, 226,
   227
Bruce, Steve   51, 52, 53, 55, 71
Burnham, Scott   80–81, 158, 162,
   165, 166

Cambridge, King's College   49–50,
   134
Canterbury Cathedral   44

238   *Index*

Cherkassky, Shura   112
Coe, Jonathan
   Middle England   133
Coleridge, Samuel Taylor   48–49, 197
Coltrane, John   213
Coventry Cathedral   31, 50, 175
Coward, Noël
   Don't make fun of the fair   170–171, 173, 174

Davies, Peter Maxwell   190, 195
Davis, Miles   213
Dawkins, Richard   9, 10, 26, 31, 72, 74
Debussy, Claude   105, 215
Dreyfus, Laurence   115
Drummond, John   187
Durham Cathedral   44, 45

Eliot, T. S.   13, 94–95
Exeter Cathedral   44, 47, 48, 49
Epstein, Jacob   50

Freedland, Jonathan   27–28
Freud, Sigmund   104
Friedman, Dustin   30
Froude, Richard Hurrell   53–54

Gilbert, William Schwenck and
   Sullivan, Arthur   129–131
Goehr, Alexander   190, 208
Goehr, Lydia   164
Górecki, Henryk Mikołaj   135, 184, 186
   *Third Symphony – Symphony of
     Sorrowful Songs*   194–195
Gould, Glenn   81, 82, 83, 112, 147, 204, 205, 206
Greene, Graham
   Stamboul Train   33
Greer, Germaine
   Female Eunuch, The   102–103, 105, 108, 111

Hamilton, Patrick
   Craven House   193
Hayes, Bill   142
Head, Dominic   2, 3, 13, 26, 48, 61, 80, 83, 102, 112, 135, 157, 170, 172
Hegel, Georg W. F.   158
Hewison, Robert   1, 20, 21, 171, 173, 175, 176
Hewitt, Angela   82, 112, 212, 215, 221
Hill, Susan   15, 19, 30, 44, 53, 54
Hitchens, Christopher   10, 24–25, 42, 72
Holden, Wendy and Růžičková, Zuzana   116
Howells, Herbert   183–184
Hurd, Douglas   113
Hussey, Walter   50
Hutchings, David and McLeish, Tom   13–14

Ivanov, Yevgeny   102

James, Henry
   Cathedrals and Castles   37–38
James, Phyllis Dorothy   38, 54
James, Skip   213
Jarrett, Keith   119–120
Jay, Antony, and Lynn, Jonathan
   *The Complete Yes Prime Minister
     The Bishop's Gambit*   40
Jenkins, David   16, 52, 58, 68, 69
Johnson, Boris   42–43
Johnson, Samuel   174–175, 178, 179
Josephs, Wilfred   183

Keeler, Christine   102

Langer, Susanne K.   100
Larkin, Philip   1
   Church Going   12, 15, 17, 23, 25, 30–31, 35, 36, 54, 74, 99
Lebrecht, Norman   20, 204
Leonhardt, Gustav   82, 83, 112

Levitin, Daniel J.   1, 18, 97, 122, 143
Lindbeck, George   64–65
Llandaff Cathedral   50
London, St Paul's Cathedral   44, 58
Lutyens, Elizabeth   179, 190, 193
Lutyens, Robert   173
Lynn, Jonathan, and Jay, Antony
  The Complete Yes Prime Minister
  The Bishop's Gambit   40

MacCulloch, Diarmaid   28–29
Mahler, Gustav   120, 149
Malcolm, David   170 *n*3
Markham, Ian   11
Marsalis, Wynton   221
Maycock, Robert   195
McCartney, Paul   188, 196–197, 228
McEwan, Ian
  Amsterdam   6–7, 8, 20, 50, 60, 62,
    83, 88–89, 89, 95, 106, 111, 123,
    126, 127, 135, 136, 138, 145,
    153, 154, 155, 156, 169, 170,
    171, 172, 173, 177, 178, 179,
    182–183, 184, 186, 187–188,
    189, 190, 191, 192, 193, 194,
    196, 197, 198–199, 200–201,
    203, 207, 208
  Atonement   2, 7, 20, 43, 52,
    109–110, 130 *n*19, 55
  Black Dogs   135, 167, 179, 216
  Chesil Beach, On   2, 4, 7, 8, 17, 18,
    19, 32, 47, 50, 63, 69, 70, 79, 79,
    88, 93, 94, 98, 99, 101, 102, 103,
    106, 108–109, 111, 112, 117,
    118, 119, 121, 122, 135, 138, 142,
    143–144, 144, 145, 147, 148,
    149, 151, 153, 155, 156, 157, 158,
    159, 160, 160–161, 162, 179,
    192, 201, 217, 218, 223
  Children Act, The   2, 4, 10, 16, 18,
    31, 32, 34–35, 45, 50, 57, 72, 81,
    92–93, 95, 96, 98, 99, 112, 114,
    117, 118, 119, 119–121, 122,
    135, 138, 140, 141, 142, 144,
    149, 151, 152, 153

Child in Time, The   2, 4, 63, 79,
    80, 81, 87, 88, 89, 90, 95, 96, 97,
    100, 102, 117, 136, 147–148,
    170, 175, 176, 199
Cockroach, The   39, 42–43, 43, 52,
    56, 56–57, 129, 139–140
Comfort of Strangers, The   80, 102,
    111, 136, 146, 148, 156
Enduring Love   4, 9, 73, 87, 100
First Love, Last Rites   2, 224
For You   7, 8, 20, 50, 60, 79, 111,
    117, 126, 136, 145, 148–149,
    153, 154, 155, 156, 169, 170,
    172, 173, 177, 178, 179, 186,
    191, 192, 193, 199, 200, 201–
    202, 203–204, 205, 206–208,
    222, 233
Imitation Game, The   17, 18, 98,
    102, 110, 114, 117, 120–121,
    122, 138, 142, 144, 155, 156,
    157, 162, 162, 163, 164, 166,
    177, 201, 213, 214
Innocent, The   129–130, 135,
Lessons   4, 9, 12, 35, 99, 102, 107,
    120, 123, 126, 127, 128, 133,
    146, 148, 152, 185
Machines Like Me   4, 24, 30, 38,
    39, 40, 44, 45, 48, 50, 52, 55, 87,
    139
Nutshell   87, 140, 158, 161
or Shall we die?   11–12, 24, 31,
    32, 33, 41, 50, 51, 55, 57, 58, 59,
    60–65, 68, 69, 70, 71, 90, 102,
    106–108, 111, 131, 172, 191,
    197, 222, 225
Psychopolis   150
Rose Blanche   89–90,
Saturday   4, 6, 8, 13, 81, 82, 83–85,
    87, 88, 92, 112, 115, 135, 143,
    148, 204, 212, 214, 217, 223
Science   10, 11, 25, 27, 69, 70, 71,
    104, 125, 197, 203
Solar   4, 8, 72, 223
Solid Geometry   72

240   *Index*

Sweet Tooth   10, 15, 32, 33, 35, 36,
    37, 38, 41–42, 47, 48, 49, 50,
    52, 53, 54, 55, 60, 73, 74, 145,
    148–149, 152, 176 *n*21, 180,
    181–182
McGregor, Tom
    Kavanagh Q.C. II   151–153
McLeish, Tom   12, 13, 14
McLeish, Tom and Hutchings, David
    13–14
Miracles, The   213
Moravec, Ivan   213
Mortimer, John
    Titmuss Regained   153
Morton, Jelly Roll   213
Mozart, W. A.
    Fantasia, K. 475   17, 18, 111,
        114, 156–158, 162, 164, 166,
        213–214
    Haffner Symphony, K. 385   118,
        149, 156, 158–161, 162
    Magic Flute, The, K. 620   111, 126,
        136, 138, 156, 212
    String Quintet, K. 593   88, 108,
        110, 156, 217

Nin, Anaïs
    A Spy in the House of Love   113–
        114
Norwich Cathedral   44, 52

Ogdon, John   112
Orwell, George
    A Clergyman's Daughter   58–59
Ostwald, Peter F.   205–206

Parry, Charles Hubert Hastings   39,
    56, 129
Paxman, Jeremy   102, 133, 186, 187
Phillips, Adam   1, 18, 91, 137, 138
Plant, Raymond   66
Preston, Simon   55
Profumo, John   102
Puccini, Giacomo   197, 215
Purcell, Henry   194

Reynolds, Joshua   96
Rochester Cathedral   52
Roosevelt, Eleanor   106
Rosen, Charles   157, 166
Rowland, Christopher   44–45
Rushdie, Salman   25
    The Satanic Verses   56
    Joseph Anton   132–133, 139
Ruskin, John
    The Stones of Venice   141
Russell, Bertrand   16, 69–72
Richter, Sviatoslav   117
Růžičková, Zuzana, and Holden,
    Wendy   116
Ryan, Kiernan   1, 17

Sacks, Oliver   17, 18, 78–79, 83,
    86–87, 89, 140, 142–143, 153,
    156, 158, 162, 164
Said, Edward   154–155
Salisbury Cathedral   44
Salzedo, Leonard   183
Saxton, Robert   208
Schemberg, Claudia   8, 109–110
Schiff, András   112, 221
Schubert, F.   109, 120, 142
    Der Erlkönig, D. 328   142
    Der Leiermann, D. 911   142,
        218–219
    String Quintet, D. 956   88
Scott, Derek B.   128
Sellers, Peter   148
Scruton, Roger   1, 9, 16, 18, 24,
    35–36, 43, 69, 73, 74, 131, 134,
    144–145, 148, 150–151, 164, 165,
    185–186
Shaffer, Peter
    Amadeus   161, 162
Shrimpton, Nicholas   61
Slay Jr., Jack   1, 92, 170
Smith, Graeme   64–65, 66, 67
Solomon, Maynard   162
Sontag, Susan   118
Spark, Muriel
    The Bachelors   32–33

Index 241

Storr, Anthony 1, 18, 93–94, 95, 100, 104, 105, 117, 119, 127, 143, 159
Stravinsky, Igor 116–117, 181, 184, 191, 215
Strauss, Richard 215
Sullivan, Arthur and Gilbert, William Schwenck 129–131

Tate, Andrews, and Bradley, Arthur 11, 24, 25
Tavener, John 46, 139, 184, 189
Thatcher, Margaret 16, 58, 60, 63–68, 69, 102, 131, 170, 172, 174, 175, 176, 177, 186–187, 195
Tippett, Michael 63, 64, 95–96, 160, 190–191, 195, 226
Turner, Barry 1, 20, 171, 173, 175, 178

Updike, John 15, 79, 103, 204
Upshaw, Dawn 194

Vaughan Williams, Ralph 16, 106, 112, 182, 184, 189, 198
Vassall, John 102

Vincent, John 66

Walton, William 184, 195
Waterhouse, Keith
There Is a Happy Land 41
Waters, Muddy 213
Waugh, Evelyn 36
Webber, Andrew Lloyd 186, 196–197, 228
Weir, Gillian 17, 78–79, 81, 89
Weir, Judith 195
Welby, Justin 26–27
Wells Cathedral 37, 44
Wells, Lynn 99, 126, 156
Westminster Abbey 27, 44, 54, 139
Wigmore Hall 4, 16, 32, 79, 82, 98, 99, 103, 108, 109, 113, 117, 145, 147, 148, 149–151, 153, 179, 192, 212, 217, 218, 221
Wilde, Oscar
The Soul of Man Under Socialism 137–138
Williams, Peter 85–86
Williams, Rowan 12, 26, 27, 28, 51, 66, 72
Wright, Tom 13